# AIMS AND METHODS OF SOVIET PLANNING

# AIMS AND METHODS OF SOVIET PLANNING

by

Mikhail Bor

*with Introductory Note by*
MAURICE DOBB

INTERNATIONAL PUBLISHERS
NEW YORK

*The text of this book was supplied to the publishers by the Novosti Press Agency, Moscow and London. While originally written in Russian, it is addressed to readers outside the Soviet Union, and its first publication is in London in the English language by Lawrence and Wishart Ltd., and in New York by International Publishers Co., Inc. The translation was made by Maxim Korobochkin, Lev Lempert and Lev Nazarov. The Index was compiled by Pat Sloan.*

*Printed in Great Britain by*
*The Camelot Press Ltd., London and Southampton*

PROFESSOR MIKHAIL BOR, D.Sc.(Econ.), has worked for more than twenty-five years in Soviet planning agencies, and is the author of over fifty works on problems of theoretical and applied economics. In 1962 and 1963 he took part in the work of a group of experts who, on instructions from the United Nations Secretariat, prepared for the United Nations the report "Planning for Economic Development".

His main books published in the U.S.S.R. are:

*Balance of the National Economy for Planning Purposes*, 1959.
*Questions of Methodology of the Balance of the National Economy*, 1960.
*Planning in the U.S.S.R. at the Present Stage*, 1962.
*Methods of National Economic Planning*, 1964.

# FOREWORD

National economic planning has been going on in one form or another for nearly fifty years in the U.S.S.R. Soviet planners have accumulated a wealth of know-how which is of great interest to many countries.

The Soviet people are now tackling many intricate problems of economic and cultural development. They are engaged in carrying out the five-year economic development plan (1966–70) and are effecting a radical economic reform in industry and agriculture. The system of agencies in charge of economic planning and management has been reorganised, methods of plan formulation have been improved and greater material stimuli to industry and material incentives to workers have been provided.

A high rate of economic growth is inherent in socialist economy, because the decisive means of production are owned by society which directly organises and controls production. The socialist economy offers vast scope for the employment of the latest methods of quantitative analysis, and for mathematical programming in particular. Modern computing techniques and mathematical methods are increasingly applied in both planning and operating the economy in the Soviet Union.

The principle of democratic centralism underlies the planned guidance of the Soviet economy. This principle, as its name implies, combines centralism and democracy. The economic reform at present being undertaken is an important step in further developing its application. The main line in improving planning and management is, on the one hand, to enhance centralised guidance of economic development, of scientific and technological progress and the scientific organisation of labour by going over to the sectoral principle of management and, on the other, to extend the functions of local agencies and enterprises in operational management. The economic independence of enterprises has been consolidated and their rights in planning and managing production and sales have been broadened. Plans contain fewer centrally-set targets.

Naturally the Soviet economy is not without shortcomings. Temporary contradictions may arise between the interests of separate enterprises and the interests of society as a whole. This may occur because plans do not provide adequate incentives or because some enterprises have a wrong understanding of their own interests. But such contradictions can be overcome in the process of economic growth.

This book aims to tell readers how national economic planning developed in the U.S.S.R. and what methods it now adopts.

M. B.

*Moscow, December 1966*

# CONTENTS

# Introductory Note

*by*

## MAURICE DOBB

Planning has been traditionally regarded as a necessary accompaniment of social ownership of the means of production (land and capital): as the essential integrating mechanism under socialism in substitution for the market mechanism that is the nerve fibre of capitalist economy (at any rate in its competitive phase). At the same time it has been traditionally regarded as constituting the major advantage of socialism over capitalism as a functioning economic system (*vide* the classic reference of Engels to the need for recognising "the social nature of modern productive forces" and for replacing "anarchy in social production . . . by conscious organisation on a planned basis"). Certainly experience has shown it to be a powerful engine of sustained economic growth and an instrument for achieving rapid structural change. So much so that few developing countries of the world today expect to extricate themselves from the quagmire of backwardness without the aid of some kind of state plan, while even older and industrially advanced capitalist countries today toy and experiment with so-called "indicative planning" (discussion of which forms the subject of the final chapter of this book).

Study of the rich experience of planning in socialist countries, in the U.S.S.R. in particular, has I believe to be approached *problematically* (looking at mechanisms and methods in the light of the specific problems they encounter and the purposes they serve), and has to be set in its *historical* context: moreover, of a continually changing context. It is, perhaps, a commonplace to say that planning in the Soviet Union did not grow up overnight. Although the planning commission (Gosplan) was constituted in 1921 as soon as the civil war and war of intervention were over, planning had to graduate through a fairly long period of partial plans and experimentation with annual "control figures" in the 1920's before the First Five-Year Plan was launched in the closing years of the decade; and only in the "years of great change" in the '30's did experience mature into effective operational annual plans, fashioned to a planning time-table, and into capacity to control and steer their implementation or fulfilment. This very maturing hinged on the increasing socialisation of the economy (agriculture included) which the process of socialist industrialisation achieved. Yet it was in the first decade of the '20's that already not only planning machinery was fashioned and tried, but the bases were laid of essential planning methodology, such as the method of balances (with their crucial input-output "norms", or coefficients) and the notion of a structural "balance of the national economy" as a whole.

Since then the very complexity of the economy has increased greatly with the progress of industrialisation (complexity of structure and the sheer number of products, product-varieties and of industrial plants). This has been reflected in increased complexity of the problems confronting planning. Moreover, during the past decade and a half policy has been increasingly concerned with harnessing the achievements of growth to the service of consumers, in order to increase the output and variety of consumers' goods and to raise the standard of life of 230 million people to an extent that was impossible in those "heroic" pre-war years when growth was the prime objective, with the most rapid possible expansion of industry (especially heavy industry) "against the clock". These two circumstances alone have introduced certain qualitative changes into the nature of planning problems, against the background of which certain changes in planning methods in recent years have to be seen in order to be understood.

In the first stages of development planning was mainly concerned with what one may call the strategic decisions on which both the balance and momentum of development crucially depend. As the structural complexity of the economic system grows, the limitation on the range of decisions that can be handled by central planning bodies, even in this age of accelerated processing of detail and calculation by computers, becomes increasingly evident. There comes about, moreover, an inevitable shift of emphasis, with transition from what has been called the "extensive" to a more "intensive" phase of development: increasing emphasis not only on anticipating consumers' needs but on constant innovation in design and technique and on achieving growth by means of constantly rising productivity of labour. Increasing prominence comes to be claimed by two problems, which one may call the problem of information (of the kind, and of sufficient accuracy and degree of detail, to enable the appropriate decisions to be taken at top levels) and the problem of both evoking and steering decision-making and initiative at the "operational" level (i.e. the plant or enterprise) within the general framework of planning of major targets and relationships. Already in the first half of the '20's the principle was recognised and established of the operational independence and responsibility of the individual enterprise, with its financial autonomy and its own balance sheet (an operational independence enthroned in that untranslatable term *khozraschot*). It stands to reason that practical day-to-day decisions (*plus* a great deal more than this) have to be taken at the plant level by those close to the actual production-situation and with the detailed knowledge and "feel" to take them surely and realistically. Moreover, it is on their judgement and initiative that a great deal depends so far as innovation and change are concerned—even if they may exhibit sectional and conservative leanings unless measures are explicitly devised to combat this.

This principle of *khozraschot* was not only reaffirmed on the eve of the First Five-Year Plan (with its strongly centralising tendencies in planning), but continued to prevail throughout the interim period, even when centralisation in planning and direction of the economy reached its peak round about the war and the immediate post-war years. True, in this past period of greatest centralisation the autonomy of the individual enterprise was increasingly fettered by the piling on of administrative directives and plan-targets of increasing detail and complexity. There was often a great deal of what Professor Liberman has since called "petty tutelage" over the enterprise, fettering its discretion and initiative, and decisions on so-called "microscopic" questions were taken by higher authorities that were ill-equipped in information or prescience to handle them. Although what may be called the "balance sheet" type of incentive (covering costs with receipts and showing a surplus) continued to hold a place, it tended to be overlaid by a series of other incentives and criteria of plan-fulfilment related to mainly quantitative fulfilment of certain targets. It is this situation that recent experiments, changes and "new mechanisms" of planning and administration have sought to rectify. This they have done by restoring operational direction and initiative to the enterprise, while at the same time freeing planners to concentrate on the more efficient handling of the major (so-called "macro-economic") structural relations and proportions and on the broader framework of "strategic" decisions within which decisions about current production policy are taken.

It was but natural that in the early days the notion of what was termed "the planning principle" and the automatic operation of a "free market" mechanism should have been counterposed, and the influence of the latter have been expected to decline and disappear with the achievement of socialism and with the extension of socialist planning to the whole economy. In *principle*, of course, planning and market autonomism are opposed in the sense that they stand to one another as alternatives; and we have spoken above about planning being substituted as an integrating mechanism for the market mechanism. Experience, however, has shown that it is incorrect to visualise the market and market-relations as entirely disappearing under socialism. There has always been a retail market for consumers' goods in the Soviet economy. This is to be regarded, indeed, as a logical consequence of the nature of wages under socialism, since wage-differences according to differing amounts and kinds of work done would lose most of their force as production-incentives if wage- and salary-earners were not free to spend their incomes as they pleased. Indeed, there has come to the fore in recent years the further question of adapting the supply of consumers' goods appropriately to the pattern of demand, so as to satisfy consumers' needs to an "optimum" extent. Again, it is wage-differentials and inducements (and *not* "direction of labour") that steer labour into the occupations and places where the jobs are available. Despite the predominance of state and co-operative trade, there has continued to be a limited sphere of free trade between town and country in the shape of the "collective farm-market" (selling produce of collective farmers' household plots as well as of collective farms). With the new economic reforms and measures there is likely in the future to be a wider sphere for direct contractual relations between state industrial enterprises themselves in procuring supplies of materials and components (*vide* Mr. Kosygin's reference in his speech of September 27, 1965, introducing the reforms of that year, to the need "to shift gradually to wholesale trade in individual types of material and equipment", with "direct ties in the future between producing enterprises and consuming enterprises" being "more widely developed").

In more recent statements and policies the relation between plan and market has accordingly been reformulated. From its very nature in a socialist economy the element of planning is, of course, dominant and that of the market is subordinate. We have spoken of the former as creating and moulding the larger framework of economic development, within which operational autonomy at lower levels operates. Yet at the same time planning uses market instruments (or "economic levers" as they have been called), such as prices, costs, taxes, interest and rental charges, credit, bonus-payments, in the course of influencing and steering these economic decisions at lower levels. Such instruments can be regarded as crucial links between the plan and its practical implementation. At the same time market indices function as "guide-lights" to production, especially so far as consumers' goods are concerned. Thus the market is not banished in the degree that planning is developed as was at one time supposed: it may be transformed, and its role changes because it is set in a quite new context; but it continues to have an essential place in the economic mechanism and to exert an influence upon the detailed functioning of the system.

This is fully evident in the changes of recent years in socialist countries: changes which are commonly described as tending in the direction of "decentralisation" because they reassert the principle of *khozraschot* (of which we have spoken), and give it greater scope by freeing the enterprise from a lot of detailed controls and directives, while at the same time substituting a unique (or "synthetic") criterion and incentive, of the "balance sheet" type, for the former multiplicity of bonuses and indices of successful performance. In this connection emphasis is laid on the importance of fusing the interests of the individual production unit with the *social* interest, as expressed in the intentions of the plan. Simultaneously other measures have been adopted to secure greater attention and responsiveness to consumers' demand on the part of producers, more efficient use of equipment entrusted to industrial enterprises and greater concern for economy of productive means. It is obvious that, especially with this renewed emphasis on (limited) autonomy of the enterprise, prices will play a crucial role in determining what is produced and by what methods, since they will influence, on the one hand, the receipts and, on the other hand, the costs of an enterprise when it decides to produce this or that commodity-line in certain quantities and to adopt this or that method of production, or combination of inputs, for the purpose. Fairly extensive changes in the structure of relative prices (although without changing retail prices or prices paid to farmers) have accordingly accompanied (or even preceded) the other economic changes of which we have spoken. For example, the Soviet price-reform of 1966–67, designed to make prices reflect more adequately the full social costs involved in production, has raised the prices of a number of so-called "capital-intensive" products (those characterised by a relatively high ratio of capital to labour in their production), principally in heavy industry, also of fuels and energy and of products of extractive industries (e.g. oil, gas, coal, ores) which it was considered had been underpriced previously, as well as allowing more price-spread for differences in quality and for novelty (cf. V. Sitnin in *Kommunist*, Sept. 1966, pp. 37–46).

With emphasis on economic efficiency has gone increased attention to mathematical methods, such as input-output analysis and what is known as 'linear programming', to the use of which in planning some reference is made below; also to cybernetics and control-systems in connection with automatic processes, and more generally with the use of computers and techniques of computer-programming in various kinds of economic calculation. The director of the leading institute concerned with mathematical economics wrote in *Pravda* a short time ago that "the elaboration of a system of interconnected economic-mathematical models, the mathematical means for their processing and the optimum solution of economic planning problems is one of the most important tasks facing Soviet economic science"; with which he coupled as a "top-priority task" the construction of "a unified system of economic planning information".

These are all signs, not of any "weakening" of planning, but rather of its maturing—its greater perfectioning, suppleness and sophistication, and its concentration on those tasks and on the kind of economic instrument than can be handled most effectively.

# I

# National Economic Planning

Man's working activity always pursues a definite aim. Man always plans his work in one way or another, estimating the available resources, the expenditure of labour and the possible results. The need for such an estimation increases when there is co-operation in labour, that is, when a few or many people work jointly. The operation of any enterprise presupposes definite aims and a programme of action determined in advance. Such a programme seeks to utilise most fully and efficiently the available resources and achieve the maximum results with the least possible effort and time.

The activity of a bee building cells in a hive is sometimes compared with the work of an architect who builds a house. A bee can create a more perfect and graceful edifice than some architects, but, as Karl Marx observed, even the worst of architects differs from the best of bees in that before undertaking the erection of a building he constructs it first on paper. He devises a plan of action, and his labour pursues a definite aim. Purposeful action, a desire to obtain the best results with the resources at hand is the most common feature of planning. This is true of any process of making a product. But the need for co-ordinated action is all the greater the greater the number of independent agents participating in one process.

For the peasant or artisan it is not difficult to perceive the direct connection between the results obtained in his primitive enterprise and the efforts exerted by himself and his family. Possible miscalculations in this "domestic" planning are not of a disastrous nature and the consequences are of a narrow local character. Hence in a society which chiefly consists of peasants and artisans, a need for general planning does not even arise. But as social production develops, the need for planning becomes more pressing, while the impossibility of planning the economy on a countrywide scale is increasingly revealed. It becomes clear that large-scale production cannot be undertaken without the strictest internal organisation, without subordinating many people to a single will. A solo musician does not need a conductor, but an orchestra must have one. Since under capitalism commodities are produced for an unknown consumer, only the market reveals whether or not co-ordination between all parts of the production machine has been achieved.

Contemporary capitalist society is characterised by the colossal scale of production, consolidation of economic ties within and between sectors and tremendous growth of the masses of goods produced for the market. At the same time the contradictions between the elements of planning in the organisation of production (as demanded by modern technology) at one enterprise and the impossibility of planning social production on the scale of a country or an economic area are growing bigger and sharper.

As far back as the early 19th century, the French philosopher Saint-Simon concluded that to plan on the scale of an entire society there must be social ownership of the main means of production. Only then will society be able to co-ordinate production with the available resources of manpower, raw materials and instruments of labour, to produce the needed things, to produce as much as is necessary for consumption and other purposes. But Saint-Simon's ideas of planning were merely brilliant surmises. National economic planning as an economic science and a system of guiding economic and cultural development came into being in the 20th century; it was created in the Soviet Union.

National economic planning is a system of guiding a country's economic and cultural development to satisfy, ever more fully, society's needs with the resources of society and in its interests, making use of objective economic laws for this purpose.

Organised and purposeful activity in planning economy and culture rests on a new social science, national economic planning. This science studies, analyses and summarises the multifarious practical work of developing the planned economy in the U.S.S.R. and other socialist countries.

The science of national economic planning is a system of knowledge based on practical experience in planned economic development and confirmed by it. It is a science of the forms and methods of the planned balanced organisation of social production, the organisation and methods of formulating a plan and verifying and securing its fulfilment.

National economic planning as a social science is an integral part of the general system of social sciences and it holds a place between political economy and the practical economics of different sectors. Political economy studies the laws governing the production, distribution, circulation, exchange, consumption and accumulation of the social product. A scientific analysis of these laws is the foundation of the science of national economic planning.

Sectoral economics (of industry, and its branches, construction, agriculture, transport, communications, trade, supply, and so on), taking as point of departure the basic propositions and conclusions of the science of national economic planning, studies the specific features of the planned balanced organisation of the reproduction process in separate sectors of the economy. At the same time the science of national economic planning makes use of the materials, conclusions and special methods of study employed by practical economics and other economic sciences.

National economic planning is possible in a society where the basic means of production are public property. As long as the state exists, state guidance, in the interest and on behalf of the whole of society, is the political basis of planning. Organisationally, national economic planning demands special planning agencies which formulate plans and secure and verify their fulfilment.

Planned economy prevails in the Soviet Union and other socialist countries. It implies social production in the interest of society as a whole, which is based on public ownership of the decisive means of production, the absence of crises and full employment of the working people, and results in the abolition of unemployment and systematic improvement in the people's standard of living.

## 2. DEVELOPMENT OF ECONOMIC PLANNING IN THE U.S.S.R.

In the very first days of the Soviet state Lenin voiced the idea of a single plan as the basis for the development of the country's entire economy.

When the decisive means of production (factories, works, land, forests, waters and transport) became public property and state agencies for directing them were organised it became possible to draw up economic plans for separate sectors and industrial areas.

In the spring of 1918, Lenin outlined a plan for laying the foundations of a socialist economy. He pointed out that the primary task was to build up the material basis of large-scale industry: to increase the production of fuel and steel, develop the engineering and the chemical industries. He stressed that the development of industry through the extensive use of the natural resources furnished the basis for the progress of the productive forces.

No sooner had the Soviet Republic come into being than it was faced with very difficult problems. Pre-revolutionary Russia held first place in the world in size of territory (one-sixth of the world's land surface) and third place in size of population (one-twelfth of the total), but ranked near the bottom among the advanced countries of the world in level of economic development. The United States, Britain, France and Germany were ahead of Russia in total industrial output. The United States with a much smaller population had an industrial output eight times greater than pre-revolutionary Russia; Germany produced almost 200 per cent more; Britain 150 per cent and France 20 per cent more.

In 1913, *per capita* steel production in Russia was 9 per cent of that in Germany and about 17 per cent of that in Britain and France; *per capita* coal production was only 5 per cent of that in Germany and 3 per cent of that in Britain; *per capita* cotton textile production was 7 per cent of Britain's.

Almost half of all the machinery and equipment used in the country was imported. More than four-fifths of metal-cutting machine tools, three-fifths of the harvesting machines and four-fifths of the mineral fertilisers came from abroad. Even ploughs, scythes and other simple farm implements were imported.

The rural population of Russia comprised 86 per cent of the total. According to the 1910 census, about 10 million wooden ploughs and nearly 18 million wooden harrows were used in agriculture. Agriculture developed lopsidedly and its efficiency was low, which inevitably led to frequent crop failures, famine and the ruin of the peasants.

In old Russia the living standard of the people was extremely low. Workers spent more than 70 per cent of their earnings on food and rent. Their diet consisted of bread, potatoes, groats and vegetable oil.

A budget survey made in St. Petersburg in 1909 revealed that about 70 per cent of the single workers rented a cot or a corner and about 43 per cent of workers with families had only one bed or a corner.

But even the semi-beggarly subsistence of the urban worker was considerably higher than that of the peasant. The countryside was steeped in darkness and ignorance. Most of the peasants were illiterate. According to the 1897 census, only 28 per cent of the population between the ages of 10 and 50 were literate. Many peoples in Central

Asia, the northern areas and other borderlands of tsarist Russia were almost totally illiterate. More than 40 nationalities had no written language of their own. In the non-Russian areas only 3·6 per cent of the population were able to read and write. The press at that time estimated that it would take at least 250 years to develop study facilities for all children of school age.

The Soviet state did not inherit even this beggarly "legacy" after the first world war, which wrecked Russia's economy. During the war, industrial production declined by 29 per cent and agricultural production by 12 per cent as compared with the 1913 level. Despite all this, Lenin had no doubt that planned guidance of the economy would enable the country to overcome Russia's age-old backwardness and build a highly developed socialist economy. In the very first days after the October Socialist Revolution, general state agencies for managing and planning the economy were set up.

The Supreme Economic Council, established in December 1917, was the first state agency for directing the nationalised economy. It was charged with elaborating general rules and plans for regulating the country's economic life. The Supreme Economic Council kept a record of available raw materials, fuel and manpower and allocated them among factories. It also set production assignments to factories and trusts. Planned regulation of the economy was undertaken in the very first months. An approximate estimate was made of the most pressing needs in major machines and consumer goods, and the possibilities of satisfying these requirements through home production were ascertained.

On this basis the Supreme Economic Council drew up the first rough draft of an economic plan. Since the country's raw material and food resources were very meagre, this draft plan was extremely modest. In 1918, it was planned to produce 5–6 million tons of coal, 1–1·5 million tons of pig-iron and 1·5 million tons of steel and to procure 200 million poods* of grain. But even this plan was not fulfilled. Foreign intervention and civil war began and major industrial and grain-producing areas were overrun by enemies of the Soviet Republic.

The Supreme Economic Council set up central administrations to manage and plan the various branches of nationalised industry in wartime conditions. There were 71 such central administrations with

* A pood equals 16·38 kg.

headquarters in Moscow, and each had a definite number of enterprises under its jurisdiction.

This system of centralised leadership of production and distribution was at that time the only one capable of ensuring the organisation of production and supply in the civil war. The system of central administration helped mobilise available resources for satisfying the country's most pressing needs, overcoming tremendous difficulties and concentrating all efforts on the main tasks.

The State Commission for the Electrification of Russia (GOELRO) was set up on the initiative of Lenin in February 1920 to draw up the first long-term national economic plan, a plan for electrification.

Lenin not only formulated the tasks of this plan, but also gave practical advice on how to draft it. According to Lenin's idea, this was not to be a narrow technical plan, it was to become a programme for transforming the entire economy.

Two hundred of the best scientists and engineers worked for ten months and drew up the first long-term plan. An analysis of the national economy showed that, despite the tremendous difficulties, the Soviet land would be able with its own forces to restore and transform the economy in a short time. Calculations were made showing how to advance the economy and to provide it with new technology on the basis of electrification.

The GOELRO plan was the first experiment in formulating a long-term national economic plan. That is why many of its targets were of an approximate nature. But it for the first time presented both a material and a financial balance of electrification, and that was a considerable achievement. The plan also contained elements of a fuel balance, balance of metal and equipment, building materials, etc. The fuel balance, for example, included estimates of the production of coal, peat and oil for ten years and also projections of fuel consumption. In addition to the general fuel balance, district balances of the fuel supply were compiled.

The electrification plan charted a firm course of building up heavy industry and envisaged a new pattern of the national economy aimed at transforming the entire country.

The proper location of the productive forces was given much attention in the electrication plan.

The GOELRO plan was approved in December 1920 by the 8th Congress of Soviets of the Russian Federation. In the same winter H. G. Wells visited Russia. And in the book he wrote immediately

after returning to Britain and entitled *Russia in the Shadows*, he related
what he had seen. In the two principal cities, Petrograd (now Leningrad) and Moscow, he saw streets with snow drifts piled high, silent
electric stations, idle factories, and boarded-up shop windows. Workers
were getting 200–300 grams of bread daily and not always that. The
civil war was not over yet. Wells spoke with Lenin, the head of the
Soviet state, who told him how a general plan for the restoration and
development of the country's economy on the basis of electrification
was being prepared: Wells listened, but did not conceal his scepticism.
In his book he called Lenin the "dreamer in the Kremlin". Eleven
years later, when Wells again visited the Soviet Union, he beheld an
entirely new country. The GOELRO plan was over-achieved and
industry, the entire economy and culture were advancing at a fast
pace. He admitted that he had erred in his judgement.

But at that time, in the early Soviet years when the economy was
devastated by civil war and foreign intervention, it was easy to doubt
the possibility of a swift recovery. Here is what the economy of Soviet
Russia was like in 1920.

|  | 1920 production | Per cent of 1913 |
| --- | --- | --- |
| Industrial output |  | 14 |
| Electric power, million kWh | 500 | 26 |
| Coal, million tons | 8·7 | 30 |
| Oil, million tons | 3·9 | 42 |
| Steel, thousand tons | 200 | 5 |
| Cement, thousand tons | 40 | 2 |
| Cotton fabrics, million metres | 100 | 4 |
| Granulated sugar, thousand tons | 90 | 7 |
| Agricultural production |  | 67 |

The level of industrial production in 1920 was about the same as in the 1870's–1880's. While in 1913 *per capita* industrial production in the United States was 13–14 times greater than in Russia, in 1921 it was 38 times as great.

In the spring of 1921 a system of planning agencies in all links of the state administration was set up under the Council of Labour and Defence. In February 1921, the State Planning Commission (Gosplan),★ was formed in February 1921. Its first economic plan was the food plan for 1921–22. In the same year sectoral plans for the steel, textile, sugar and rubber industries were compiled. Next came a long-term plan for the restoration of agriculture in the areas which suffered most from famine, and the first annual plan for the development of industry. Annual control (target) figures for the development of the entire economy of the Soviet Union were drawn up for the first time in 1925.

The GOELRO plan formed the basis of all these economic plans. After the end of the civil war, the New Economic Policy (NEP) was introduced in Russia. It was aimed at laying the foundations of a socialist economy, using for this purpose commodity-money relations (money, trade, market) and allowing private trade under state control in order to develop socialist industry to the utmost, consolidate its ties with the peasant farms and gradually draw the peasantry into socialism via co-operatives.

With the transition to peaceful construction the development of agriculture became one of the most difficult problems in the country's economic life. The Soviet state, naturally, could not directly plan the output of more than 24 million small peasant farms. During the restoration period it regulated agriculture and steered it into the necessary channels by utilising various measures of an economic and political nature. These were:

(a) legislative measures which determined the use, management and rent of land;

(b) economic measures (taxes, prices, credits, insurance, and so on);

(c) cultural measures—propaganda of agricultural knowledge, agricultural education, activity of seed selection stations, pedigree farms, nurseries, model experimental fields, etc.

A network of machine-renting stations was set up in agriculture. All trade in farm machinery and implements was in the hands of the state. Almost the entire production of agriculture for the market was

★ *Gosplan* is a Russian abbreviation of *Gosudarstvennaya Planovaya Komissia*. This term is used throughout this book.

bought by the state and co-operatives. The Government, by setting relatively higher prices, sought to accelerate the increase in the production of grain, cotton, flax, sugar-beet and other crops. The regulation of prices and the growth in state and co-operative purchases were combined with the planned supply of manufactured goods to the main districts producing grain and industrial crops.

From the very outset of the New Economic Policy private trade was controlled by the state. The Government actively supported and encouraged state and co-operative trade, seeking to restrict, oust and then gradually abolish private trade.

In 1926, the pre-war (1913) level of industrial production was exceeded by 8 per cent, while the output of agriculture was 96 per cent of that level. Noting these achievements, the 4th Congress of Soviets of the U.S.S.R., held in April 1927, instructed the Government to draw up a five-year national economic development plan. To provide a scientific groundwork for the first five-year plan the Gosplan and economic People's Commissariats held special conferences on various national economic questions. These conferences, attended by leading scientists and practical workers, played an important part in verifying that the targets were realistic, technically and economically, taking into account the latest achievements of world science and technology. At the conference on the iron and steel industry, for example, scientists and technicians proved the fallacy of claims that the planned growth rates in this industry were not feasible.

The first five-year plan specified assignments for all sectors of the economy and for manpower, trade, cultural development and finance. While the GOELRO plan had summary assignments for 17 branches of industry, the first five-year plan set definite assignments for about 50 branches of industry.

One of the big merits of the first five-year plan was the elaboration of a definite calendar programme with a breakdown of production and construction assignments for each year. The first five-year plan had annual targets for the growth of total output in industry and agriculture, new construction, and the major reconstruction projects, growth of the national income, capital investments in all sectors and the budget. It indicated the scale and pace of development in separate sectors, thereby ensuring proportionality in the development of the national economy and co-ordination of separate sides of social reproduction (production and distribution, accumulation and consumption).

The first five-year plan for the economic development of the

U.S.S.R. was approved by the 5th Congress of Soviets of the U.S.S.R. in April–May 1929.

Collective farms were organised on a large scale in the first years of the first five-year plan period. This made it possible to introduce a state sowing plan in the spring of 1930. It contained direct assignments for the sowing of different crops, estimated their yield and outlined measures for the organisational and economic strengthening of state farms and collective farms. These assignments which had the force of law were broken down for each state and collective farm.

The drafting of national annual plans began in 1930. The first annual plan (1931) for the first time set industry a range of technical and production targets and outlined major measures for achieving the targets in each branch of industry. The annual plan included assignments for building new and reconstructing old enterprises. It also elaborated qualitative performance indicators. For the first time targets were set for increasing the power and technical facilities of agriculture. The manpower plan included the annual programme of the allocation of manpower and the training of personnel. The entire annual production programme was so drawn up as to single out the state and co-operative sectors and also the assignments for Union Republics, territories and regions.

The first five-year plan of industrial production was fulfilled in 4 years and 3 months. During this period the output of large-scale industry grew by 130 per cent, key industries which played a decisive part in the economy were created, the GOELRO plan was fully fulfilled and a basis was laid for completing the technical reconstruction of the entire economy.

The objectives of the second five-year plan were outlined in 1932. To prepare and scientifically verify its aims and targets the Gosplan convened 24 scientific and technical conferences in 1932 and 1933. Thousands of scientists in the most diverse spheres and all mass organisations took part in formulating the second five-year plan. Major scientific problems were examined at joint meetings of the Gosplan and the U.S.S.R. Academy of Sciences.

While the GOELRO plans set concrete production assignments to 17 branches of industry and the first five-year plan to about 50 branches, the second five-year plan covered 120 branches.

The programme of capital construction was elaborated in greater detail. It specified the location and construction of over 1,000 heavy industry enterprises, including many large electrical stations, engineering works, metallurgical works, collieries, large ore mines, oil industry enterprises, cement works, etc. The construction programme of the plan also included about 350 light industry factories. The capital investment plan contained a detailed programme for transport facilities, public utilities and cultural and service establishments. It listed the construction projects, and fixed the dates for their commissioning.

The second five-year plan was elaborated in detail not only by sectors and People's Commissariats but also for each Republic, territory and region. All parts of the plan, given by sectors and territories, were much better co-ordinated. The method of balance co-ordination was used more extensively. The method of checking the feasibility of plans by technical and economic data was improved.

Plans were drawn up by areas. Definite targets for industry, agriculture, transport, capital construction, culture, etc., were set for each area.

Intra-factory planning was further developed during the second plan. Comprehensive technical, industrial and financial plans embracing all activities of enterprises were drawn up. They came to be known as the *Tekhpromfinplan* (TIF plans). A system of organisational and technical measures was incorporated in these plans. TIF plans were drawn up with the wide participation of workers, engineers and technicians, who helped tap the internal potentialities of enterprises.

All the major targets of the second five-year plan were over-fulfilled. Industrial output increased by 120 per cent and the main economic task—completion of the technical reconstruction of the entire economy—was accomplished. Agriculture too made headway.

The third five-year national economic development plan for 1939–42 was to be an important stage in the country's advance. But its implementation was cut short by the Nazi invasion in the summer of 1941.

The table overleaf shows the leap made by the Soviet Union during the years of peaceful development.

The attack of Nazi Germany on the U.S.S.R. interrupted the peaceful life and constructive endeavours of the Soviet people. The country's entire forces and resources were concentrated on defeating the enemy. A week after the war broke out the Soviet Government adopted a mobilisational national economic plan for the third quarter of 1941. In August 1941, the war economic plan for the fourth quarter of 1941 was approved. In 1942, plans were adopted for the economic development of the regions free from enemy occupation—the

| | 1940 output | 1940 as compared with 1913 | 1940 as compared with 1920 |
|---|---|---|---|
| National income | | 5·4 | |
| Industrial output | | 7·7 | 5·5 |
| Electric power, million kWh | 48,300 | 24 | 96 |
| Coal, million tons | 165·9 | 5·4 | 19 |
| Oil, million tons | 31·1 | 3 | 8 |
| Steel, million tons | 18·3 | 4·3 | 94 |
| Cement, million tons | 5·7 | 3·2 | 160 |
| Cotton fabrics, million metres | 3,900 | 1·6 | 39 |
| Granulated sugar, million tons | 2·2 | 1·6 | 24 |
| Agricultural production | | 1·4 | 2·1 |

Volga area, the Urals, West Siberia, Kazakhstan and Central Asia.

The war economic plans of 1942, 1943 and 1944 were of great importance in shifting the productive forces to the eastern areas, in restoring and expanding production, especially of armaments and war materials.

Planning in war-time was highly centralised, its aim being to ensure the satisfaction of all the needs of the front. But even in those hard times, work on long-term plans was not stopped. In 1943, a plan for the development of industry and transport in the Urals for 1943–47 was prepared. In 1944, plans for the restoration and development of the iron and steel, non-ferrous metals, coal, oil and electric power industries for 1945–46 were drawn up.

As Soviet territory was liberated plans for the economic restoration of the liberated areas were prepared.

The war took millions of lives and inflicted colossal damage on the entire economy. In the course of the war

1,910 towns, more than 70,000 villages and over 6 million buildings were destroyed

about 25 million people were left homeless

31,850 industrial enterprises, 4,100 railway stations and 65,000 kilometres of railway track were destroyed

40,000 hospitals and other medical institutions, 84,000 schools, technical schools, universities, colleges, and scientific institutes, 43,000 public libraries were looted and destroyed

98,000 collective farms, 1,876 state farms and 2,890 machine and tractor stations were looted and destroyed

7 million horses, 17 million head of cattle and 29 million sheep and goats were confiscated by the invading troops or driven off to Germany.

In 1945, the year when the war ended, the economic level of the U.S.S.R., compared with 1940, declined as follows: national income, 17 per cent; industrial production, 8 per cent; production of electric power, 11 per cent; coal, 11 per cent; oil, 40 per cent; steel, 33 per cent; cement, 68 per cent; cotton fabrics, 60 per cent; sugar, 78 per cent; agricultural output, 40 per cent.

After the war ended the fourth (first post-war) five-year plan for 1946–50 was drawn up; then came the five-year plans for 1951–55 and 1956–60 and the seven-year plan for 1959–65.

Despite the tremendous war damage, the Soviet people, by their all-out effort and drawing on the advantages of a planned economy, succeeded in regaining the pre-war level of industrial production in about two and a half years, and of agricultural production in five years.

The early fulfilment of the fourth and fifth five-year plans and the successful accomplishment of the plans for 1956–58 and the seven-year plan made it possible greatly to exceed the pre-war level of economic development and leave far behind the level of old Russia. Overleaf are some figures.

In 1965, real incomes of factory and office workers (per employed person) increased 2·3 times and of collective farmers 3·4 times as compared with 1940.

The restoration of the economy and its continued rapid growth brought about changes in the organisation and methods of national

|  | 1965 as compared with 1913 | 1965 as compared with 1940 |
|---|---|---|
| National income | 36 | 5·9 |
| Industrial output | 61 | 7·9 |
| Electrical power | 258 | 10·6 |
| Coal | 19·9 | 3·5 |
| Oil | 24·3 | 7·8 |
| Steel | 21·1 | 5·0 |
| Cement | 40·2 | 12·7 |
| Cotton fabrics | 3·0 | 2·0 |
| Agricultural output | 2·4 | 1·8 |

economic planning. But at the same time, the excessively directive nature of planning and the system of managing industry and construction restricted and fettered the initiative of the republics and local organisations. This resulted in inadequate use of internal potentialities and irrational transportation of goods, and upset production ties within and between areas.

The state plans had too many targets of a directive nature for the development of separate sectors, Republics and areas. The nomenclature of industrial goods centrally planned in 1953 was twice as large as in 1940 and the number of indices in the capital construction plan trebled. Targets for the production of small ancillary establishments were also of a directive character. Detailed targets of a directive nature were elaborated for the development of agriculture, which led to serious mistakes in crop growing and livestock raising in various areas.

Since 1954, measures have been consistently taken to eliminate the excessively directive character and the over-centralisation of economic management and planning. A large number of enterprises and construction sites were placed under the direct jurisdiction of the Union Republics, and the rights of enterprises and local economic agencies were broadened. Planning of the activity of the educational system, health services and public utilities was fully handed over to the Governments of the Union Republics.

Management of industry and construction was reorganised in 1957. The sectoral ministerial system of guidance was replaced by management of industry and construction based on the territorial principle through the Councils of Ministers of the Union Republics and Economic Councils set up in economic areas.

Plans drawn up by the enterprises became the basis for preparing national economic plans and ensuring their fulfilment.

Measures were taken to improve the use of available fixed assets and operating capacity and to bring to light additional productive potentialities. Mention should also be made of the general re-evaluation of fixed assets, accompanied by an ascertainment of their physical and moral depreciation, and a simultaneous inventory of productive capacity in industry.

The system of planning capital construction was reorganised and essential changes introduced in the forms and indicators of the capital construction plan. A new procedure for formulating plans was instituted with the object of better ascertaining what was practicable in the way of scale of production, construction and freight turnover, growth rates of labour productivity and reduction of production costs. The framing of production plans at enterprises and construction sites, and in U.S.S.R. ministries and departments, had to be preceded by drawing up a plan of new technology.

But though these measures were important, they were not decisive. They dealt with specific questions, without making serious qualitative changes in the system of management and planning. The Directives of the 23rd Congress of the Communist Party of the Soviet Union for the five-year national economic development plan of the U.S.S.R. for 1966–70 pointed out that the serious shortcomings in some sectors of the economy revealed in the course of fulfilling the seven-year plan were caused by the discrepancy between the greatly increased scale of production and the existing methods of planning and managing the economy and the system of material stimulation. The operation of objective economic laws had been underestimated in planning and directing the economy. Damage had resulted from "subjectivism", arbitrary changes of proportions in the development of sectors and the taking of a number of decisions affecting the economy without properly ascertaining the objective conditions governing them. Plan

assignments had concentrated the efforts of enterprises chiefly on meeting quantitative targets. Profit, bonuses, credits and other economic
instruments were little utilised in planning and managing the economy.

The decisions taken by the Central Committee of the C.P.S.U. at
its plenary meeting in September 1965 and the laws promulgated by
the 6th Session of the U.S.S.R. Supreme Soviet in the same year
initiated an all-embracing economic reform in managing, planning
and stimulating industrial production. This economic reform is
designed to solve fundamental, vitally important problems of socialist
industry. Its aim is to create the organisational prerequisites and
economic conditions for the advance of industry to a new, higher
stage.

The reorganisation of economic management and the rationalisation
of the organisational structure of industry involves a whole system of
scientifically-based measures, which are now being introduced carefully
and without haste. How is the planning system being improved, what
are its new features?

It has been decided substantially to reduce the number of centrally-
approved plan indicators. Instead of the existing overall indicators of
"gross output" and "commodity output", which fixed in money
terms the volume of output by an enterprise, one overall indicator of
"output sold" has been introduced. Enterprises will no longer be given
compulsory targets as regards the number of workers to be employed,
labour productivity and the average wage level. Nor will assignments
be set for the reduction of production costs.

But however significant the cut in the number of obligatory targets,
something else is more important. The main thing is that the system
of indicators is being fundamentally changed. These are to become
criteria by which industrial enterprises should be guided in their
operation and which should serve as the basis for assessing their work.
A new system is being devised which encourages enterprises to raise
the efficiency of production and improve the quality of goods, and
stimulates the interest of an enterprise as a whole and of each worker
in bigger and better results of operation. For industrial enterprises the
following targets and indices retain their directive character:

(1) volume of output sold;
(2) targets for the major nomenclature of goods;
(3) volume of centralised capital investment;
(4) commissioning of productive capacity and assets built with
centralised investments;

(5) targets for the development and introduction of new technology (manufacture of new models, introduction of new manufacturing processes, mechanisation and automation, etc.);

(6) assignments for the delivery of raw materials and other supplies and equipment;

(7) wages fund;

(8) profit (volume and level of profitability);

(9) indices of relations with the budget.

All other indices of economic activity will be planned by enterprises independently.

The change in the methods of planned guidance is designed to ensure the combination of centralised state planning with broad economic initiative and greater economic stimulation of industrial production. Enterprises must work on the basis of full *khozraschot*, or economic accounting.* In conformity with this, the results of the operation of enterprises will be evaluated by the output sold.

In the same rank with these primary indices we now place the profit of an enterprise or the profitability of its output and also the fulfilment of assignments for the delivery of major kinds of goods. Remuneration of the labour of workers in industry is made directly dependent not only on the results of their individual efforts, but also on the general results of an enterprise's operation. The principle of reciprocal material responsibility underlies the economic relations between enterprises. The new system of planning and economic stimulation makes the personnel of enterprises personally interested in the setting of higher plan targets which provide for the full use of the productive assets, manpower, material and financial resources and improvement in the technique of production and the quality of the goods.

The economic reform, preserving and developing the element of

* *Khozraschot* is an abbreviation of the words *khozyaistvenny raschot*, meaning economic accounting. It is a term describing the system of operational economic independence of an enterprise within the single state plan and single policy in technology, capital investments, price formation, wages, finances and statistics.

An enterprise operating on the *khozraschot* basis is given by the state assets for its economic activity, and with the income from the sale of its output it has to cover fully all outlays and also obtain a profit. Part of the profit is handed over to the state and some of it remains with the enterprise and is allocated to the technical development fund, housing and cultural construction fund and incentive fund. On the basis of the obligatory assignments approved by the state (they are few now) the enterprise itself draws up a detailed plan, concludes economic contracts with other enterprises; it may accept orders for goods over and above plan if that does not interfere with carrying out the state assignments.

centralisation in planning industrial production, ensures a radical change in the role of indices which stimulate the interest of collectives of workers and of each worker individually. This aim is served by the profit index. Profit must now act as one of the decisive targets in the general system of the industrial plan indices.

Without an account of profit it is impossible to determine how well or badly an enterprise is managed and what contribution it makes to the national income.

But profit does not cover all the aspects of an enterprise's activity. The index of profitability and the mass of profit depend on the influence of factors determining the level of production costs and those determining the movement of prices.

Under socialism, profit cannot be the sole criterion of productive activity. But neither must it be underestimated.

Profit has a number of important advantages as compared with other end-result criteria of the industrial plan. In contrast to the cost of production, the profit index reflects more fully the increase in output, the extension and renewal of the assortment of products and improvement in quality. Profit reflects in the most graphic form the contribution an enterprise is making to the common fund for the development of Soviet society; at the same time it links most effectively the interests of the whole of society with the interests of the personnel at the given enterprise, because an increase in profit will mean higher remuneration of the personnel. This is how the principle of democratic centralism is co-ordinated with the initiative of enterprises seeking to operate profitably.

It is clearly impossible to enhance the role of profit in the system of economic stimuli without a radical improvement of the existing price system, which is still (1966) defective, because wholesale prices have not been revised for more than ten years. The price system needs to be revised so as to make enterprises more interested in developing new technology and bettering the quality of their output and also to create definite advantages for the industries consuming these goods. The main trends in revising wholesale prices of industrial goods are now (1966) being charted so as to introduce the new prices in the next year or two.

Experience in developing modern large-scale industry also shows that the maintenance of high growth rates in production and labour productivity is impossible without a progressive and economically effective technological policy, an improvement in the sectoral structure of industry and rational organisation of the entire process of material production. That is why it became necessary to replace the territorial principle of economic guidance by the sectoral principle of managing the economy through ministries.

But high rates of scientific and technological progress and of expansion in the production of goods cannot be ensured by proceeding *only* from the sectoral principle of management. Guidance of the economy must ensure the efficient solution of a number of intersectoral and territorial problems, especially problems such as specialisation and integration of production, comprehensive development of economic areas and the full and rational use of raw material, power and labour resources. Consideration for specific features in the economic development of the national republics is an important element of territorial economic guidance directly linked with the national policy of the Soviet Government. That is why combining the sectoral and territorial principles of management is of fundamental importance.

To ensure rational territorial planning and the comprehensive use of resources the governments of the Union Republics are required to prepare plans for the development of production throughout the entire territory of each Republic, including industries of Union-Republican or Republican ministries.

Great flexibility and operational skill is required in planning and managing production at the present stage. It is necessary promptly to take account of the swiftly changing economic situation, to manoeuvre with resources, to co-ordinate production with the growing needs of the economy and the changing demands of the population and make immediate use of scientific and technological achievements. This determines the main line in developing planned guidance, namely, to ensure organic unity of centralised planning with the economic independence of enterprises.

Greater economic independence and initiative of enterprises is ensured by setting up at all of them funds from part of the profit (a production development fund, a material incentive fund and a fund for cultural and social measures) and also by giving enterprises much greater rights in regulating production and economic relations. To manoeuvre with resources, co-ordinate production with the needs and demands of the population on the spot, and rapidly introduce the achievements of science and technology has become imperative in planning and managing production.

The establishment of direct economic ties between enterprises is an important form of their economic independence. Such relations make it possible to establish economic proportions in greater conformity with the objective needs of different industries. This is one of the prime advantages of direct ties. Their main purpose is to pool the efforts of the personnel of inter-connected enterprises for solving many problems of technological progress and raising, on this basis, the quality of goods and the efficiency of social production.

# 2

# How National Economic Plans
# are Drafted

### I. A SYSTEM OF PLANS OF DIFFERENT TYPES

A system of interconnected and co-ordinated plans is needed to encompass and guide the multifarious and intricate economic life of a country with all its internal and external ties and relations. Indeed, the economic organism of such a large and economically developed country as the Soviet Union consists of many industrial, agricultural, construction, transport, trading and other enterprises—economic cells, as it were, of the social organism. These "cells" are combined in larger groups—associations, firms, and sectors.

The specific features of each consecutive stage in the aggregation of economic activity, naturally, demand a special method of action. Each economic cell and each aggregate has its specific aims which it strives to attain. In drawing up a plan for an individual enterprise, data respecting each single lathe should be considered. A firm in its calculations uses groups of similar machine-tools—lathes, drilling, milling machines, etc. A plan of an enterprise cannot be formulated without counting each commodity it produces, but the plan of a firm or central administration of a ministry cannot be drawn up unless an aggregated assortment is used. Hence the need to differentiate plans by the nature of their indices.

It is one thing when the plan maps out the activity of an enterprise for a day, a month, three months or a year, and another when the plan covers the activity and development of an enterprise over several years. The shorter the plan period, the fewer the changes in the capacity or nature of the enterprise and in the sectoral or territorial structure of production. At the same time the entire process of production and sale of goods can be determined in more detail and more fully when the plan period is shorter. On the other hand, in a plan designed for several years more place is given to indices dealing with changes in the structure and location of production, and the efficiency of the productive machine, while the targets will be set in lesser detail. Consequently, plans should be differentiated by the duration of the period they cover, that is, current plans and long-term plans.

In economic activity several specific forms and stages can easily be singled out. These are, first of all, the production of various goods and also the building of new enterprises and installations; then come such forms of activity as the transportation of goods, sale of goods, the supply of enterprises with all the materials and machines needed for production. There is also the satisfaction of the personal needs of the individual members of society (which includes the delivery of the goods they need, the satisfaction of their intellectual requirements, the development of education, of the health services, science, culture, the provision of houses, etc.). Lastly, there is the provision of finances and credits to serve society's productive and non-productive spheres.

Plans are differentiated by their

(1) function; plans of production, construction, transportation, technological progress, manpower, expenditure on production and circulation, supply and sales, advance of living standards, financial and credit plans;

(2) degree of aggregation: plans of enterprises, construction sites, state farms and collective farms, economic associations (combines, trusts and firms), ministries and departments; overall plans of economic areas, cities, regions, territories, Autonomous and Union Republics; overall sectoral plans; national economic plans;

(3) period of operation—operative (a day, ten days, a month, three months); current (for a year or two); long-term (for five or seven years); general plans (for 15–20 years).

All these types of plans are interconnected and form a single system of plans.

In practice we always have to deal with comprehensive plans for the development and activity of an enterprise or an association of enterprises or a totality of enterprises, in one territory—district, city, region, Union Republic, and the Soviet Union as whole. The plan of each such sub-division is an overall plan because it includes production, construction and supply. Moreover, it also deals with questions of raising the living standards of the people, education and the movement of financial and credit resources. At the same time the plan of each economic sub-division can be either current or long-term.

Great importance attaches to the proper combination of long-term and current national economic planning in the Soviet Union. We have said that a planned economy needs plans for a longer period, for a number of years, and also for shorter periods, for the immediate future. This is explained above all by the fact that national economic planning is continuous because the production of material goods cannot be stopped: since society cannot stop consuming it cannot stop producing.

National economic planning organically combines current and long-term plans. This is an important requisite for fully reflecting scientific and technological achievements in the national economic plans. And it helps to bring to light and tap potentialities for expanding production and to maintain proper proportions.

It is impossible to plan production, the development of technology, capital investments and labour outlays without fully considering all sides and prospects of society's development. Each annual plan must be an organic part of the long-term plan. At the same time the long-term plans must be solidly "tied to the ground" and correctly adjusted with the help of annual plans and their actual fulfilment.

There must be continuity in planning. Indeed, capital accumulation made in the given period (in the form of capital construction, an increase in circulating assets and stocks) determines the volume, growth rate and structure of production in the next period. The volume and composition of the national income used in the current year determines next year's level of consumption and the scale of accumulation. The training of personnel at the given moment predetermines the possible manpower resources for various sectors of the economy and areas in future, and so on.

Long-term plans underlie the entire planning system. Their leading role is determined by the fact that a sufficiently long period of time is needed for radical changes in the structure of production and consumption, for major achievements in technological progress and for solving national economic problems.

Each enterprise must visualise the perspective of its development for years in advance. Construction and transport organisations, scientific, cultural, educational and public health establishments must have similar perspectives.

Several types of long-term plans have been elaborated in the Soviet Union in the practical work of planning:

(a) general long-term plans for the development of the economy and culture of the country as a whole for many years ahead;

(b) general long-term plans for the development of separate areas, centres and sectors of production;

(c) plans for the development of the country's economy and culture in the next several years.

Long-term planning in the U.S.S.R. developed primarily on the basis of formulating and fulfilling five-year plans. The choice of a five-year period was not accidental. It is explained, first, by the fact that five years is approximately the period sufficient for building and commissioning large industrial enterprises, hydro-electric stations, big canals and irrigation and land reclamation systems and railways. During this period important measures can be carried out for the technical reconstruction of economic sectors, the training of personnel and effecting other changes in economic life, which make up the essence of long-term planning.

In formulating a plan for five years it is also possible to determine the trend and foresee the economic results of developing technology and, consequently, to frame a fully definite production plan. The five-year plans offered a suitable framework for the socialist organisation of the people's efforts in accomplishing major tasks of economic construction.

But plans for five or seven years cannot accomplish economic tasks for the radical reconstruction of the existing material and technical basis of production. For this purpose plans for a longer period are needed.

The GOELRO plan was the first general long-term plan in the U.S.S.R. It was designated for 10–15 years and mapped out the way for restoring and reconstructing all sectors of the economy on the basis of electrification.

Shortly before the late war the U.S.S.R. Gosplan was commissioned to draw up a general plan for the development of the U.S.S.R. over 10 or 15 years (the war prevented the formulation of this plan).

The U.S.S.R. and other socialist countries have also had long-term plans for periods of less than five years. But these were plans for separate sectors or for solving specific economic problems.

A general plan for the electrification of Soviet railways, a general plan for the development of Moscow and other similar plans were drawn up and approved in the post-war period.

The programme of the C.P.S.U., adopted by the 22nd Party Congress, outlined the main tasks of national economic development for 20 years, from 1961 to 1980. During this period the country's social product is to increase 5 times, industrial output 6·2 times and agricultural output 3·5 times. Capital investments of 2,000,000 million roubles are to be made, labour productivity in industry is to rise 4–4·5 times and in agriculture 5–6 times, and the U.S.S.R. is to attain the highest living standard in the world.

Long-term plans can only approximately take into account changes in machinery, manufacturing processes and productive organisation, political changes and economic shifts which might occur in the world. That is why they are adjusted in the course of their fulfilment.

They are carried out with the help of plans for shorter periods which, in their turn, are based on the targets of the long-term plans.

The need for current planning is determined by the fact that it makes it possible: (a) to amplify the targets of the long-term plans; (b) to specify and adjust the targets of the long-term plans by taking into account the changes in both the external and internal conditions of society's development; (c) to exceed long-term plans on the basis of the resources created in the course of fulfilling them, thanks to the effort and the initiative of the people and the application of the best know-how; to direct efficiently the development of the economy.

Current plans may also envisage the solution of new problems which arise in the course of fulfilling long-term plans (for example, a big expansion in the production of farm machines, the building of instrument-making and other factories, etc.)

In long-term plans the range of indices is smaller. A big place is held by indices of the overall results to be aimed at and accounting indices. Aggregated balance calculations and aggregated rates and standards are used more widely.

Current plans have a more detailed and wider range of indices which are based on a diversified system of thoroughly integrated and sub-stantiated balances and technical and economic calculations.

Before and during the late war annual, quarterly and monthly plans for the entire economy were drawn up and approved. But this system has outlived itself. Between 1947 and 1963, current plans were only annual plans; the first two-year plan was approved for 1964–65.

## 2. HOW A PLAN IS FORMULATED

The formulation of a plan for the entire national economy demands the concerted work of all links of the planning system, and work on drafting plans proceeds almost simultaneously in all links. Planning is based on five-year plans with a breakdown of assignments by years, sectors, Union Republics, ministries, enterprises and construction sites.

Extensive preparatory work precedes the drawing up of a national economic plan for a definite period. The "preparatory programme" is usually formalised in a government decision which lays down the procedure for drafting the plans and the dates for presenting them.

Several stages can be singled out in preparing a plan: elaboration of the form of tables, the range of the plan indices and methodological instructions for them; summing up the results and analysing the fulfilment of the plan for the current (basic) period; elaboration of the main trends and preliminary estimates for the long-term plan; formulation of the national plan; approval of the national plan; passing down the assignments of the national long-term plan to the Union Republics, All-Union and Union-Republican ministries and departments; adjustment and approval of the long-term plans for the development of the Republics, territories, regions, areas, ministries and departments; adjustment and approval of the long-term development plans of enterprises.

This division of plan formulation by stages is conventional and is done mainly for methodological purposes. Actually it is often difficult to separate one stage from another. For example, in analysing plan fulfilment for the preceding period the main indices for the planned period are outlined; while working out the plan indicators, the expected results of plan fulfilment in the preceding period are specified.

Let us examine in greater detail separate stages of plan drafting.

The first question planners have to tackle when they undertake to formulate a long-term or current national economic plan is, how to reflect most fully in the plan the aims facing the economy in the given period and the ways of achieving these aims.

A national economic plan is a very intricate structure. To erect it, one must choose the architecture and the bricks or blocks from which it will be built. In the case of a plan these are first of all its indices, the combining of these indices into interconnected groups, tables (forms of the plan) and sections of the plan.

Let us continue the comparison of plan formulation with the erection of a big building. For the building not to collapse in the process of construction there must be uniform rules for performing separate jobs which are obligatory for all builders, and reciprocal co-ordination between the construction elements. For planners such uniform and binding rules are the system of plan indices and methodological instructions for the formulation of a national economic plan.

The range of the indices, forms of tables and structure of the plan by sections and the methodological instructions are drawn up for each new long-term plan.

In the case of current plans this work is usually limited to correcting the existing forms, indices and methodological rules. These modifications can be more or less essential, depending on what changes in the economy or forms and methods of management must be taken into account.

It is the duty of the U.S.S.R. Gosplan to elaborate the forms of the tables, plan indices and methodological rules for them.

The binding nature of the forms, plan indices and methodology of calculation for all planning links makes it possible to ensure their comparability in drawing up plans by sectors of the economy both for the country as a whole and for Republics, economic areas, territories, regions, cities, etc.

The system of plan indices includes indices of different kinds: indices in physical terms and value terms, quantitative and qualitative indices, approved indices and accounting indices.

Indices in physical terms are given in definite physical units of measurement (tons, pieces, metres, and so on). They cover assignments for the production of industrial goods in physical terms (types, assortment, etc.), the volume of goods carriage and average daily loadings, the commissioning of capacity, labour productivity in physical terms and purchases of agricultural produce. These indices are of great importance for dovetailing the development of separate sectors and categories of production. For example, material balances are based on indices of industrial output in physical terms. Planning of the carriage of various goods combines the development of industry and transport; planning of productive capacity ensures conformity in the development of production and construction.

The system of indices in physical terms, however, does not offer the possibility of establishing the total expenditure of social labour, of determining and comparing the general results of activity in separate sectors, economic areas, enterprises and their associations. That is why planning the volume of production and construction, the commissioning of fixed assets, trade, production costs and profitability is done in value terms, in terms of money.

Value indices (volume of industrial output, size of capital investments, volume of trade, national income, etc.) are measured in monetary units (roubles) and are determined by evaluating indices, given in physical terms, in operative prices. This is necessary for co-ordinating the planning of production with the planning of manpower, of production costs with finances, and of supply both with financing of trade and with the population's incomes.

These indices must ensure the possibility of analysing the plan in three major aspects—sectoral, territorial and departmental.

The *sectoral* aspect reflects the grouping of targets by sectors of the economy: industry as a whole (including the steel, fuel and engineering industries), agriculture, transport, etc. These targets fully cover the given sector, irrespective of the location of production on the territory of different republics and regions and also the jurisdiction of separate enterprises. The sectoral structure of the plan enables economists to build into it the production ties and proportions for the balanced dovetailing of separate sectors both in the country as a whole and in republics and economic areas.

The *territorial* aspect of the indices reflects above all the grouping of the state plan targets by Union Republics which bear responsibility for fulfilling their shares. The territorial aspect of the plan also includes the breakdown of assignments by economic areas. This section is elaborated by Republican Gosplans and approved by the Councils of Ministers of the Union Republics. In the long-term plan of the U.S.S.R. targets are broken down not only by Union Republics but also by territories and regions (for example, targets for the purchase of agricultural produce, the lists of the biggest construction projects).

Moreover, in formulating the national economic plan for the U.S.S.R. as a whole some indices are also calculated for big economic and geographical areas. These calculations are needed to ensure the comprehensive development of the main economic areas.

The *departmental* aspect reflects the grouping of indices by ministries and departments.

Another important grouping of indices is by sections of the national economic plan.

Indices of the national economic plan are grouped in sections proceeding from the social division of labour and the existing structure of the economy. Account is also taken of the existing organisational structure of the economic planning agencies, the administrative-territorial division of the U.S.S.R. and also the geographical location of the country's productive forces. All these sections of the plan are thoroughly integrated and in their sum-total make up the single state plan for the economic development of the Soviet Union. The national economic development plan of the U.S.S.R. for 1966 included the following main sections:

    (a) overall section of the plan (main synthetic indicators);

    (b) sections of separate trends and sectors, including:

        (1) industry;

        (2) development of specialisation in industry and construction;

        (3) agriculture and forestry;

        (4) transport and communications;

        (5) capital construction;

        (6) geological prospecting;

        (7) manpower and personnel training;

        (8) material and cultural standards of the people;

        (9) expenditure on production and circulation;

      (10) trade;

      (11) material supply plan;

      (12) territorial section—economic development plan of the Union Republics and economic areas.

Throughout the history of socialist planning the system of plan indices has been constantly improved. The new economic tasks which face the country, the progress of science and technology, changes in the sphere and methods of economic management—all imperatively dictate improvement of the system of indices.

In the first years of national economic planning when only separate sectoral plans were drawn up, definite assignments were set for a small range of sectors and the numbers of indices was very limited. The system of plan indices was in the main created only when the GOELRO plan was drafted. Subsequently it developed from one plan to another.

Let us stress one highly important aspect in developing and improving the system of indices of the industrial plan which was true up to the present economic reform.

The changes affected mainly the quantitative side of the indices. Indices of the industrial plan were formed mainly during the first and second five-year plans and were preserved essentially without serious qualitative changes until recently. The changes were mainly of a quantitative order, the number of indices was cut or increased, the indices were differentiated or aggregated, but their system was not essentially altered.

The main, characteristic feature of this system was that it concentrated efforts only on the quantitative side of production. In conditions of dynamic development and high economic growth rates, when the prodigious, intricate tasks of converting a backward land into a highly developed industrial country were being accomplished, chief attention was paid to the quantitative side, to indices of the volume of production and to a system of indices for industry in line with these demands.

But a new stage in the development of the U.S.S.R. has set in, new economic conditions have arisen, making obvious the inadequacy of the existing system of industrial planning and the need to go over to other criteria in assessing the operation of enterprises, to indices which would promote the optimum development of the country's economy as a whole and of industry as its major and decisive part.

Essential shortcomings in the planning system as a whole, specifically in the system of industrial production indices, alongside shortcomings in the organisation of management and economic stimulation, prevent fuller and more comprehensive use of the advantages of socialism for raising the efficiency of social production.

The economic reform now being carried out in the U.S.S.R. in industry meets the vital requirements dictated by the new stage of development.

The objective prerequisites of this reform, as pointed out at a plenary meeting of the Central Committee of the C.P.S.U. in 1965, are the huge increase in the scale of production, capital investments and size of productive assets, the increasingly complex economic ties in the national economy and the acceleration of scientific and technological progress. The present-day scientific and technological revolution has posed many intricate problems. To raise to the utmost the efficiency of social production has become a focal problem. Rational, economically sound management has acquired decisive significance, especially in industry. And all this dictates a radical change in the system of indices.

The new system of indices now being introduced in Soviet industry is based on the close interconnection of the following three groups of indices:

(1) Value index of the scale of production (volume of goods sold).
(2) Target for the production of goods in physical terms.
(3) Profit index.

As pointed out earlier, value indices alone are insufficient for co-ordinating demand and production. Production which is at the same time productive consumption objectively demands concrete, qualitatively definite goods for satisfying the demand. Of course, the demand made on various industrial goods differs. Output satisfying personal non-productive needs is one thing and goods satisfying the needs of production is another. In the case of goods which satisfy personal non-productive needs, present-day conditions dictate abandonment of the policy of setting a detailed nomenclature and assortment by way of a directive. The detailed assortment must be determined on the basis of direct contacts with trading organisations representing the interests of the consumer. *The Statute of Socialist Enterprises* (approved by the U.S.S.R. Council of Ministers on October 4, 1965) says that enterprises should alter the nomenclature and assortment of consumer goods in conformity with the demand and change of orders by trading organisations, and that such alterations need not be sanctioned by higher agencies.

The situation is different in the case of means of production. The high growth rates of the Soviet economy and its intricate tasks make it essential to preserve for a certain time a more detailed nomenclature and assortment as obligatory assignments for industrial enterprises. For this reason, the nomenclature of output for consumer goods will, as a rule, be of an aggregated nature, with a more detailed breakdown of the assortment in the plan of enterprises themselves, while in the case of means of production the same obligatory nomenclature of output as existed until now is preserved in the main.

A combination of an aggregated value index of the volume of production and a more or less detailed nomenclature of major kinds of goods in physical terms ensures the necessary co-ordination of production and demand.

The essence of indices in industry and other sectors of the economy will be further examined in Chapter 4.

### 3. THE ROOT SOURCE

Important though it is, determination of the indices, forms and methodology for the formulation of a plan is only the first step in planning. The next stage is the working out of a draft plan. It begins with summing up the results and analysing plan fulfilment in the current (basic) period.

Precision in determining growth rates of a sector for the planned year, the proper establishment of ties both within a sector and between sectors and ascertainment of the production, material and manpower possibilities of separate sectors, etc. depend on how precisely economists calculate the expected plan fulfilment in the pre-plan period.

At this initial stage wide use is also made of the statistical analysis of the production level and growth rates, average daily output and total volume (as compared with the past periods and with the plan). Possible overfulfilment of the plan for the output of goods and of qualitative targets is foreseen by calculation of the use of productive capacity. Account is taken of the raw material, power and labour resources of the sector and also of intra-sectoral and inter-sectoral co-operation.

Next comes the elaboration of the main trends of national economic development for the planned long-term period. Here it is necessary to formulate the main assignments for the basic indices and to ensure co-ordination of the projections of production and capital investments with the possible resources of raw materials, fuel, supplies and equipment. But before the choice of the main trends of the plan can be made, recommendations must be worked out on the introduction into the economy of the results of scientific research. For example, the Soviet Government, undertaking the preparation of the five-year plan for 1966–70, instructed the U.S.S.R. Academy of Sciences to sum up the results of scientific studies and, on the basis of these, to determine the main trends of technological progress in different branches of industry in 1966–70. Ministries and state committees* examined measures for the technical re-equipment of enterprises, intensification of manufacturing processes, introduction of new technology, development of specialisation and increase in capacity of specialised categories of production.

Summing up all these data, they submitted their recommendations to the Gosplans of the Union Republics for working out draft proposals on the main trends of the plan.

Simultaneously institutes of the U.S.S.R. Academy of Sciences prepared for the U.S.S.R. Gosplan proposals on such important aspects of the long-term plan as the growth rates of social production and the structure of production most favourable to economic growth, growth rates of labour productivity and rational utilisation of manpower resources, lay-outs for the location of production by sectors, raising the efficiency of production and capital investments, and so on.

Making use of these recommendations, industrial enterprises, state

---

* Alongside ministries there are also central governmental departments which guide activity in separate sectors (for example the State Planning Committee, State Committee for Material Supply, State Committee for Science and Technology, etc.).

farms and collective farms submitted their proposals for possible increase in production, improvement in the quality of goods, rise of labour productivity, reduction of costs, etc.

These proposals and draft plans prepared by industrial enterprises, construction sites, state farms, collective farms, research, designing and other organisations, provided the basis of the general state plan.

Republican ministries and other economic organisations, having received and summed up the proposals of separate enterprises, determined the possible expansion of production together with the operating capacity, and prepared their proposals for additional capacity, volume of capital investments and other plan indices.

On the basis of proposals by Republican ministries and departments, Republican Gosplans prepared summary proposals for the basic trends in developing the economy and culture of the Union Republics, giving projections of the major plan indices for five years.

This is how proposals for the main trends were received by the U.S.S.R. Gosplan. Simultaneously the All-Union and Union-Republican ministries and departments, institutes of Academies of Sciences and sectoral academies worked on proposals for the main trends in the respective sectors of the economy and culture, in the major branches of the sciences, in the location of production, etc. Of particular importance were the draft overall plans for the development of key sectors drawn up by the ministries.

On the basis of the proposals received, the U.S.S.R. Gosplan drew up a preliminary variant of the main trends of the five-year plan, a variant of the major national economic proportions, a provisional balance of the national economy for planning purposes, and made thorough preparations to examine and discuss the proposals of the Union Republics in all their major aspects. This ensured the co-ordination, at the requisite scientific and practical levels, of different variants of the main trends and the choice of the best one.

After the directing bodies had approved the main tasks of economic development in the plan period, the U.S.S.R. Gosplan prepared control (target) figures for the ministries, departments and Union Republics, setting the preliminary volume of production, capital investments, and material supply. This serves as the basis for the next stage—preparing a full-scale draft five-year plan for all indices and for each year, with a breakdown of targets by sectors, Union Republics and economic areas.

D

## 4. HOW FACTORY PLANS TURN INTO A GENERAL STATE PLAN

We have stated earlier that plans drawn up by enterprises underlie all the different types of state national economic plan.

The technical, industrial and financial (TIF) plan is the plan for the operation of an enterprise in the current year, encompassing all aspects of activity: technical, economic, and financial. It furnishes the answer to three main questions. What goods and what financial results an enterprise has to produce? What resources it needs for this purpose? What measures have to be carried out to fulfil the plan?

The content of TIF plans varies in different branches of industry, depending on the specific features of the given branch. But there are main sections which, as a rule, are elaborated at each enterprise.

*Production Programme.* This is the leading section of the TIF plan. It indicates what goods, in what quantity and in what period an enterprise has to produce in the given year. Here the indices of quality are fixed and provision is made for deliveries, by way of production co-operation, to other enterprises and for the manufacture of new kinds of goods.

*Technical Development Plan.* This includes a programme for the introduction of new technology and manufacturing processes, mechanisation and automation, and determines the nature of research and experimental work connected with the development and organisation of production of new kinds of goods. It also includes a plan for the production of equipment, modernisation, manufacture and testing of new models, etc.

*Plan of Organisational and Technical Measures* (OTM plan). This is closely linked with all sections of the TIF plan. It lists all the measures which have to be carried out to increase output and improve quality, raise labour productivity, cut costs and increase accumulations.

*Supply Plan.* This determines the needs of an enterprise in raw materials and other supplies, fuel and power. It also indicates the need in articles and semi-manufactures, repair of equipment and experimental work, and the dates for delivery of the necessary supplies.

*Labour Plan.* This contains assignments for labour productivity, calculation of the wages fund and the number of workers and other employees. It also includes a programme for training and raising the skill of the personnel.

*Production Cost Plan.* This includes assignments for the reduction of costs, an estimate of production costs and calculations of the cost of separate goods.

*Capital Construction Plan.* This is drawn up by enterprises engaged in new construction. It lists the projects to be built, the period of their construction and dates of commissioning, the cost of construction and measures for reducing it, and also an estimate of the needs in building materials, equipment and building workers.

*Financial Plan.* This reflects all the activities of an enterprise in a generalised way. It lists all income and expenditure, shows how much profit will be received, how it will be utilised, what payments have to be made to the budget and what sums will be received from the budget.

Preparations for drafting the plan at each enterprise start long before the beginning of the plan period. First of all, work in the current period is analysed and potentialities which could be tapped in future are brought to light. The expected plan fulfilment for the current year is estimated.

The framing of the plan is divided into several stages. The first starts and finishes at the enterprise itself, usually in June, when the results of plan fulfilment for the first six months are summed up and the assignments up to the end of the year are specified.

Special teams of workers, technicians and engineers are organised to suggest important measures for technical development and the elimination of bottlenecks, and to prepare suggestions for the production programme, especially if it is to undergo essential changes. These teams pay special attention to suggestions for innovations and inventions to overcome current difficulties.

The next step is the drawing up of the technical development plan or the OTM plan. This indicates what new goods will have to be produced at the enterprise, what machinery and equipment is to be introduced and what machines are to be modernised with an eye to the latest technological developments. At large enterprises with an intricate range of work, the OTM plan consists of several sections. The following can be named:

(1) Introduction of new machinery and manufacturing processes.

(2) Mechanisation of labour-intensive processes and manual jobs.

(3) Organisation of the manufacture of new articles.

(4) Elimination of spoilage and improvement in the quality of goods.

(5) Saving of materials, supplies, electric power and fuel.

(6) Easing working conditions.

The OTM plan fixes the dates and names the persons responsible for carrying out each measure; and indicates the expenditure on its implementation and the saving to be expected, together with the effect of each measure on all the economic indices of production: volume of output, cost of production, labour productivity, and so on.

Such OTM plans are prepared for each section, shop and the enterprise as a whole. They are drawn up on the spot at the work places, and the entire personnel takes part in this activity. Such plans make it possible to bring to light all potentialities for increasing production and to define measures for improving the operation of the enterprise as a whole.

Simultaneously a drive for technological innovations is organised. Production engineers, technicians, workers and economists examine these proposals. The most important of them are discussed at production conferences. Expected saving and the bonus to be paid to innovators is estimated for each measure. Then the total expected saving is calculated. The examined and approved measures are incorporated in the plan.

The draft plan is discussed in the shops, sections and teams and at meetings of Party members and general meetings of personnel. When complete, the TIF plan is the programme of the enterprise for next year. It shows what goods the enterprise can give the economy, what materials will be required and what the profit will be. Formerly the TIF plan of each enterprise had to be examined by the body under whose jurisdiction the enterprise was placed. Now the TIF plan has to be approved only by the management of the given enterprise.

On the basis of proposals received from enterprises under the jurisdiction of a definite ministry, a comprehensive plan for the development of each sector of the economy is drawn up. This includes a system of indices characterising all aspects of the sector's development. In addition to indices of output in terms of money and physical terms and of specialisation and co-operation of production, the plan of any industry also has indices for the introduction of new technology, capital investments, wages fund, material supply, etc. The comprehensive plan also includes indices, approved now by the enterprises themselves, of labour productivity, cost of production, quality of goods, and also a number of technical and economic indices: assets per worker, the output asset ratio, power consumption per worker, unit capital investments, etc. In present-day conditions these are important qualitative performance indices.

In drawing up comprehensive development plans of Republics, account is taken of the specific features of planning the separate sectors of the economy. Finally, on the basis of draft plans of the Union Republics the U.S.S.R. Gosplan draws up and submits a draft five-year national economic development plan. Its targets are broken down by years, by separate sectors, Union Republics and economic areas and are dovetailed with the material balances of the major kinds of raw materials, supplies, fuel, equipment and machinery for the entire economy.

Following the examination of the draft state plan by the Soviet Government it is submitted for approval to the U.S.S.R. Supreme Soviet. The approved plan is forwarded to the Union Republics, ministries and departments which, in their turn, send it to the individual enterprises. Now that the volume of centralised appropriations for capital investments, the programme for the production of goods, targets for the growth of profitability, the introduction of new technology and so on, are definitely known, the major indices of each enterprise's plan are specified.

The next stage of planning work is shifted to the shops and sections of each enterprise. The factory management passes on to the shops their main targets, affording them every opportunity to display initiative in exploring internal resources.

The sections of a shop plan coincide in the main with the corresponding sections of the factory plan, but they are much simpler. For example, the supply plan of a shop is an estimate of the needs in materials, power, etc., without indicating where they are to come from. For the shop gets everything necessary from the factory warehouses and is not directly connected with the suppliers.

Plan assignments for teams are drawn up on the basis of the production programme of the given shop. Assignments to individual workers are usually given by the foreman, who takes into account the skill and abilities of each worker and also the need for the fullest use of equipment at each workplace.

To fulfil the annual programme well, quarterly plans are usually broken down in detail for ten-day periods, weeks, days, and in many cases even hours. To ensure guidance of plan fulfilment and to control the work of each section and shop is the most important and most difficult thing in the management of an enterprise. Large factories have special production-dispatcher departments whose task is to regulate the work and ensure rhythmical production of goods, not allowing interruptions or rush work. In the long run the successful work of the entire personnel in carrying out the state plan depends on their ability to organise emulation and help each worker cope with his output standard. In this, mass organisations play a very big part.

# 3

# Methods and Techniques of Calculating Long-term and Current plans

## I. HOW THE UNITY OF DIFFERENT PLANS IS ENSURED

In view of the number of different plans embracing all major aspects of the country's economic and cultural life, how do planners ensure the unity of this entire system? How do they manage to fit each plan into the others and place it in the general system, just as each brick is laid in its place in the wall of a building? Of course, the country's economic life itself is the common factor in all the different plans, which makes them parts of a single whole. The diversity of plans is a reflection of the diversity of forms of economic activity, diversity of economic ties and reciprocal dependencies. But although correct, this statement does not provide a full answer to the question. For there are many cases when the existence of a common factor does not lead automatically to unity of action. It is only when the single basis of any sphere of social relations is understood and the main scientific concepts are formulated in the same language that there can be unity and co-ordination in the work of different agencies taking part in a joint action.

The initial postulates, on which the formulation of all plans are based, are called methodological principles. These are the intrinsic demands and conditions for properly taking into account and using the objective laws governing economic development.

The following primary methodological principles of national economic planning can be singled out:

(1) democratic centralism;

(2) unity of politics and economics;

(3) scientific character of planning;

(4) proportional development based on singling out the key links of the economy;

(5) comprehensiveness and unity of the plan;

(6) stimulation of the personal and collective moral and material interest of the working people in the results of their labour;

(7) unity in formulating, verifying and securing fulfilment of the plan.

Let us consider each of these principles.

(1) Planning by the principle of *democratic centralism* implies the need to determine scientifically the general scale and growth-rate of production, the development-rate of sectors and districts and the decisive proportions in the economy, while leaving the detailed elaboration of the plan to enterprises and groups of enterprises. The active democratic participation of the working people makes it possible to study the best experience more fully and introduce it more swiftly, and to apply more efficiently ideas and projects engendered in the course of daily practical activity.

The combination of centralised state guidance with wide constructive initiative of local agencies and of the personnel of enterprises which have full operational independence in management ensures a unity between the general state plan targets, which encompass the main trends of economic development, and the plan projections of enterprises, districts, regions and Republics which take into account local possibilities and resources for the further growth of production and construction.

Development of the principle of democratic centralism in planning implies that the role of plans and proposals coming from below, beginning with the enterprises, will increase in the single national economic plan. At the same time, the role of centralised state guidance will be reinforced, because only such guidance, resting on the single state plan, can ensure the most rational and efficient use of the country's internal resources.

(2) The principle of *the unity of politics and economics* signifies that all questions of developing the economy and culture must be considered from the point of view of general state interests and of the interests of the entire economy. In socialist production the interests of a separate area, ministry, firm or enterprise do not run counter to the interests of the national economy as a whole, because each enterprise is an integral part of the whole. The unity of economics and politics is the leading principle of planned guidance of the entire economy. This unity, bringing change in policy because of changes in the economy, is expressed in national economic plans in the form of the unity and interdependence of the political and economic tasks which are set for the given planned period.

This postulate is of great importance for national economic planning and for the formulation of state plans, because a political approach to economic questions is a requisite for the proper organisation of planning and the successful carrying out of state plans.

Directives for the formulation of national economic plans, adopted at Congresses of the C.P.S.U., define the main links of the plan, the growth rates of key sectors, the scale of production in the main industries, etc. They ensure unity of purpose in drawing up the plan and introduce the necessary uniformity in work on the plan for the entire country from top to bottom.

The unity of politics and economics in planning is emphasised by the directive character of the major plan targets. Plans are a system of economic and political assignments which are set by the Communist Party and the Soviet Government and are aimed at building communism. Hence the purposeful and mobilising nature of these plans. National economic plans are obligatory state assignments. They are approved by the Supreme Soviet of the U.S.S.R. and assume the nature of law. Centralised guidance would be a mere wish if national economic plans did not have the force of law and were not obligatory.

(3) *The scientific character of planning* demands that plans be based on the utilisation of the objective laws governing social development and on a realistic account of the available resources and existing social-economic development level, and also of the resources which will be created in the course of plan fulfilment. The use of electronic computers and mathematical methods is of essential importance for raising the scientific level of planning.

Scientific planning is incompatible with "adventurism" and "hare-brained projects" in planning, with ignoring real conditions and accumulated experience. It is also incompatible with a mechanical "re-distribution" of plan targets when enterprises which fail properly to utilise their resources are given easier assignments.

The importance of enhancing the scientific level of planning was stressed in the decisions taken by the Central Committee of the C.P.S.U. at its plenary meeting in September 1965. They pointed out that the present scientific and technological revolution has placed in the forefront such questions as the technological level, the quality and reliability of equipment and its efficient use. Reflection of scientific and technological progress in plans is regarded as a prime condition for raising the efficiency of social production. Plans must be based on prospects of scientific and technological progress. They must provide for swift industrial application of scientific and technological achievements. A scientifically-based system of rates and standards for planning must be created.

The scientific character of planning, especially for long periods, is ensured by the wide enlistment of scientists, engineers, agronomists and technicians of different specialities in drafting plans. For example, more than 300 eminent scientists, including 72 members and corresponding members of the U.S.S.R. Academy of Sciences, took part in the work of the commissions set up by the U.S.S.R. Gosplan for formulating the major sections of the seven-year plan for 1959–65. More than 1,000 specialists took part in drawing up the development plan for the metallurgical industry; more than 800 for the electric power industry, and about 1,500 for the oil and gas industry.

The main purpose of scientific planning is to ensure the maximum saving of social labour and to raise the efficiency of the economy. The implementation of this principle means:

(i) to develop scientifically-based rating of the expenditure of labour, material and financial resources in production and distribution;

(ii) to bring to light and tap all the internal resources and potentialities of the national economy;

(iii) to eliminate all unproductive outlays, losses and extravagances in production and distribution;

(iv) to make the best use of commodity-money relations.

(4) *Ensuring adequate proportions in the economy by singling out the key links in economic development* is a primary methodological principle of scientific planning.

The proportions and ties in the national economy are diverse and intricate. They may be divided into the following main groups:

(i) general economic proportions (proportions between production and consumption, means of production and consumer goods, consumption and accumulation, incomes and consumption, the replacement fund and the national income);

(ii) proportions between sectors of the economy (between industry and agriculture, production and construction, production and transport, production and supply);

(iii) territorial proportions (between economic areas and within areas);

(iv) proportions within sectors of the national economy (extractive and manufacturing industry, engineering and metallurgy, crop-growing and animal husbandry, rail, water and road transport, etc.).

Proportionality in the development of the economy can be ensured only if it proceeds from the established key links of the national economic plan and the major economic problems of the plan period. By singling out the key links of the plan, the necessary resources are concentrated on the priority development of those sectors or areas which are decisive in the given period.

Applied to the aim of national economic planning, the postulate of the key link implies the demand to single out at each given moment the most important sections of the plan which are decisive for fulfilling the programme as a whole. A scientifically-based plan presupposes scientific choice of the principal key link of the plan.

This can be either an entire sector or separate sections of the economy, whose accelerated development makes it possible to cope with the main tasks of the plan. In selecting the key link it is very important that sectors of the economy be chosen which are in the main stream of scientific and technological progress, so that their development can help promote a general rise in the productivity of social labour.

Everything that can promote maximum growth rates in key branches of modern industry and agriculture is taken into account when drafting plans today. Other sectors are planned in conformity with the leading sectors. This is how the advance of the entire national economy and proportional combination of its sectors are achieved.

The principle of the key link is likewise a general principle of economic planning for the Union Republics, economic areas, industries and individual enterprises. In the case of a Republic, for example, it is determined on the basis of the general tasks of its economy, the Republic's economic and natural peculiarities, its specialisation in the national economy of the U.S.S.R., etc.

(5) *The principle of the unity and comprehensiveness* of plans was formulated by Lenin as follows: "All plans of separate sectors of production must be thoroughly co-ordinated and interlinked and make up the single economic plan we need so much." To apply this principle in planning means to use a single system of indices of the national economic plan, a single methodology of working out the plan targets.

Undertaking the formulation of a long-term plan, the U.S.S.R. Gosplan draws up general obligatory forms and indices of the plan, decides the dates of its preparation, and also the methods for working out plan projections, and forwards them to all the Union Republics, ministries and departments.

The principle of the unity and comprehensiveness of plans is realised by co-ordinating the plans of the Union Republic, ministries and departments through the system of balances and also with the help of elaborating and establishing proportions between sectors, areas and industries.

A few years ago attempts were made to implement the principle of the unity and comprehensiveness of the plan through the so-called "joining" of the plans of the Union Republics. Under this scheme, the U.S.S.R. Gosplan did not set any guide-lines in advance, but enterprises themselves, on their own initiative, drew up plans which were then combined and specified in the plans of Economic Councils and in the overall plans of the Union Republics. It was only at the concluding stage that the plans, finished in the main, were brought together in a single national economic plan. But life has demonstrated the insufficiency of such a simplified approach.

In the new conditions of planning and management comprehensive single and optimum plans for each link of the economy are drawn up on the basis of preliminary assignments received from the central planning agencies for the production of the major kinds of goods, the development of new technology and the volume of capital investments. Much attention is paid to stimuli aimed at bringing to light internal potentialities for raising the efficiency of production and the full *khozraschot* independence of enterprises in their operational economic activity.

(6) The successful accomplishment of the tasks which face national economic planning directly depends on how each production collective and each worker is interested in improving the activity of his section, shop, enterprise and sector as a whole. Hence the need to be guided by the *principle of stimulating the personal and collective, the material and moral interest of the working people in the results of their labour.*

In the Soviet Union at all stages of economic development much attention has been paid to combining the initiative of the masses with the maximum use of material stimuli to make the working people interested in developing production.

The general interests of the people, expressed in the national economic plans, can be realised only through the activity of enterprises which are the basic links of the country's economy.

What is of need and benefit to society must also be economically beneficial for each enterprise, for its personnel and for each worker. To be guided in planning by the principle of material incentive means to utilise such forms and methods of planned guidance and management as would stimulate enterprises to explore more efficient ways for satisfying the interests of the entire people. The recent decision on the economic reform of industry outlines a programme of action for the utmost development of economic stimuli. Let us mention some of the major components of this programme:

(i) a qualitatively new system of industrial production indices which orients enterprises on raising the efficiency of production instead of the old system which oriented enterprises on expanding production;

(ii) sharp reduction in the number of indices of a directive character and extension of the economic rights of enterprises in planning, use of their fixed and circulating assets, making capital investments, utilising manpower and rewarding their workers;

(iii) strengthening the direct link between the size of the wages fund and material stimulation funds (incentive fund, fund for social and cultural measures and housing construction), on the one hand, and the volume of goods sold and profit obtained, on the other.

This system of assessing and stimulating activity makes an enterprise directly interested in fulfilling high plan assignments and, consequently, in fully and efficiently using productive assets, manpower and financial resources.

The principle of providing material incentives to the worker follows from the law of distribution according to work which operates under socialism: "From each according to his ability, to each according to his work." Distribution according to work makes the working people materially interested in the results of production, stimulates labour productivity, helps to improve the workers' skill and the technology of production.

Socialist society has a method of distributing necessities and benefits in which the share of every one in the distributed social product is determined by what he contributes in socially useful work. Socialism implements the economic law of distribution according to work, which expresses the intrinsic connection between the labour contributed to society by each worker individually and the size of the remuneration he receives from society. The more productive the labour of the worker, the more material and spiritual wealth he creates, the more he receives from society and the higher the well-being of all the people.

(7) The formulation of a plan, even of a perfect one, is only the first step in national economic planning.

Ensuring plan fulfilment is an important aspect of planning. The *principle of unity in formulating, verifying and ensuring fulfilment of plan* is one of the most important methodological principles of scientific economic planning. Constant verification of plan fulfilment, the use of verification for introducing corrections in the plan and rectifying mistakes, the disclosure and tapping of new resources and internal potentialities in the course of verification in order to fulfil the plan— these are obligatory conditions for guaranteeing plan fulfilment.

Verification of plan fulfilment makes it possible to bring to light and take into account not only existing resources which for some reason or other fail to be used, but also the resources for economic and cultural development which are created in the course of carrying out the plan.

## 2. TECHNIQUES OF CALCULATION FOR PLANS

We have examined the main methodological principles of planning. Closely associated with them are methods and systems for calculating and co-ordinating plan indices, methods of analysing plan fulfilment by separate sectors and indices.

The methods of planning include not only the techniques of calculating the single national economic plan, but also the calculations needed for planning separate sectors and areas, separate elements of production, distribution and exchange, and the use of the product and income. For this reason the experience of allied economic sciences is utilised in the general and specific methods of planning. These include an analysis of economic activity, bookkeeping, mathematical and economic statistics, sectoral economics and economic geography. Mathematical methods have been increasingly employed in recent years.

Several main methods of formulating, checking and analysing plans have been developed. These include:

(1) analysis of economic activity;

(2) technical and economic calculations;

(3) balance method for co-ordinating all sections and indices of the plan to ensure proportionality in the development of separate sectors and branches of the economy;

(4) mathematical methods and models.

Technical and economic calculations, the balance method and mathematical methods are inseparably connected through the use of systems of rates and standards of production, exchange, consumption and accumulation of goods, rates for the expenditure of means of production, manpower and financial resources and rates for the organisation of production.

Let us describe these methods.

(1) *Methods of analysing economic activity.* The initial point in the process of drafting a plan is the analysis of the state of the economy in the period preceding the plan. That is why a deep and thorough study of the initial level, summing up the practical experience in the pre-plan period, precedes the work of calculating the plan for the next period.

The main task in analysing the initial level is to reveal new potentialities, whose tapping will make it possible to accelerate the country's economic growth. These potentialities are taken into account when drawing up national economic plans and, what is most important, in the course of their fulfilment, in order to exceed the state assignments.

The analysis of the existing proportions in the development of separate sectors and the ascertainment of their tendencies are of a comprehensive nature because progress of a sector or an area is studied from the viewpoint of the needs of the entire economy, in comparison with the results of operation in allied sectors and branches. The purpose of such an analysis is to ensure conformity between (a) the concrete needs of the given area or sector, (b) the needs of the country as a whole and (c) the resources for satisfying these needs, so as to establish the degree of conformity between production and consumption.

An analysis of development of the national economy includes a study of the existing proportions within each sector, between allied sectors, within the bounds of separate Republics and economic areas, and, lastly, proportions between areas. This makes it possible properly to co-ordinate allied sectors, and to reveal the needs in capital construction, development of transport, etc.

In analysing existing national economic proportions comparisons are not limited to the material elements of production. The wages fund and other incomes of the population are compared with the output of consumer goods, with the volume of goods available for the market and the paid services rendered to the population.

A study of proportions brings out the general and particular tendencies of national economic development and makes it easier to influence them purposefully in one or another direction. This is how the Soviet Government, on the basis of an analysis of the level of economic development, takes measures to change national economic proportions.

Of great importance is comparison of interdependent data on productive activity in allied sectors and enterprises of the same type, an analysis of reserves for better use of productive capacity, raising labour productivity and saving raw materials and fuel. Such a study concretely shows how fully the needs of the economy are satisfied and to what extent the requirements of planned proportional development are observed.

Economic analysis encompasses a wide range of questions pertaining to the activities of enterprises, organisations and institutions, territorial economic agencies, separate sectors, etc. To draw up a plan it is necessary to have not only an all-round analysis of fulfilment of plan assignments by an enterprise, sector, etc., in the current period, but also an analysis of the changes in ties and proportions.

An analysis, of course, is not confined to examination of average indices, results, actual rates, etc. It is differentiated by groups of enterprises of one type, groups of collective farms, etc. The experience of leading enterprises which have achieved the best results is carefully studied in order to work out how to get the best results in drafting the next plan.

To set plan assignments for industry, construction and transport it is very important to analyse the maximum level of production, goods transport, etc., achieved in the period under review.

An analysis of a country's economic situation in the pre-plan period is completed by a general assessment of the level of economic development and the living standard of the population. This assessment proceeds from the country's real natural-economic potential as compared with similar data from other economically-developed countries. For example, the available natural resources and the degree of their use, the productive capacity and the demand for corresponding goods, commodity stocks and level of consumption are compared. Again, a comparison is made between the scale of production and other economic indices. Such comparisons of the scale, rates and proportions at later stages of planning make it possible to find criteria and optimum boundaries of plan targets.

The working methods used in an analysis are comparisons, employment of a system of interconnected analytical indices, selective study of the operation of separate enterprises, comparative analysis of kindred enterprises, aggregation, price substitutions, balance dovetailing of indices, calculation of indices, calculation of correlation coefficients and also other statistical methods.

(2) *Methods of technical and economic calculation.* All projections of production growth in separate sectors are based on detailed technical and economic calculations of both the demand for the given goods and the possible output.

To work out assignments for production growth in each sector planners use specific technical and economic calculations.

In industry such calculations include:

(a) improvement in the use of available capacity and increase in capacity of operating enterprises through reconstruction, intensification of production processes and improvement of productive organisation;

(b) commissioning of new enterprises and shops;

(c) improvement in the use and increase in the resources of raw materials and other supplies, fuel and power and the use of substitutes instead of the main raw materials;

(d) rise in labour productivity;

(e) change in the number of workers;

(f) reduction of production costs,

and many other calculations.

In agriculture determination of the volume of output is ensured by the following calculations:

(a) increase in cultivated agricultural land, in the sown area and in the head of livestock;

(b) increase in the yield of crops and productivity of livestock.

To bring out the economic efficiency of producing some or other goods in different areas the unit labour expenditure is calculated.

Assignments for the main activity in sectors (production, construction, goods carriage, etc.) are obtained by technical and economic calculations of productive capacity, supplies and the number of people engaged in productive labour. The checking of production assignments in relation to financial resources is of great importance.

Detailed calculations are also needed to set plan assignments in socio-cultural development. These assignments are based on rates or standards which regulate all sides of activity of the establishments and organisations in this sphere.

Calculation of the economic efficiency of introducing new technology, mechanising and automating production processes and organising

E

new categories of production hold a special place among the technical and economic calculations used in national economic planning.

(3) *The balance method.* The balance method has been put forward as the leading method in formulating national economic plans both by practical experience and by the theory of national economic planning.

The balance method in planning, statistics and accounting signifies a sum-total of methods used to ensure the dovetailing and co-ordination of interconnected indices. However different these indices, the purpose of this method is the same—to achieve balance between the interconnected indices.

The balance method is widely used in the most diverse spheres of science, technology and the economy in the form of balance calculations or special tables which are called "balances". It is an important instrument for bringing to light disproportions in the economy, and for determining the necessary proportions and growth rates of the economy.

In practice, the use of balance methods in planning requires the working out of a system of balances which encompass all sections of the national economic plan. In their sum-total the indices of the balances must reflect the proportions and ties of the national economy not only statistically but also dynamically.

A plan at any level (enterprise, association, ministry, Republic, the national economic plan) can be constructed only by using a widely ramified system of various balances. This system, utilised in formulating, verifying and ensuring the fulfilment of a national economic plan, includes (a) balances of the material elements of production, consumption and accumulation, (b) balances of manpower, and (c) financial balances.

(a) The system of balances of the material elements of production, consumption and accumulation is the best developed. This system includes, first, balances of natural resources; second, balances of productive capacity; third, balances of fixed assets and, fourth, material balances as such.

*Balances of natural resources* express the state of and changes in the major natural conditions of social production. Balances of all land, agricultural lands, ploughland and water resources serve as a point of departure in drawing up agricultural development plans. Balances of the reserves of metallic and non-metallic minerals, forests, water resources, etc., underlie plans for the development of the extractive industries.

*Balances of productive capacity* express the situation in the sectors of the economy and changes during the plan period. They ensure the connection between the resources of productive capacity and the needs of the national economy for the most important industrial goods; and between the resources and needs of the economy in power capacity.

The balance of productive capacity is drawn up in two variants: for establishing the construction programme of the national economic plan and for establishing the production programme of industry.

The balance of productive capacity for different sectors is the main planning document on which are based capital investments and their allocation between branches of industry or between sectors of the economy. The proper allocation of capital investments is impossible without verified and detailed balances characterising the resources of productive capacity, the need in capacity, its availability and use.

The second variant is balances of the use of productive capacity, which express the level of utilisation of available capacity and capacity to be commissioned during the operation of the plan.

*Balance of fixed assets.* This is a system of interconnected indices characterising the process of reproducing fixed assets. This system includes indices of assets at the beginning of the period, commissioning of new assets, deduction of obsolete assets and assets available at the end of the period. Indices of depreciation of assets and capital overhauling are of great importance.

*Material balances proper* are most widely represented in national economic plans, and are divided into two groups depending on their economic designation: (a) balances of the means of production and (b) balances of consumer goods. Such a classification is, naturally, in part conventional.

Material balances used in framing national economic plans cover only industrial and agricultural goods of key significance for the major economic tasks of the state plan. Material balances for planning purposes are drawn up for rolled steel, major non-ferrous metals, coal, oil products, main types of machinery and equipment, electric power, basic chemicals, timber and building materials, manufactured goods and foodstuffs and agricultural raw material. Balances of production and consumption of major material resources in the Union Republics, economic areas, regions, territories and cities are acquiring ever greater importance.

*Manpower balances* are widely used in drawing up national economic plans. To fulfil a production programme and meet the quantitative and qualitative assignments of the plan a sector must have the necessary production personnel of requisite skill. Manpower balances ensure co-ordination of the requirements of separate sectors and areas with the resources of labour power and skilled personnel.

Lastly, *financial balances* make up the third major group of balances in the national economic plan.

With their help it is possible to secure an all-round tie-up between production, distribution and circulation of goods in their material form, on the one hand, and the formation and use of the incomes of enterprises, collective farms and the population, on the other.

The main financial balances are: the state budget—the country's principal financial plan; the balances of the income and expenditure of enterprises, departments and ministries, the cash and credit plans of the State Bank and specialised banks; the balance of the money income and expenditure of the population; the overall financial plan of the state.

The preparation of balances is not an aim in itself but a means of complying with the requirements of socialism's objective economic laws. The role of the balance method in planning must not be over-estimated; the main thing is the content of the balances themselves.

(4) *Methods and models of mathematical economics.* Planning agencies increasingly employ mathematical methods in their economic planning and calculations, and also modern computation techniques which have created the possibility of drawing up optimum plans. Greater emphasis on elements of quantitative analysis and the employment of mathematical methods in economic science helps to improve planning. The use of these methods enables scientists to solve definite tasks of economic management and planning with much greater precision.

The use of modern mathematical methods in the economy presupposes the preliminary elaboration of macro-economic models which contain the main quantitative and qualitative characteristics of the studied processes and phenomena and are usually expressed by a system of equations. Of course, a model is always a simplified reflection of reality, since models take into account only those forms of the process which are most important in the given concrete conditions.

A provisional balance of the national economy, inter-sectoral balances of production and consumption of goods, matrix models of sectoral plans and plans of enterprises are the most important macro-economic models used in planning.

Various methods can be employed for finding solutions with the help of macro-economic models. Thus, the finding of the limit of a function is now done with the help of methods of linear programming.

Linear programming has been introduced in planning quite recently, but some experience has already been accumulated and the range of problems successfully solved with the help of linear programming has been established.

First of all these are problems of production planning, the drawing up of an optimum programme for the output of goods with the given manpower and material resources or the optimum use of the productive capacity of an enterprise. The optimum can be either the cost of processing the goods, the time the equipment is used or the volume of output which has to be brought up to the maximum figure through the most efficient use of the equipment. If the assortment of produced goods is diverse, if the equipment or the combination of operations is periodically changed, an optimum solution of such problems is achieved only with the help of linear programming, which makes it possible not only to improve the use of productive capacity but also to enhance the precision of planning by strictly dovetailing the contemplated scale of production with the optimum possibilities of the enterprise, with its resources.

Sectoral planning presents a similar problem, i.e. the problem of distribution of the planned assortment of goods between enterprises in the given sector, taking into account their productive capacity and other production distinctions (for example, the distribution of orders by enterprises in the serial production of machinery). A specific group of production problems is presented by the rational cutting of industrial materials (timber, glass, steel sheet, pipes, etc.) or the making of mixtures used in many branches of industry that produce alloys, mixtures and compounds —the metallurgical, chemical, food and other industries.

Methods of linear programming are most effective in determining dietary standards, in planning changes of prices, and in working out measures designed to raise the living standard of the people and increase consumption.

Great possibilities are held out by the use of linear programming when planning agricultural production for distributing the sown area between different crops, national planning of crop rotation, calculation of an optimum combination of sectors in agriculture, determination of the best composition of the livestock herd, the most efficient feed rations for livestock, and so on.

The so-called transport problem of linear programming is of great practical importance (it is elaborated in particular detail and there are special simplified methods of solution). A model of a transport problem is successfully applied for planning the shipment of coal from several deposits to places of consumption; cement from cement mills to the consuming areas; sea transportation of oil and oil products; air transportation of passengers and freight; optimum transportation within big cities (transportation of building materials to construction sites, various mass-consumption goods from warehouses to shops, removal of excavated earth, etc.).

Another variant of the transport problem makes it possible to choose the best location of new enterprises: calculations for the most favourable location of cement mills, factories producing building materials and mineral fertilisers or processing industrial and agricultural raw materials (coke plants, oil refineries, food factories), as well as other calculations for the location of warehouses, etc. This list of the applications of linear programming in planning is far from complete.

The Lagrangian multiplier, simplex (basic solutions), distribution, graphic, potentials and matrix methods are the most widely used linear programming methods for planning purposes.

The graphic method is the simplest and most illustrative. But it is useful only if there are two variables. Three variables complicate the solution and four make it impossible. That is why this method is little used.

The full possibilities of linear programming can only be realised by employing electronic computers.

Electronic computers perform all elementary arithmetical operations (addition, subtraction, multiplication and division); they are capable of performing at tremendous speed any operation performed by mechanical calculating machines. But alongside arithmetical operations electronic computers can automatically perform various logical operations. The ability automatically to pass from some arithmetical operations to others and from arithmetical operations to logical and vice versa allows the solution of the most diverse mathematical problems, including those that cannot be solved with the help of ordinary calculating machines because of the colossal expenditure of time.

Another major field of applying electronic computers is in the automatic control of manufacturing processes, shops, factories, electric power stations and transport systems.

The method of *variation approximations* which has been applied in planning for many decades holds a special place.

Its essence is as follows. The compilers of a long-term plan for one or another sector have to deal with many unknowns. They do not know the demand for the articles of the given sector because there is as yet no plan for the development of the consuming sectors. Nor do they know the raw material possibilities and the available capital investments. All sectors are in a similarly uncertain position because each one is connected with many other sectors, and for the solution of all the problems in the given sector it is necessary to have the entire national economic plan. Therefore, at first, a very approximate draft plan is drawn up by sectors, starting with the extractive industries. The planners proceed from the most favourable conditions. Naturally, the calculations are made not for all branches of industry and agriculture but for a group of the key branches. In the process of further work these original programmes by sectors are altered on the basis of balances which reveal the ties of the sectors with the national economy. Before an acceptable plan, in which all sectors are co-ordinated, is finally drawn up several variants of the plan are usually prepared. From the mathematical viewpoint the variation method is in effect a method of successive approximations.

When imbalance of the resources of production (and imports) of some goods and the needs of the national economy (and exports) is revealed, successive adjustments are made by changing the plans of sectors which produce or consume these goods to restore the balance. Inasmuch as a change in the production plan of some sector leads to a change of its demand for other goods, it is necessary, when achieving balance for one kind of goods, to undertake the balancing of others and from them return to the first.

The estimating of resources serves as the common basis between the balance method, the method of technical and economic calculations and the variant method. Estimating means establishing general obligatory limits of the unit production inputs or utmost limits of the consumption of goods. No planned economy is possible without this.

### 3. CALCULATING RESOURCES AND CONSUMPTION

The ultimate aim of all national economic plans in the U.S.S.R. is the fullest satisfaction of society's needs. But what are "the needs of society"?

In the most general way they can be defined as the conditions objectively needed for living. They are expressed in a definite sum-total of material and spiritual necessities and comforts and reflect the intrinsic tendencies of society's development at a given level of science, technology, culture and social life.

In the U.S.S.R. planning of the economy is comprehensive and rests on a thorough assessment of the people's current and long-term requirements. People need many things and they are also concerned with the fate of succeeding generations. That is why Soviet planners, while calculating present-day requirements, always take into account, first, how these needs will grow in future and, second, what part of the created income and material resources must be expended in the form of accumulations to ensure the future.

An essential element of society's needs is first of all the need of material production itself. A considerable part of society's productive capacity and labour time must be expended to operate the numerous enterprises in the extractive industry and agriculture. The goods produced by these enterprises go chiefly for productive consumption in the form of fuel burned by factories, electric power stations, locomotives and ships; of electric power which sets into motion diverse mechanisms; metals, building materials and chemicals which go for the making of installations and machines for the extractive sectors.

Social needs include the need to accumulate resources for the expansion of production, because without this society cannot develop, and also the need to accumulate insurance stocks and reserves to protect the country from any exigency.

The satisfaction of needs presupposes the existence of appropriate resources. Since the production of goods requires a certain combination of the instruments of labour, materials and workers, the potentialities for satisfying the growing requirements largely depend on elements which are included in the overall concept of society's resources, namely, operating and potential productive capacity; the available and potential increase of raw materials and other supplies; the size of the population, its growth and changing composition; and labour productivity.

The resources which society possesses in the planned period consist of two main items: (a) resources available at the beginning of the period, and (b) resources created in the course of plan fulfilment. For a current plan, designed for one or two years, the volume of such resources as productive capacity and the size and composition of the population can be reduced to the first item (although for separate sectors and separate areas the accretion in the course of the year can be considerable in the balance of resources). It is equally obvious that for a long-term plan, especially for a general plan covering a period of 15 or 20 years, the second item is of great importance.

The planned organisation of the economy in the U.S.S.R. allows for the rational use of labour in the interest of the whole of society. It makes it possible to estimate in advance the needs of the national economy (separate sectors, enterprises, areas) in manpower and correspondingly to take measures to satisfy them.

The use of manpower resources in the U.S.S.R. is characterised by:

(i) the systematic increase in the number of people employed in the national economy;

(ii) systematic qualitative changes in the composition of the working people: cultural and technical advancement of the workers, systematic improvement of skills, etc.;

(iii) the planned steady improvement of the working and living conditions of the working people.

Rational allocation and efficient use of manpower resources in the national economy is a primary task of planning. It is accomplished in the U.S.S.R. with the help of manpower balances.

The economy of the U.S.S.R., which is steadily and proportionally developing on the basis of public ownership of the means of production, ensures a swift growth of the population engaged in social production.

The 1959 census returns show that from 1939 to 1959 the population engaged in social production increased by 12·2 per cent, while the total population rose 9·5 per cent. The employed population in the U.S.S.R. constitutes 47·5 per cent of the total, while in the United States, for example, it is only 35 per cent.

Employment of the population in the working age-groups is considerably higher in the U.S.S.R. than in the United States. In 1959, almost 90 per cent of the able-bodied population were gainfully employed or were studying, while in the United States the corresponding figure was about 70 per cent (in 1958).

The planned proportional development of the national economy in the U.S.S.R. makes it possible to ascertain in good time the need for manpower, systematically to organise the training of personnel and rationally to allocate the workers by sectors of the economy and production sections on a countrywide scale.

In addition to labour resources, the potentialities for economic growth are also determined by the capacity of the productive machine in major sectors of the economy and the natural raw-material and power resources.

A balance of productive capacity is a primary instrument in drawing up the production programme of industry. The balance is calculated at each enterprise by the Republican Gosplans, and for key industries by the U.S.S.R. Gosplan.

Technological progress and directly related capital construction are the main sources for the growth and improvement of production. In socialist society the main aim of technological progress is to ensure the utmost saving of social labour, to ease work and, on this basis, attain high growth-rates of social production. For this purpose diverse measures are annually applied in industry, construction, agriculture and transport. All of them can be combined in several groups, each characterising a particular trend in the development of technology. The main trends of development are electrification and chemicalisation of production processes, mechanisation and automation of production. Such trends as the application of electronics, of rocketry and, especially, nuclear technology have increasingly emerged in recent years.

Each of these trends of technological progress is assigned specific tasks in the state plans.

The plan for the development of new technology and the production programme are interconnected in the state plan. On the one hand, technological progress is a primary element in the production programme; on the other, the planning of technological progress depends on such indicators of the production programme as the growth rates of the engineering, chemical and other industries.

How are society's needs determined? We have said that the social needs include:

(a) the need for means of production for the current process of material production;

(b) the need for means of production and consumer goods to ensure in the future period the expansion of production and also an increase in reserve and insurance funds;

(c) the need for consumer goods to satisfy the requirements of the population;

(d) the need for consumer goods to maintain administrative and scientific establishments.

The need for means of production for current material production, capital construction and reserve and insurance funds is determined on the basis of the production and construction programmes of the plan and also of the consumption rates. Planners utilise as rates aggregated national economic coefficients and aggregated sectoral rates which characterise the full magnitude of unit inputs in each sector, taking into account the sum-total of ties in the national economy. The national economic coefficients are established by analysing the balances for a number of years and by studying possible tendencies in the plan period as regards changes in coefficients owing to technological progress and the introduction of new materials.

To determine the need for consumer goods to satisfy the demands of the population is a matter of prime importance.

The needs of the population grow continually. This law of growing needs, which operates in the economy, is objectively based, above all, on the development of production, which brings about a rise in the efficiency of production, intensification of labour, changes in living conditions and consolidation of ties between countries and between areas within a country. The expansion of production changes the working and living conditions of the people, gives rise to new requirements and alters the composition of needs. Broader and stronger ties between countries and nations are an important factor engendering new requirements. The cultural advance of the population essentially affects the nature of requirements. As needs rise, consumption steadily grows.

The overall growth of people's needs in socialist society has two specific features: (a) high growth rates of needs among *all* sections of the population, and (b) gradual *elimination of differences* in the pattern and level of needs of the intelligentsia, factory and office workers and peasants.

At the present level of socialist society's development, needs are expressed in the value (monetary) form as effective demand. The continuous increase in the demand for consumer goods is a feature of the Soviet economy. It is illustrated above all by the dynamics of retail trade. It we take the volume of state and co-operative retail trade in 1928 as 100, it was (in comparable prices) 233 in 1940, 257 in 1950, 758 in 1960, and 1,016 in 1965; in 1970 it is expected to be 1,458, about 44 per cent above the 1965 level.

Simultaneously, the gap between the level and composition of demand in town and country is being steadily closed. The ratio of retail trade per urban and rural resident in pre-revolutionary Russia was 16 : 1; in 1928 it was 9·2 : 1; in 1940, 5·2 : 1; in 1960, 3·4 : 1; in 1964, 2·9 : 1. The goods composition of rural retail trade is strikingly changing. In 1924/25, salt, paraffin oil, matches, laundry soap and cotton goods claimed 35 per cent of all retail sales in the countryside. In 1963, the share of these five items was only 5 per cent, though their total sales had increased tremendously. In 1964, the rural population bought 6·4 million clocks and watches, 1·5 million wireless sets and radiograms, 547,000 TV sets, 123,000 refrigerators, 319,000 motor-cycles and motor scooters, 1·9 million bicycles and mopeds, and 780,000 sewing machines. Between 1952 and 1963 the sale of sugar increased almost 5 times, various tinned goods 5·5 times, and salted herring 4·5 times.

An increase in consumption is accompanied by deep qualitative changes in the composition of demand. Here are some figures:

| | 1940 | 1950 | 1960 | 1964 |
|---|---|---|---|---|
| Total sales | 100 | 110 | 326 | 396 |
| All foodstuffs | 100 | 94 | 264 | 332 |
| of which | | | | |
| milk and dairy products including cheese | 100 | 94 | 567 | 726 |
| sugar | 100 | 128 | 420 | 538 |
| flour, bread and bakery products | 100 | 90 | 169 | 182 |
| All non-food goods | 100 | 140 | 434 | 505 |
| of which | | | | |
| Silk fabrics | 100 | 220 | 979 | 945 |
| knitted goods | 100 | 116 | 515 | 706 |
| wireless sets | 100 | 637 | 27 times | 29 times |
| furniture | 100 | 96 | 692 | 1,100 |
| bicycles and mopeds | 100 | 342 | 15 times | 17 times |

The relationship between the retail demand for raw materials and semi-manufactures and for manufactured goods is changing. In 1928, the ratio of retail sales of fabrics to clothing and knitted goods was 3 : 1 while in 1963 it was 1 : 2·4. In 1925/26, the demand for leather was five times bigger than for ready footwear, while now there is no retail demand for it at all. In 1928, the demand for flour was greater than for bread, while in 1962, it was about 22 per cent of that for baked bread.

The steady growth of needs dictates, first, a swift increase and improvement in the production of consumer goods, and second, a steady extension of their assortment. At the same time the structure of production of consumer goods must ensure definite proportionality in the development of separate sectors, which applies above all to allied inter-connected sectors. Thus, the development level of the clothing industry must bear a definite relationship with that of the textile industry; of the footwear industry with the leather industry; of the food industry with agriculture, etc.

In determining the size of the consumption fund for a long-term period economists start with an analysis of the so-called initial (or basic) consumer's budget of one person. This is a special balance calculation based on processing data of the balance of the population's money income and expenditure, the balance of commodity resources and trade and the balance of agricultural produce.

The consumer's budget is elaborated *per capita* of population and also separately for the urban and rural population, for workers and peasants and for separate groups with different income levels. A budget for a long-term period is calculated on the basis of the initial period. For this purpose planners utilise data on consumption rates of foodstuffs as required for health, rational consumption rates of non-food goods and also standards for the adequate provision of services by cultural and other establishments.

Such maximum rational rates of the main consumer goods which, according to contemporary scientific ideas, satisfy, within reasonable bounds, the requirements of society's members, figure in planning as *general long-term consumption rates*. They are elaborated within the bounds of the feasible increase of production and purchasing power in the next 15 or 20 years. For some consumer goods these rates can be attained in the near future, and for other goods in more distant periods.

Alongside the general long-term rates, rational *planned consumption rates* are drawn up which are to be achieved at each definite period of the plan in conformity with the possible level of production and of incomes. These planned rates are consecutive steps for the gradual attainment of the general long-term consumption rates.

General long-term rates are not, however, immutable, given once and for all. As social production expands, the people advance culturally, the scientific study of consumption is further developed, and consumption rates are adjusted and changed.

Two groups of factors are considered when working out rational consumption rates:

(a) socio-economic factors—level of production, level of technology and labour productivity, the class composition of the population, the level of incomes, professional composition and cultural level;

(b) natural historical conditions—the physiology of man, climatic features of separate areas, the traditions of peoples and nationalities.

To take fuller and more correct account of different factors which determine consumption, economists differentiate consumption rates by groups of population and also geographically (territorially). *Per capita* consumption rates can be established only as average weighed differentiated rates, taking into account the future composition of the population and its future territorial distribution.

Scientific consumption rates of foodstuffs represent a scientifically-based diet which is fully adequate for nutrition and takes into account differences resulting from climatic conditions, distinctions of national food habits, etc.

Consumption rates of clothing and footwear are differentiated for three climatic zones: (a) cold, (b) temperate and (c) warm.

To take into consideration distinctions in clothing, footwear and other consumer goods, alongside general consumption rates (for the U.S.S.R. as a whole), additional rates are elaborated for separate Union Republics and areas.

National rates represent the quantity of consumer goods the population needs to buy annually to restore the worn-out part of its clothing, footwear, etc.

Rational rates are calculated on the basis of an approximate outfit of clothes and footwear for a family of four. Proceeding from the periods of the physical wear and fashion-obsolescence of articles, economists ascertain the quantity of fabrics, knitted goods and footwear needed for replenishing the annual wear and tear.

Rational consumption rates are worked out by summarising the available statistical and practical data, and also on the basis of appraisals by scientists and experts repeatedly verified by experiments and discussions. Materials of budget surveys play a large part in substantiating consumption rates.

An idea of the rational consumption rates of foodstuffs and of non-food goods can be gained from the table on the next page.

The expenditure on science is determined on the basis of the plan for research in science and engineering and the plan for applying the results of these studies in the national economy. Development of the social and natural sciences is planned by the U.S.S.R. Academy of Sciences and of the technical and agricultural sciences by the ministries. The State Committee for Science and Technology holds a leading place in planning the development of the respective spheres. The outlays on science grow very swiftly both relatively and absolutely.

| Foodstuffs | Unit of measurement | Annual consumption per capita |
|---|---|---|
| Meat | kg | 87 |
| Fish | ,, | 16 |
| Milk and dairy products | ,, | 467 |
| Sugar | ,, | 44 |
| Eggs | pcs | 365 |
| Potatoes | kg | 120 |
| Non-Food goods | | |
| Cotton fabrics | sq m | 37·4 |
| Woollens | ,, ,, | 5·1 |
| Silk fabrics | ,, ,, | 10·3 |
| Linen fabrics | ,, ,, | 5·2 |
| Total | | 58·0 |
| Non-spun fabrics | ,, ,, | 2·0 |
| Knitted underwear and garments | pieces | 8·25 |
| Leather footwear | pairs | 3·3 |

The following data illustrate the growth of the Soviet Union's expenditure on science.

*Expenditure on Science and the Training of Personnel in Higher Educational Establishments Covered by the Budget of the U.S.S.R.*

| | 1940 | 1950 | 1960 | 1964 |
|---|---|---|---|---|
| Science, million roubles | 113 | 539 | 2,339 | 3,971 |
| per cent | 100 | 480 | 2,100 | 3,450 |
| Higher Educational Establishments (million roubles) | 288 | 721 | 1,167 | 1,450 |
| per cent | 100 | 250 | 400 | 500 |
| Total, million roubles | 401 | 1,260 | 3,506 | 5,421 |
| per cent | 100 | 310 | 870 | 1,360 |

In determining the scale of the expenditure, account is taken of the trends of research in science and engineering not only in the Soviet Union but in all highly developed countries.

In contrast to the outlays on science, the expenditure on the maintenance of administrative institutions is steadily reduced relatively (in the total expenditure) and also in absolute figures.

After determining the potential resources for economic development and calculating social needs of every kind, comes a job of great importance and complexity—co-ordination of resources and needs.

Several variants of the balance of the given resources are drawn up and verified and ways of reaching the optimum in production and consumption are outlined. Mathematical methods and electronic computers assume ever greater significance in this work. Since the co-ordination of resources and needs includes all kinds of resources—material, manpower and financial—and needs of every kind, a multifarious system of balances is brought into action, specific, synthetic and global balances. At the initial stages of drafting national economic plans, the dovetailing of resources and needs and the establishment of the most efficient proportions in the economy are attained through the extensive use of economic models for planning purposes.

Let us see what economic models are utilised in planning.

### 4. THE USES OF MODELS

The method of simulating or modelling designed machines, devices or structures has long been used in industry and construction. Apart from making it possible to visualise his project as a finished product, the model enables the designer to put it through its paces and to check its behaviour under realistic operational conditions. A thorough test of a model may minimise the unforeseen in the operation or maintenance of structures, machines, devices, etc. Simulation or modelling is used very extensively in many fields of production, science and engineering.

To construct an economico-mathematical model means to express the functional dependences of a given economic process in mathematical terms.

To be able to do so we must ascertain the quantitative relationships between the economic indices of the process under study. Now, these involve the qualitative aspect of any economic process. Therefore, a qualitative socio-economic analysis of it must be basic to its economico-mathematical model. Most often it is practically impossible to express mathematically the influences and interactions of all factors involved without exception. Therefore, the model is restricted to the key factors, to decisive relationships and dependencies. Even then the mathematical model of an economic problem, or economico-mathematical model, constitutes as a rule a highly complex set of equations and several conditions expressed by inequalities. Such a model may be a system of interrelated tables with a series of initial data and quantities to be determined.

Naturally, an economico-mathematical model is always simpler or poorer than the actual economic problem the model represents. Yet all kinds of experiments can be made on such a model, it can be analysed, and finally the best solutions can be found.

It is the analysis of the economico-mathematical model with the aid of mathematical techniques that constitutes the main stage of the treatment of an economico-mathematical problem. A vast volume of computations characteristic of this class of problems is effectively done with powerful digital computers.

The simplest model is a function of economic parameters. A number of economic dependencies can be expressed by a function of one variable—linear, parabolic, hyperbolic, exponential, logarithmic, etc. Each of these functions represents a definite type of quantitative dependence. Functions of one variable as well as of several variables are used. The model-function applies to an economic process which depends on one or several basic factors. For example, the consumption of a commodity by identically composed families depends mainly on their income.

When it is found difficult to establish immediately the dependence between certain variables, recourse is had to establishing the dependence between these variables and their increments. This leads to differential equations by which the dependencies between the functions themselves can be found.

More intricate economic processes are modelled by a set of equations. Sets of linear algebraic equations are usually used for describing statistical processes (e.g. the distribution of available resources).

Techniques furnished by the theory of probability and mathematical statistics have long been extensively used in Soviet economic planning. Linear programming and inter-sectoral input-output analysis are now being effectively developed and applied with the aid of electronic computers.

Highly promising methods of dynamic programming have been developed in recent years. Suppose the problem is to determine the maximum output of automobiles over a long-term period, taking into account the input-output relations of automobile building with other sectors. The problem can be solved in many ways. A lot of steel can be put immediately into the production of automobiles. Alternatively, more steel can first be put into the expansion of automobile-building enterprises to produce more vehicles somewhat later. An important feature of such problems is the development of the best procedure to obtain the best results.

The major economico-mathematical models applied for planning the Soviet national economy are: (a) the preliminary or provisional input-output table of the national economy and (b) the inter-sectoral input-output table of national production and consumption.

Let us consider the application of the provisional table to planning.

The most general targets of the national economic plan for a certain period are determined quantitatively by developing the input-output table of the national economy.

The table is a system of several input-output subtables co-ordinating the entire set of aggregate economic indicators describing the process of socialist production and its results for the period accounted or planned.

The input-output table of the national economy is used for determining the scale and rate of development of production for a planned period and projecting the proportions, corresponding to general economic laws and specific targets of production, between the state sector and the collective-farm and co-operative sector, between sections of society, and between the two subdivisions of production (I, the production of producers' goods and II, production of consumer goods).

The basic structural components of the table are:

(1) A summary selection including a summary table, a reproduction table for basic sectors, a table of fixed assets, and a table of levels, proportions and rates of national economic development.

(2) A table of production, distribution and consumption of products, with tables of means of production (producers' goods) and objects of consumption (consumer goods).

(3) A table of production, distribution and final consumption of the national income, with tables of financial relations between the state, co-operatives, collective farms and private persons and a table of private cash incomes and expenses.

(4) A table of labour resources.

The development of the national-economic plan, which is, essentially, a plan of socialist economic reproduction, is impossible without determining the necessary proportions and relations in the economy for the period planned.

It is only by the summary input-output table of the national economy that all major national-economic proportions can be computed in their dynamics, mutual relation and inter-dependence.

In long-term national planning the provisional input-output table projects the national plan, determining its main items: the rate of growth of industrial production, its structure (group I and group II), capital investment, the effectiveness of accumulation, private incomes and the volume of trade.

The method of variant approximations and the provisional input-output table enable the development of sectoral plans to rest on a thorough study of the level of economic development, its relations and proportions, the interdependence of different sectors of production and its variation over the period planned.

When input-output calculations have projected the direction and rate of development, the levels of development of the key sectors, and the volume of saving and consumption, individual sectoral targets, can be elaborated and co-ordinated.

The provisional table is an economico-mathematical model of a country's national economy for a period assigned. It includes the following compact group of closely interrelated items:

National product
    including:
    subdivision I
    subdivision II
Industrial product (this consists of outputs for different sectors).
    including:
    subdivision I
    subdivision II
Agricultural product
National income
Capital investment
Accumulation fund
    including:
    Production-accumulation fund
    Non-production accumulation fund
Consumption fund
Real private incomes
Volume of trade.

The absolute magnitudes of the above items are given as from the beginning and the end of the period planned. At the same time the average annual rates of variation of these quantities are also determined.

The determination of the parameters of the economic model of social production for a period planned is based on the analysis of the national product accounts, actual proportions and relations, the reserves for increasing output and raising the effectiveness of production, and above all those reserves which originate from technical progress, efficiency and a more rational distribution of manpower.

The input-output calculations made on the strength of the data furnished by accounts yield a dynamic series of intersectoral coefficients. This series makes it possible to pass from accounts to the calculations of targets for a year planned. The usual procedure is as follows. Out of the entire set of sectors an industry is isolated as the main sector. Having determined the inter-sectoral input-output coefficients for several years ahead, the industrial output is computed for the year planned. For this purpose recourse is made to the index of the volume of fixed productive assets in the industry as of the beginning of the next year and the yield of assets per unit output.

Since the coefficients of the use of fixed productive assets and the structure of the use of industrial output for two subsequent years (the plan and the account year) can practically be assumed to be equal, having calculated the industrial output in the plan year, we can determine from the table of input-output relations all basic indices of the use of social output in the same year (industrial output, the volume of capital construction, the volume of transportation haulage, the consumption fund, etc.). Thus, we can calculate the economic model for the next year.

However, this method is not applicable to the calculations of the model for a long-range period. Three basic methods for the development of the provisional input-output table for a long-range period have been evolved in the practice of long-range planning. These methods, complementing and controlling each other, are conventionally labelled: (a) the method of the "saving input-output table", (b) the method of the "labour input-output table" and (c) the method of the "consumption input-output table".

The *first method* of development of the provisional input-output table is based on the calculation of an objectively possible volume of saving in production and the assets-output ratio (by which is meant the ratio of the value of productive assets to that of annual output). In the determination of long-range targets, analysis is first of all made of the trends and possible changes in the rate of production saving, and then of the trends of the effectiveness of saving.

The problem of the relation and dependence between the rates of growth of production, the saving of productive assets and the assets-output ratio of output growth is solved in its general form with the aid of a theoretical analysis of the process of reproduction. This analysis warrants the conclusion that the rate of growth of output equals (other conditions being equal) the quotient from dividing the rate of the production saving of social output by the assets-output ratio or, to put it differently, the product of the rate of production saving by the effectiveness of saving.

To apply this conclusion to planning the rates of growth of production for a certain specific period, the following trends are investigated in the development of a long-range plan: (a) change of the capital-output ratio, (b) change of the proportion of national income in national product and (c) change of the proportion of savings of productive assets in the national income as a whole and for each major sector.

Naturally, when plan targets are worked out for a year, i.e. when the planned year is compared with the current year, the relations of the previous year can be assumed to be stable for the planned year as well, taking into account the fact that structural changes within one year will not be so considerable as seriously to affect these relations. However, this applies only to preliminary drafts. The Soviet economy develops at such a high rate that intra-sectoral and inter-sectoral structural changes may be considerable even for such a short period of time as a year.

Still less is it permissible to extend automatically the relations evolved in the account period for any long-range term. For planning at long term it is necessary to investigate the trends in the pattern and development of these relations.

First of all, a study is made of the capital-output ratio or the ratio of fixed capital to the national product.

The more important factors responsible for the effectiveness of the use of fixed capital include: (1) change in the sectoral structure of industrial production, (2) change in its territorial structure and (3) mechanisation of labour-intensive processes.

Let us discuss these factors in more detail.

(1) The priority growth of the sectors of the group I and in particular the accelerated development of the generation of electric power, mining, oil extraction and the production of gas as well as ferrous and non-ferrous metallurgy and the chemical industry are objective factors of the growth of the capital output ratio. However, it is necessary to

take into account the opposite trends in the variation of the sectoral structure. The rapid development of sectors like organic synthesis, the production of light metals and semi-conductors, electronics, etc., appreciably decreases the capital–output ratio.

Increases in the capital–output ratio are neutralised to a certain extent by savings on current expenses as well as increases in the productivity of labour in the national economy as a whole.

(2) An extensive programme of investment in economically less developed areas inevitably increases for a while the capital output ratio. However, the introduction of the richer deposits of less developed areas is bound to raise considerably the effectiveness of investment.

(3) The complete mechanisation of labour-intensive processes in all sectors will entail important economic consequences. The effectiveness of investment connected with the initial introduction of mechanised processes is determined not by the resulting increase of output but by reduction in the number of employees and lower production costs. It should be noted that the complete mechanisation of production, the transition from partial to overall mechanisation and integrated automation is bound to increase substantially the effectiveness of investment.

The factors directly conducive to the effectiveness of investment are technical progress in all its forms, the expansion of production by the reconstruction and technical renovation of operating enterprises and a better use of fixed and circulating capital as a result of technical progress and the development of the creative initiative of employees. Of essential importance is the improvement of the structure of capital construction in productive sectors: a higher proportion of equipment and a lower share of construction work.

All the factors mentioned above operate simultaneously, but the results of their interaction differ at different stages of economic development. To determine correctly the variation in the capital–output ratio is a complex and laborious problem. However, no absolutely accurate and complete registration of all changes is necessary for a preliminary examination of the rates of growth. Rather is this a problem to be settled at subsequent stages of planning.

Both theoretical activity and practical planning indicate that the rates of investment can in socialist society be determined in planning as effectively as the demand and output of some products. Objectively possible rates of investment for a long-range period can be determined by calculating the following basic factors:

(a) the proportion of national income in national product,

(b) the proportion of the fund of investments in national income,

(c) the proportion of investment in productive assets in the total fund of investment (in some cases of investment in fixed productive assets), and

(d) the capital-output ratio of production (in some cases fixed [productive] funds are taken for the ratio).

The quantitative measure of these factors is determined on the basis of the input-output accounts of the national economy with allowances for possible changes of these factors in the period planned.

To determine the rate of development of each sector, it is highly important to ascertain the changes in the proportion of this sector in production and the proportion of investment in productive capital in this sector with respect to the entire investment fund, or in other words that part of output which will be channelled into the investment in productive assets of this sector. The part of the aggregate product invested in any sector in the form of productive capital can be expressed in units of output of this sector. If the proportion of the sector in total output is 1 : 2, each unit of aggregate output can be equated to 2 units of output of the sector under consideration. Having expressed the investment in productive assets in a given sector in units of output of this sector, we can compare and analyse the relation between the productive assets and output of the sector under consideration.

Thus, to determine the rate of development for a sector, the following quantities must be calculated additionally:

(a) the proportion of the saving of productive assets in the sector under study with respect to the total amount of saving, and

(b) the proportion of the output of the sector under study in total output.

The decrease of the capital-output ratio owing to a higher yield of fixed productive assets, a saving in the use of circulating capital, quicker returns on circulating capital, etc., tend to increase the rates of growth. An increase in the proportion of investment also operates in this direction.

The Soviet economy has an important advantage: objective possibilities for ensuring a planned rate of growth. Making use of this advantage of the socialist system, stemming from social ownership of the means of production, the state establishes and maintains the required rate of development of each sector of the national economy.

The deliberate establishment of rates of development of production as a whole as well as of its specific sectors requires an obligatory plan and a provision of labour resources necessary for the development of production and the maintenance of steady growth in the productivity of labour.

The *second method* of development of the provisional input-output table is closely connected with the first one. The second method proceeds from calculations of the input-output table of manpower resources for a long-range period and of an objectively possible growth of the productivity of labour. The total population number and the number of able-bodied population are determined on the basis of demographic calculations. Then possible manpower resources are calculated, including those resources which can be drawn into industries, cultural activity, services, and management and administration.

The national product results from the operation of two factors:
(a) the number of those engaged in material production, and
(b) their efficiency (the productivity of live labour).

The calculations of the summary labour input-output table make it possible to establish at long term the number of those to be engaged in material production. The calculations are performed in approximately the following order:

1. Total population numbers: Determined taking into account the average annual coefficient of natural population growth

2. Number of able-bodied population: Determined on the basis of demographic calculations

3. Number of people above the pension age and under full age engaged in the national economy: Determined taking into account their ratio to the number of able-bodied people in the previous years

4. Number of those engaged in household work: Determined taking into account the reduction of this number

5. Number of those engaged in studies without discontinuing gainful employment: Determined on the basis of input-output tables for training manpower

6. Number of those engaged in productive and non-productive sectors: All resources of gainfully employed are determined (those engaged in all spheres minus those engaged in household work and studies)

7. Number of those engaged in non-productive sectors: Determined for basic fields (education, public health, cultural activities, services, administration); standard ratings are used in the calculations

8. Number of those engaged   All engaged in the national economy are taken
   in the productive sphere:   into account minus those engaged in the non-
                               productive sectors

Employees are distributed between the productive and non-productive spheres taking into account the need to meet more and more effectively the material and cultural requirements of the population as well as the need for the growth of the productivity of labour to increase the proportion of employees engaged in the non-productive sphere.

The determination of a possible number of employees in the productive sphere is followed by the long-term calculation of the growth and level of the productivity of labour. The calculation must take into account the data for previous periods and establish a multiple correlation between the indices of fixed capital per first-shift employee (the ratio of fixed capital to the number of employees engaged on the first shift):

—the consumption of power per employee, and

—labour productivity or net output per employee.

Then the prospects for the growth of fixed capital per first-shift employee and electric power per employee are estimated. Having established these two factors, we determine the prospective size of output and the rate of its growth. All further calculations of the prospective national income, its structure, the volume of capital investment, etc., are based on an analysis of input-output relations in the national economy.

The *third method* is based on determining the fund of consumption and input-output relations between subdivisions I and II of national production. The consumption fund is computed on the basis of the population's consumption budget for previous years. The population's consumption budget is drawn up by analysing family budgets, sets of selected foodstuffs and consumer goods, and official housing, service and cultural standards. The population's consumption budget helps to determine the total fund of consumption. The calculation of this fund and the corresponding stock of consumer goods makes it possible to establish the volume of output of subdivision II. Then the entire volume of national output is calculated by analysing summary input-output tables of the national economy for previous years and determining input-output coefficients between subdivisions I and II.

The above methods of calculating the provisional input-output table of the national economy are applied simultaneously. The combination of all three methods in planning ensures proper quantitative parameters of the basic proportions in long-range plans. After that the development of particular input-output plans for material, financial and manpower resources can be proceeded with.

The model of a country's economy in the final year of a period planned, set out as a provisional input-output table of the national economy, should then be expanded into a system of national economic input-output plans. Of major importance at this stage is the development of the inter-sectoral input-output plan for output, distribution and consumption.

Several fundamental investigations into the inter-sectoral input-output plan have been carried out in the Soviet Union in recent years. Mention should be made firstly of the investigations performed by the Central Statistical Board of the U.S.S.R. into the inter-sectoral input-output account of production and the inter-sectoral input-output labour plan in 1959, as well as the investigations carried out by several laboratories for area inter-sectoral input-output tables of production (the Mordovian, Tatar and Karelian autonomous republics and the Kaliningrad Region).

The Economic Research Institute and the Computing Centre of the U.S.S.R. Gosplan (the state Planning Committee of the U.S.S.R.) have developed an inter-sectoral input-output table for 1966 to 1970 from data of the national economic plan of the U.S.S.R. for 1962 and 1963.

A general scheme of the inter-sectoral input-output table of production, distribution and consumption in physical terms can be represented as shown on page 91.

The inter-sectoral input-output table in physical terms describes flows of physical units into and out of the sectors of material production. The entire volume of output (coal, pig iron, steel, electric power, etc.) in the national economy in the year planned (produced output, imported output, etc.) is channelled into the consumption of the corresponding sectors of the national economy, into export, nonproductive consumption (consumer goods) and savings. Summing up, we obtain the "final output" of the corresponding sector.

By proper economic analysis we can calculate the coefficients (standard rates, quotas) of the material expenditure of output produced by sector A, for example, for the production of unit output in those sectors which consume the output of sector A. These are the coefficients of direct expenditures. Their economic meaning is quite simple: at a given technical level, there are definite quantitative relations between

| Sectors Units | Resources | | | | Distribution of Resources | | | | | | |
| --- | --- | --- | --- | --- | --- | --- | --- | --- | --- | --- | --- |
| | | | | | Material Consumption in Production | | | | Final Output | | |
| | _Production_ | _Import_ | _Others_ | _Total_ | _Sector A_ | _Sector B_ | _Sector C_ | _Export_ | _Consumption outside production_ | _Savings_ | _Total for distribution_ |
| Sector A | | | | | | | | | | | |
| Sector B | | | | | | | | | | | |
| Sector C | | | | | | | | | | | |

interrelated sectors of production, i.e. definite quantities of output produced by allied sectors are expended per unit output of a given sector. Any change of output in one sector requires adequate changes of outputs in other technologically allied sectors or else changes in the rates or quotas of expenditure of output of these sectors per unit output of a given sector.

The matrix of coefficients of direct expenditures makes it possible to describe quantitatively the direct input-output relations between different sectors.

However, a knowledge of the direct inter-sectoral relations alone is insufficient for economic control. Indirect expenditures on the output of any product must be taken into account.

Direct plus indirect expenditures make up total expenditures. Here is an example based on the data of the input-output table for 1959. The production of 1 ton of pig-iron required 29 kg of coal directly, and 870 kg of coke (which is equivalent to 1,241 kg of coal), then 1·8 kWh of power (which is equivalent to another 9 kg of coal); other indirect expenditures on 1 ton of pig-iron in terms of coal amount to 133 kg, which makes a total of 1,383 kg of coal. Consequently, total expenditures of coal per ton of pig-iron amount to 1,412 kg (29 kg + 1,383 kg) i.e. nearly 49 times as much as direct expenditures.

To obtain the matrix of total coefficients, the matrix of the direct coefficients is inverted with the aid of electronic computers.

A flow of output of a sector which is represented in physical terms in the above inter-sectoral input-output table can also be expressed in money.

The pricing of the inter-sectoral input-output table makes it possible to describe not only the flows of output as a movement of goods but also the amount and type of expenses on the output in a given sector. Common measuring units make it possible to superimpose two input-output tables: the table of output flows and the table of expenditures on output.

The inter-sectoral input-output table in terms of cash is a complex matrix of approximately the following form:

*General Scheme of the Inter-Sectoral Input-Output Table of Production, Distribution and Consumption (in money)*

| Distribution of resources | Material consumption in production | | | National income | | | |
|---|---|---|---|---|---|---|---|
| | Sector A | Sector B | Sector C | Output for export | Consumption fund | Fund of savings and reserves | Total output |
| Resources | | | | | | | |
| Sector A Sector B Sector C etc. Depreciation | First quadrant | | | Third quadrant | | | |
| Total | | | | | | | |
| Wages fund Incomes of enterprises | Second quadrant | | | | | | |
| Total | | | | | | | |
| Grand total | | | | | | | |

The inter-sectoral input-output table in terms of cash is a three-quadrant table. The first quadrant describes the inter-relations of all sectors of material production, and the total gives the fund of replacement of the means of production consumed in the process of production. The second quadrant gives the wages fund and the gross incomes of enterprises, their sum being equal to the national income.

Summing up the totals of the first and second quadrants (by columns) we obtain the sum of all expenditures on the output of each sector as well as the national economy as a whole. This sum indicates the structural sectoral pattern of the national product and national income.

The data of the third quadrant of the table give the export of output and the use of national income for consumption and savings.

Treatment of the table of direct coefficients and the solution of the corresponding set of equations with electronic computers yield the inverted matrix or the matrix of total coefficients of expenditure. In contrast to the matrix of direct expenditures, the matrix of total expenditures shows the entire output of sectors expended on a certain output of another sector both directly as well as via the outputs of other sectors. It is very important that total expenditures should be related to unit final output. By final output is meant the output constituting the material content of accumulation, consumption and export.

A proper appraisal of the possibilities for applying the inter-sectoral input-output table in planning shows that it is an important tool of national economic planning. The sphere of application of the inter-sectoral input-output table is very wide. It can be effectively used at the preliminary stage of planning, during the development of a plan as well as during its progress.

The provisional input-output table of the national economy is specified on the basis of the inter-sectoral input-output table approximately in the following order:

(1) The total size of national output and national income is determined for a period planned (i.e. the quantities $x$ and $y$) on the basis of calculations of the provisional input-output table of the national economy.

(2) The sectoral structure, $x$, is determined from the calculations of the provisional table. This structure may, of course, contain aggregated items only. These are above all aggregated for the following sectors: industries, farming, construction, transport and communication. The analysis of the effectiveness of savings, the trends in the productivity of labour, the dynamics of the consumption budget and the structure

of capital investments makes it possible already, at the stage of a preliminary input-output table, to determine possible outputs of the sectors producing metal, electric power, machines, chemicals, cement, and consumer goods.

(3) Trends are then determined in the variation of the coefficients of direct expenditures versus technical progress. The matrix of the coefficients of direct expenditures of the previous period reflects the relevant proportions evolved over this period. They have been affected by both progressive and regressive processes, and these coefficients cannot be extended to the period planned. The concrete proportions and relations (and these are reflected by the coefficients of direct expenditures) depend not only on changes in equipment and technology but also on qualitative changes in the structure of production.

(4) The physical composition, $\gamma$, i.e. consumption, accumulation (savings) and export, is determined on the basis of data on the structure, $x$, and the plan matrix of direct expenditures. As for the general amounts of consumption, savings and export, these are given earlier by the provisional input-output table of the national economy.

The above four stages yield for a planning agency a provisional (preliminary) inter-sectoral table of production and consumption of 30 to 40 columns and lines. This input-output table is a sound basis for subsequent more elaborate sectoral and area plans involving the entire set of input-output calculations, material, manpower and financial.

The role of the inter-sectoral input-output table especially increases after the draft has become a national plan; the table becomes a tool for preserving proper proportions in economic development under any changes introduced as the plan is realized. Using the input-output table, the plan may incorporate (taking fully into account all national economic input-output relations) adjustments throughout a period planned as different factors of economic development change over this period.

Apart from the provisional input-output table of the national economy and inter-sectoral input-output plans, several more specialised economico-mathematical models have been developed. These include the economico-mathematical models of the optimum distribution and specialisation of production in different sectors.

# 4

# The State Economic Plan of the U.S.S.R.

In the preceding chapters we dealt with the methods, the organisation and the techniques of calculating long-term and current plans. Let us now examine the ultimate product of the planning agencies' and their numerous helpers' efforts, the drafting of the centralised economic plan of the U.S.S.R.

We can do this best by resorting to the recently drafted long-term economic development plan for 1966–70, known as "Directives of the 23rd Congress of the C.P.S.U. for the U.S.S.R. Five-Year Economic Development Plan for 1966–70". These directives emphasise the following sections of the long-term state economic plan.

—the principal results of the economic development of the U.S.S.R. in 1955–65;

—the main tasks of the economic development of the U.S.S.R. in 1966–67;

—industry;

—agriculture;

—transport and communications;

—capital construction;

—higher living standards and a higher cultural level for the people;

—siting of productive forces and the development of the economy in the Union Republics;

—foreign economic relations.

Approximately the same is the structure of other long-term plans. The annual economic development plans of the U.S.S.R. have a more detailed structure, including material balances, distribution plans, plans of inter-Republican deliveries, and others.

Let us see how plan assignments are fixed for the basic divisions of the long-term plan.

## I. RESULTS OF THE DEVELOPMENT OF THE ECONOMY

We mentioned already that the determination of the initial level of the country's economic development was among the main issues in the entire work of plan drafting.

We also pointed out that the main problem in analysing the initial level was to bring out new economic reserves, the use of which would provide the opportunity of stepping up the economic development of the country. The reserves brought out show sources for meeting the newly appearing needs of society.

In planning practice we distinguish the reserves available in the entire national economy from those in the various economic sectors, areas and within the enterprises.

The adequate siting of productive forces and adequate proportions between the sectors of the national economy are a source of *nation-wide reserves*. These reserves are taken into consideration in mapping long-term plans.

*Reserves within economic sectors*—these are the reserves which are of significance for the development of sectors subordinated to a Union or Union-Republican ministry in the spheres of industry, agriculture, construction, transport, etc. These reserves involve the intensification of specialisation and the development of co-operation of enterprises, the concentration and integration of production.

Production development reserves may be of particular importance for raising the economic level of a republic, territory or region. These *intra-regional reserves* are created by raising the production organisation level and promoting intra-regional relations between enterprises of various industries.

It is the wide range of *internal reserves of enterprises* that is of a particularly mass nature. They are connected mainly with improving the efficiency of utilising fixed and circulating capital and the enterprises' labour and financial resources. All these reserves can be brought out and utilised only on the basis of long-term and current plans which permit prediction of economic development tendencies and the mapping out of measures designed to take advantage of them.

The Directives on the 1966–70 five-year economic development plan, in the chapter on the results of the foregoing seven-year plan, point out that the considerable growth of the country's economic potential, of the people's prosperity and culture, and of defence potential, are the principal results of that period. The net national product used for consumption and accumulation increased by 53 per cent in the course of 1959–65. Industrial output increased by 84 per cent.

The industries which form the foundation of the retooling of the entire economy and of steady technological progress—power engineering, machine building and the chemical industry—extended their share in the total industrial output from 27 per cent in 1958 to 35 per cent in 1965. Radical changes took place in the country's fuel balance. The share of oil and gas, which accounted for 32 per cent in 1959, increased to 52 per cent in 1965. Qualitatively new production machinery was built up; fixed productive assets in the national economy as a whole increased in the seven years by 90 per cent, and in industry they were doubled. The seven years saw the construction and the commissioning of more than 5,500 big industrial enterprises. This means that in the course of seven years Soviet industry built up the same amount of productive capacity as had been created previously in the course of many decades of economic development.

The Soviet Union is leading the world in the development of certain key branches of science, technology and production (space exploration, nuclear physics, mathematics, electronics, radio engineering, metallurgy, rocketry, aircraft building and some other fields).

The growth of production and the creation of the necessary resources made possible some major measures to raise the living standards of the people.

The real incomes of the working people increased. The minimum basic wages of factory and office workers were raised, as were rates and salaries for low- and medium-paid employees. Income tax was either abolished or reduced for a considerable section of factory and office workers. Pensions were established for collective farmers. Minimum pensions for some categories of pensioners were raised. Benefits to war invalids were expanded. The grants and benefits received by the population out of public consumption funds were 74 per cent greater. The working day was reduced to seven hours or even six hours for some categories. Housing construction got under way on a large scale. Ninety per cent more housing was built and commissioned than in the foregoing seven years (1952–58) and almost as much as had been built in all the years prior to 1958.

Consumption of manufactured goods and foodstuffs increased. The plan for the development of pre-school institutions was overfulfilled.

All these indisputable facts are vivid proof of the Soviet Union's successful economic development. But an objective appraisal of the results of the previous plan period includes not only the positive aspects of work. It must also take into account the most marked shortcomings in planning, management and utilisation of resources.

The successes scored, no matter how significant, do not satisfy the Soviet people. In order to carry out successfully the programme of building the material and technical foundation of communism, to ensure the world's highest level of labour productivity and to attain the highest living standards for the population as compared with any developed capitalist country, it is essential to speed up the rate of economic development, to improve the efficiency of production management, and to obtain the best results with the least possible input.

An analysis of Soviet economic development in the recent years has shown that there was a drop in growth rates, a deterioration in the efficiency of capital investment, and a certain worsening of qualitative indicators in industrial development. Here are some data.

*Average Annual Rate of U.S.S.R.'s Industrial Development*

|  | 1952–58 | 1959–65 |
|---|---|---|
| Increment of industrial output including: | +12·0 | +9·2 |
| Output of means of production (group A) | +12·8 | +10·3 |
| Production of consumer goods (group B) | +10·7 | +6·6 |
| Growth of labour productivity in industry | +7·6 | +5·2 |

The successes of the national economy of the U.S.S.R. could have been more considerable had more adequate use been made of the objective opportunities inherent in the Soviet socialist system. The output of staple farm produce in the U.S.S.R. is growing. However, the rate of this growth in 1961–65 was lower than in the foregoing years. The result was that the seven-year plan assignments for agricultural development failed to be carried out.

Considerable shortfalls in the output of agricultural produce were connected, first and foremost, with a deceleration of the growth of output by group II industries and with the widening gap between the increment-rate in groups I and II in industry.

The growth of production by group I surpassed the rate of growth in group II in 1951–58 by 20 per cent. The target figures for 1959–65 provided for 28 per cent, though actually this gap increased in that period by 56 per cent. Group I was delivering a diminishing share of its output to the industries producing consumer goods. In 1950 means and objects of labour for group II accounted for 28 per cent of the total output of group I, whereas this share diminished on the average to 18–20 per cent in the course of 1961–65.

The errors made in economic planning, as well as a random arbitrary approach to the solution of intricate economic problems, led to infringements of important proportions in the development of the Soviet economy. The result has been that the development of the oil and gas industry and of the light and food industries lags behind the targets planned. The lag in the development of agriculture and industries producing consumer goods led to disproportions between the growth of effective demand and the stocks of commodities and supply of services. This had an adverse effect on the growth rate of the population's real incomes and on material incentives. The development of industry was inhibited by shortcomings in capital construction. There were delays in commissioning certain items of productive capacity, a scattering of capital-funds among construction-projects, and a considerable growth in the cost of the enterprises commissioned.

The fact that plans for the introduction of new equipment and techniques in industry were regularly underfulfilled and that important scientific discoveries were being put into practical use only after considerable delay had an adverse effect on development rates in industry.

All these shortcomings were due to the inadequacy of the industrial management system and to defects in the sphere of planning and economic incentive, which together prevented the complete utilisation of the advantages of a socialist economy.

The Directives on the 1966–70 five-year plan point out that a lack of balance had developed in recent years between the sharply increased scale of production, on the one hand, and planning methods and the economic management and material incentive system on the other.

Another important circumstance was that the aggravation of international tension caused by the activities of the United States government, which unleashed armed aggression in various areas of the world, required additional funds in order to guarantee the country's defence potential.

The analysis of the principal results of the country's development in the foregoing plan period leads, naturally, to considering the targets of economic development under the new plan.

## 2. MAIN TASKS OF THE ECONOMIC DEVELOPMENT OF THE
### U.S.S.R. IN 1966–70

This part of the Five-Year Plan Directives determines the lines of the country's economic and cultural development and the targets to be obtained in the next five years.

The main economic task of the 1966–70 five-year plan is to secure a further considerable growth of industry and high stable rates of agricultural development and, on this basis, to obtain a considerable rise in the people's living standards and a more complete satisfaction of their material and cultural needs. The directives state the decisive means towards solving this problem, namely, the utmost utilisation of the achievements of science and technology, the industrial development of all social production and the enhancement of its efficiency, and increase of the productivity of labour.

The formulation of the main target of the long-term plan contains a concise expression of the plan's basic content. This section of the plan normally includes instructions on what must be done to attain the targets. Thus, the Directives point to five such basic points:

(1) to increase industrial output by about 50 per cent in the five years; to provide for the further technical re-equipment of all sectors of the national economy and to ensure the accelerated development of consumer goods production;

(2) to increase considerably the output of farm products;

(3) to enhance the efficiency of production through technological progress, improvement of the organisation of labour and production, better use of productive assets and capital investments, improvement of the quality of goods, and stringent economies;

(4) to speed up scientific and technological progress by expanding scientific research, applying its results to production and utilising inventions in industry;

(5) to improve the management of the country's economy through the improvement of planning, economic stimulation of production, extension of the initiative and economic independence of enterprises, and enhancement of the working people's material interest in the results of their labour; and to secure a correct combination of centralised planned management with economic initiative and independence of industrial enterprises.

The chapter "Main Tasks of the Economic Development of the U.S.S.R. in 1966–70" plays an important part in the plan. It includes some of the general plan assignments which were outlined at the

23rd C.P.S.U. Congress by A. N. Kosygin, the head of the Soviet Government, in his report. Here are some of the assignments which characterise in a general way the trends and rate of the U.S.S.R.'s economic development for 1966–70.

| | |
|---|---|
| Growth of the gross national product | by 40 per cent |
| Growth of fixed productive assets for the country as the whole | by more than 50 per cent |
| including: | |
| industry | by 60 per cent |
| agriculture | by 90 per cent |
| Growth of national income | by 38–41 per cent |
| Increase of consumption fund | by 36–39 per cent |
| Rise of *per capita* real incomes | by 30 per cent |
| Growth of gross industrial output including: | by 47–50 per cent |
| output by group "A" | 49–52 per cent |
| output by group "B" | 43–46 per cent |

The quantitative assignments are contained in a more detailed form in the so-called "Summary Section" of the state economic plan drafted on the basis of the Directives of the C.P.S.U. Central Committee. This section or summary table of basic indices concentrates the most important key indices of the economic plan, which express the scope and rates of production growth for individual sectors, as well as the most important conditions for the further development of production and for raising the living standards of the population. What indices are these?

They are, first and foremost, the indices of the rate of growth of the national income, of industrial output (on the whole and separately for the industries which produce means of production and consumer goods), of the commissioning of productive capacity and fixed assets, of the volume of government capital investments, of the growth of labour productivity, of the increase of real wages, of retail trade turnover, of revenues of the state budget, and some other indices.

The index for the growth of national income provides the most general expression of the growth of production and living standards. In Soviet planning practice, national income is defined as society's aggregate income used for non-productive consumption and accumulation.

In order to calculate the volume of the national income, the sum total of the growth of output by all branches of production is calculated in actual prices and in comparable prices (prices functioning at the beginning of the long-term plan period are taken usually as comparable prices; for the 1966–70 five-year plan they will be the prices operating on January 1, 1966), and the sum total of raw materials, fuel, electrical power and other means of production is excluded, these being calculated in the same actual and comparable prices.

The continuous growth of the national income in the U.S.S.R. guarantees the steady rise of the people's living standards and the rapid expansion of production.

The index for growth of national income and the other indices included in the Summary Section of the state plan must provide the answer to the question of how the targets fixed for the long-term plan period are being reached.

It is the transition to communism that is the main target of the U.S.S.R. today, while the building up of the material and technical foundation of communism is its chief economic task.

In order to attain this target, it is essential that the current and long-term plans should provide for and maintain the most efficient possible proportions between the sectors of production and the areas of the country, between accumulation and consumption and, consequently, must fix and maintain the relevant rates of development for the given sectors and areas.

How do we interpret the term "proportions" in economic planning?

A proportion is the concrete quantitatively fixed interdependence of production, economic sectors and aspects of the social process of reproduction, in which the elements in such interdependence are in due conformity one with another. Within one period this conformity is of a more or less stable nature.

"Disproportion" is the opposite conception. It is also a more or less stable relationship to be observed in certain conditions between industries, sectors and reproduction spheres, and is characterised by lack of balance between elements which ought to be connected and interdependent.

In the U.S.S.R., production is organised by the state in a planned way with the aid of a centralised economic plan. In drafting economic plans, both long-term plans and current plans designed for a year or two, the state proceeds from the needs of society and from the real possibilities created in the process of social development. By fixing in the economic plans assignments for the production of various kinds of material wealth, as well as of the implements of labour essential for creating this wealth, distributing the labour resources of society throughout the sectors of social production and setting the necessary and really feasible level of labour productivity and, at the same time, the level on which the needs can be satisfied, the Soviet state deliberately changes the proportions and ratios in the national economy.

Proportions in the social production process are flexible and are constantly changing with the development and change of the mode of production and the economic system. Changes in society's level of economic development lead to an alteration in the proportions between production and consumption, between production and the accumulation of the national product, between the individual economic sectors (and, first and foremost, between such vital sectors as industry and agriculture), and between the incomes and consumption levels of the various groups of the population.

The technico-economic aspect of proportions and links of production finds its concrete expression:

(a) in the rates (actual and planned) of the input of labour, raw materials, other supplies, fuel, and electric power per unit of production or work;

(b) in the rates for the utilisation of equipment, machines and production space;

(c) in consumption rates for industrial goods, foodstuffs, etc.

In order to maintain the continuity of production, it is essential to provide for adequate proportions between the demand for means of production in the given sectors and the extent of production of these means in other sectors. A wide range of economic balance tables are drafted for this purpose.

The proportional nature of the U.S.S.R.'s economy is not an aim in itself; adequate proportions are essential not for their own sake but as the fundamental paramount condition for guaranteeing a high and stable rate of continuous expansion of production. The establishment and maintenance of a certain system of proportions is always subordinated to the solution of the problems of economic policy for the period under plan.

All this involves investigating and, if necessary, changing the proportions existing at the commencement of one or another period, so as to establish new proportions that are desirable from the viewpoint of the problems to be solved in the plan period. This is the chief content of the problem of proportion planning.

The problem of rates and proportions in the development of economic sectors and areas and of correlating the various elements of the reproduction process in the interests of steady economic and cultural development has always been the chief problem of planning the national economy.

The proportional development of the economy does not presuppose identical growth rates for all economic sectors. On the contrary, if the rates were identical proportions would be immediately violated. Indeed, the national economy can develop successfully only when the industries and economic sectors that are most important for the given plan period develop at a faster rate and ensure the economic efficiency of all the elements of production. With reference to the present conditions of the U.S.S.R.'s economic development, this applies to such industries as power engineering, radio electronics, the manufacture of computation facilities, instrument-making and some other branches of machine building, and the chemical industry.

The purposeful (supported by the consideration of objective economic laws) establishment of proportions and ratios among the productive branches and areas of the country in distributing implements of labour and manpower requires the establishment of corresponding development rates both for individual sectors of production and for social production as a whole.

Stable and rapid economic development and continuity of this development are indispensable features of the Soviet economic system. This is connected with the operation of several permanent factors. Here are the most important of them:

(a) planned development of the entire economy, which excludes disproportions that are inevitable in a non-planned economy;

(b) prevention of unproductive use of the national income;

(c) maintenance of a high rate of productive accumulation;

(d) personal material and moral interest of productive personnel and intellectuals in the growth of social production.

In the U.S.S.R., active research is under way into finding the objective laws which govern the changes of major proportions and, in particular, into such important practical problems as the ratios and dependence between the growth rate of production and accumulation of productive assets and their efficient use, between the growth rates of output and labour productivity, and between the rate of output of means of production and the manufacture of consumer goods.

These serve as the basis for calculating the preliminary input-output table of the national economy, which we mentioned above.

Once the basic lines of economic development in the plan period and the vital proportions in the economy are fixed, detailed calculations of the chief plan targets are made for economic sectors, Republics and economic areas, as well as the assignments for consumption and accumulation. Since the scale of the potential growth of public consumption depends on gross output, it is the assignments under the plan's production programme that are set first of all.

### 3. PRODUCTION DEVELOPMENT PLAN

The planning of production underlies the state economic plan. The plan's production programme includes indicators for the production of industrial and agricultural products and determines all the other divisions of the plan.

Industry plays the leading role in the U.S.S.R.'s national economy. This role is determined, first and foremost, by the fact that industry creates the bulk of the national product and of the national income in the U.S.S.R. Further, industry is the material foundation of technical progress throughout the entire economy. By providing the national economy with machines, equipment and instruments, as well as with fuel, power and staple raw-material resources, industry determines to a considerable extent the development of the entire economy, the scale and rate of all social production and, consequently, the raising of living standards.

The following data illustrate the growth of industry in the U.S.S.R.'s economy:

#### Share of Industry in the U.S.S.R.'s Economy in 1964
#### (in per cent)

| | |
|---|---|
| In fixed productive assets | 49·5 |
| In personnel engaged in material production (construction included) | 42·5 |
| In the country's national product | 64·1 |
| In the national income | 53·6 |
| In capital investments into productive sphere | 54·0 |
| In power consumption | 68·0 |

Industry consists almost exclusively of enterprises which are state or national property, and it employs the overwhelming majority of the working class. Another criterion of the leading part played by industry is the fact that it serves as the basis for enhancing the U.S.S.R.'s defence potential.

The overall industrial development plan includes the production programme, a plan for the development of the technological and organisational aspects of production, a plan for capital construction, a plan for labour and wages, a plan for materials and equipment supplies and sales of products, a plan for production costs, and a financial plan.

The production programme of industry is an important component of the overall industrial plan. It includes assignments for the scope, assortment and quality of goods put out by the sectors and industries, proportions among the branches within industry, as well as between industry and the other sectors of the national economy.

The following are the basic indices of the production programme for industry: value indices of production volume in permanent and current market prices, output in physical terms (including assortment and quality indicators), technico-economic standards, indices in specialisation, co-operation and integration of production.

The indices (partly obligatory, and fixed by higher-level agencies, partly only calculated) in capital construction, development and introduction of new equipment, in materials and equipment supplies and sales, in productivity of labour, strength of personnel and wages, in cutting production costs and in finances are reflected in other sections of the centralised economic plan—the plan of capital investments, plan for labour, etc.

In conformity with the economic reform now being carried out in industry, the indices fixed for industrial enterprises by higher-level bodies as regards production output will be limited to the following:

(1) Total volume of sales in operative wholesale prices. The index of goods transported may be used in some industries if necessary.

(2) The more important types of output in physical terms (with a reference to goods for export) and indices of goods quality.

In 1966–68, the annual plans will include fixed indices for gross and marketed output which, as industrial enterprises change over to new conditions of planning and management, will turn into calculated indices, while the sales index becomes the general obligatory state assignment.

The gross output index is used now for measuring the physical volume, dynamics and growth rate of industry as a whole, for its individual branches and for the areas (it will still be used in accounts when it stops being a plan index. This index serves as a basis for calculating proportions between industrial and agricultural production, between the industrial output of group "I" and group "II", and other proportions.

Gross output is planned in stable (comparable) prices. Since January 1, 1966, the wholesale prices of enterprises (i.e. without turnover tax) are operating as such prices.

Gross output includes the value of commodity output, of non-paid raw materials and other supplies of the customer, changes in the carry-over of semi-manufactured goods, tools and devices produced at the given plant (and in some industries, also the carry-overs of non-completed production if the duration of the production cycle exceeds two months).

Both marketed production and gross output are determined by the enterprise method. But in order to co-ordinate the plan of marketed production with the cost of production, with the sales plan and with the financial plan, the former is planned not in comparable prices, but in prices operating at the moment of the drafting of the plan.

Industrial output in physical terms is presented in the centralised economic plan in the form of assortment or a list of the most important products (it includes the obligatory products distributed under inter-Republican delivery plans, i.e. for deliveries from one republic to another, and the products used for building up reserves, for exports, and various all-Union needs).

The Directives include the following basic indicators for the development of industry in 1966–70 (in per cent of 1965).

| | |
|---|---|
| Total Industrial Output including: | 147–150 |
| Output of industries manufacturing means of production (group I") | 149–152 |
| Output of industries making consumer goods (group "II") | 143–146 |
| Oil | 142–146 |
| Gas | 173–185 |
| Electrical power | 164–166 |
| Rolled Steel | 134–138 |
| Chemical industry | 200 |
| Machine-building and metal-working | approximately 160–170 |
| Light industry | approximately 140 |
| Food industry | approximately 140 |

In addition, there are separate assignments for the production of 40 items of goods in physical terms and eight types of goods in their summary value in millions of roubles.

The estimation of the scope and growth rate for industrial

production is accompanied by fixing assignments and drafting measures for improving the assortment and quality of goods. Assignments for the whole assortment are included in the enterprises' plans on the basis of contracts between producers and consumers within the general scope of output for each plan item (assortment). Since this must take into account both the requirements of the national economy and the possibilities of industry, the assortment of industrial output is constantly changing. Some items are substituted for others, the output of new goods is launched and the production of obsolete goods is stopped.

Quality indices play an important part in planning industrial output.

Along with the general principle that the plan must envisage the output of up-to-date and high-quality goods, there are more concrete assignments for each individual industry. Thus, for instance, the oil-refining industry is to manufacture no less than 80 per cent of its total diesel fuel with a sulphur content of not more than 0·5 per cent, to bring the output of high-octane petrol to 55–60 per cent of the total, and to employ efficient additives in the production of diesel and motor oils, etc. The chemical industry is to improve the quality of plastics, extend the production of polymer materials, enlarge the production and assortment of extra-pure chemicals, etc.

The production programme for industry is drafted according to the sectoral principle. The state economic plan singles out 12 basic industries (ferrous and non-ferrous metallurgy, the fuel industry, power generation, etc.).

The indices of industry's production programme are also grouped along departmental (for the ministries, boards and departments) and territorial (for the Union Republics, economic and geographic areas, economic administrative districts and regions) lines.

In planning the volume and growth-rate of industrial output, the priority development of machine-building, chemistry, power engineering and other key branches and the provision of adequate proportions throughout industrial production are of primary importance.

Along with an increase of production by group I industries as a whole in 1964 by 9·7 times, as compared with 1940, the output of the chemical industry increased by 13·6 times, of machine-building and metal-working by 14·8 times, and of power generation by 10·9 times. In 1966–70, parallel with a planned 47–50 per cent growth of industrial output, the output of the machine-building and metal-working industry will increase by 60–70 per cent, power generation by 65–70 per cent, and the production of the chemical industry is to double.

Of primary importance is the establishment of adequate proportions between the output of means of production (group I) and the output of consumer goods (group II). The high level of economic development reached by the U.S.S.R. permits it now to develop the industries both of group I and group II at a fast rate simultaneously. The Directives envisage that the growth-rate of group II should be brought closer to that of group I. In 1959–65 the average annual growth rate for the manufacture of means of production was higher than that for the production of consumer goods by more than 50 per cent, whereas in 1966–70 this rate will be but 10–15 per cent higher.

Under conditions when the growth rates for groups I and II are coming closer, the part played by heavy industry acquires a new meaning. Heavy industry must, as before, play the leading part in guaranteeing the building of a strong material and technical economic basis, intensive technical progress and enhancement of defence potential. However, due to the rapid growth of the industries which turn out consumer goods, investment in the enlargement of enterprises turning out means of production for the light and food industries, agriculture and housing construction, and in cultural and other services for the people, is steadily growing. Heavy industry enterprises turn out larger quantities of goods for cultural and household purposes.

In this light, the development of the chemical industry offers excellent prospects. For the chemical industry the Directives envisage 150–200 per cent enlargement of the output of various high-quality chemicals and other articles for domestic use, while in the "non-ferrous metallurgy" section a threefold increase of consumer goods output is planned. Similar targets were set for all branches of heavy industry.

Along with the planning of rates and proportions for industries, of major importance is the planning of industrial output for the Union Republics and economic areas.

The production programme of industry in a long-term plan (for five years and more) is calculated on the basis of estimating the national economy's needs for goods produced by a given industry; of analysing the achievements of Soviet and foreign enterprises which produce similar goods; and of long-range estimation of technological progress in the given industry. The latter includes calculations of the prospective balance of productive capacity, in view of the long-term plan for the development of economic ties with enterprises, organisations and institutions which consume the given goods, and calculations for the development of the raw material, fuel and power basis of the given industry.

Current (annual) programmes are drafted on the basis of rough estimates for the relevant year of the long-term plan, taking due account of newly explored resources and of the needs of the national economy, as well as the permanent economic bonds between a given industry or department with other ministries, etc.

The drafting of industry's production programme involves an appraisal of the national economy's requirements for industrial goods in the plan period, calculation of the enterprises' productive capacity and of the quantities of raw materials and other supplies, fuel and power necessary to provide for the planned output of industrial goods. Productive capacity balances are important tools in drafting the production programme of industry. These balances are compiled by every enterprise, by every ministry, by the Republican Gosplans and, for the key branches of industry, are generalised by the U.S.S.R. Gosplan.

The balance of productive capacity is drafted according to a pre-fixed range of goods (pig-iron, steel, coal, oil, etc.) according to the following model pattern.

|  | Basic period | Plan period (for years of long-term plan) |
|---|---|---|
| 1 | 2 | 3 |
| Operating capacity at the beginning of period | | |
| Increment of capacity: | | |
| by commissioning capacity at newly built enterprises | | |
| by enlarging operating capacity (through improving production processes, reconstructing equipment, mechanising and intensifying production and carrying out other organisational and technical measures) | | |
| by building new capacity and plant at operating enterprises | | |
| Retirement of capacity | | |
| Operating capacity at the close of plan period | | |
| Average annual capacity | | |
| Production of goods | | |

Productive capacity is defined as the maximum possible production of a certain assortment of goods with the maximum use of the equipment and floor space, in keeping with the planned operation cycle, using advanced production techniques and progressive forms of production organisation and rates of utilising resources. It is measured by the amount of products in physical terms. Thus, the productive capacity of an automobile plant is measured by the number of automobiles, of a cement factory by the amount of cement, and of a weaving mill by the number of metres of fabrics.

Calculation of productive capacity includes all the available production equipment at the disposal of an enterprise (both operating equipment and equipment inoperative at the given moment due to breakdowns, repairs, modernisation, etc.).

In the practice of economic planning, the results of productive capacity calculations are used, first and foremost, as a basis for the draft plan of industrial production, as well as for planning capital investments, for drafting balances and plans of equipment distribution, and for planning specialisation and development of intra- and inter-regional co-operation.

The designing and construction of new enterprises and the enlargement of operating enterprises requires the setting up of an adequate raw-material basis. That is why the state economic plan includes assignments for the development of mineral and raw-material resources and for the accumulation of a necessary reserve of prospected mineral deposits.

The needs of the national economy in industrial goods are determined by input-output tables for the most important kinds of raw materials and other supplies, fuel, electric power, equipment, as well as consumer goods. These calculations are based on rates for the expenditure of material resources, which ensure their most efficient utilisation. Priority is given to requirements in materials and equipment connected with the development and introduction of new equipment.

The scope of production and construction, included in the calculations of material balances, must be in strict conformity with the scope fixed in the relevant sections of the plan.

In the initial stages of plan drafting, as well as in drafting general plans for a long period, the requirements in producers' goods are determined by the method of aggregated economic coefficients. These coefficients are summarised sector-wise standards which characterise the total input per unit of production in each sector, with due account for the needs of all the adjacent sectors which supply it with raw stuffs and other materials, fuel and power (according to the 1959 inter-sectoral balance the total expenditures exceeded the direct expenditures on the production of diesel locomotives by 130 per cent, of electric locomotives by 90 per cent, and of coal by 20 per cent). Using aggregated economic coefficients the planning agencies establish the requirments for means of production, taking due account of the sum total of ties in the national economy. Thus calculated aggregated standards are regularly defined, with due account for technological progress in individual industries and the introduction of new materials. In the next stages the requirements are defined and corrected by the direct count method on the basis of more detailed standards for goods and of balance calculations. Long-term plans contain assignments for cutting the input of raw materials and other supplies, fuel and electric power. Thus, the Directives make provision for cutting the expenditure of rolled steel in machine-building and metal-working by approximately 20-25 per cent. The consumption rate for fuel in industry is to be cut by no less than 8-10 per cent and that for power by 6-8 per cent.

In conformity with the classification of means of production into implements and objects of labour, two groups of balances are employed in determining the demand for them:

(1) balances of industrial goods used chiefly as implents of labour, among them balances of equipment—machine-tools, forge-press equipment, turbines, rolling stock, etc.;

(2) balances of industrial goods used chiefly as objects of labour, among them balances of raw materials and other supplies, ore, pig-iron, steel, rolled stock, soda, fuel, electric power, building materials, etc.

Material balances are drafted first for the raw material, fuel and power-producing industries and for machine-building, and then for the other industries.

On the next page is the standard pattern of material balance adopted for the national economy as a whole.

Summary inter-sectoral input-output tables are compiled for the most important kinds of products whose range is fixed by the state plan (ferrous and non-ferrous metals, building materials, oil products, fuel, agricultural raw materials, main types of equipment).

Republican balances with divisions by districts and district balances are drafted on the same pattern, but for a wider range of goods. They

*Material Balance*                          *for 196 . . .*
(name of product)

| Resources, total | Distribution of total |
|---|---|
| including: | including: |
| (a) production | (a) production and operational needs |
| (b) imports | (b) construction |
| (c) other revenue sources | (c) market fund |
| (d) carry-over at suppliers at beginning of year | (d) exports |
| | (e) state reserves |
| | (f) current reserves |
| | (g) carry-over at suppliers at end of year |

are drafted after the funds for each Republic have been allocated and the plan of inter-republican deliveries fixed.

Adequate appraisal of the population's requirements in manufactured consumer goods calls for a comprehensive study of the commodity pattern of the population's demand. The planning of the industrial output of consumer goods is closely co-ordinated with the planning of turnover, its volume and commodity pattern, and with the production programme of agriculture—the chief supplier of raw materials for the light and food industries—as well as a wide range of important goods used directly by the population without being industrially processed.

The planning of various funds is required for the retail goods-turnover plan. This planning is done on the basis of material balances worked out for the most important foodstuffs and non-food commodities. Draft summary balances for the basic kinds of products put out by the light and food industries (dairy and meat products, flour, groats, sugar, textiles, furniture, soap, etc.) are drafted to approximately the pattern shown overleaf.

The intensive development of industry brings about major changes in its structure, which enhance the efficiency and productivity of social labour. In present conditions new branches which guarantee fast technological progress receive particular attention. The less efficient types of fuel and power, raw materials and other supplies are being steadily ousted by highly efficient ones, and the all-round use of these is rapidly expanding. The share of synthetic materials and metals and

*Pattern of Balance for Light and Food Industry Output*

| Resources | Distribution |
|---|---|
| 1. Carry-over at beginning of year<br>2. Supplied by industry<br>3. Imports<br>4. Supplied from earlier reserves<br><br>5. Supplied from other sources | 1. Market fund<br>2. Industrial processing fund<br>3. Extra-market fund<br>including:<br>  industrial consumption fund<br>  fund of organisations financed<br>  by budget<br>  fund of industrial clothing and<br>  footwear<br>  other purposes<br>4. Exports<br>5. Reserve |
| | Total to be distributed |
| | Balance |

alloys with new properties is increasing. New types of machines, instruments and apparatus connected with automation and electronics are coming into increasing use.

The structure of industry reflects the quantitative ratios between its component parts—the branches, types or various groups of production, as well as the forms of the social division of labour. The change of these ratios in favour of the more progressive sectors characterises the process of the development and perfection of industrial production. This presupposes priority development of those industries which determine the trends and rate of technological progress and the higher efficiency of social production; the development of production specialisation, co-operation and integration; and co-ordination of the development of industry and its component parts with the development of all the sectors of the national economy.

The Directives give instructions for enhancing the level of specialisation and co-operation of enterprises, involving the development of economically expedient forms of integration of production, which guarantee the better utilisation of raw material resources. The cutting of production costs and expenditures on the transportation of raw materials and finished goods is an important criterion for determining the size of an enterprise and the degree of its specialisation and integration.

The planning of specialisation in industry is performed along three basic lines:

(1) Item specialisation, characterised by the concentration of the output of certain finished goods at special enterprises (machine-tool and automobile plants, shoe and textile factories). The plan for item specialisation is drafted for the most important items of industrial output.

(2) Element specialisation, which involves the division of the manufacturing process into the individual production of elements, units and parts (ball-bearing plants, piston factories, etc.).

(3) Process specialisation, characterised by singling out certain stages of the production process (foundry enterprises, spinning and weaving factories). The planning of process specialisation applies to the most important kinds of ingots, shaped steel castings, forgings and stampings, as well as to certain other processes, such as repair jobs.

The long-term plan for specialisation development is drafted according to years for industries and kinds of goods, singling out specialised plants, factories and shops. Specialisation plans for the ministries include specialising shops and enterprises.

Specialisation of industrial production is inseparably connected with co-operation. Specialisation divides the production process into its component parts, whereas co-operation unites it into a single whole.

Co-operation is a form of organising production in which a number of individual enterprises establish close productive relations for the manufacture of a certain complex product. A characteristic feature is the establishment of productive relations between enterprises in the process of carrying out a common production task.

Co-operation is also planned along three lines corresponding to and proceeding from the lines of specialisation.

In drafting production plans for individual enterprises, industries and Republics much attention is given to mapping measures for the further development of industrial production integration. This is based on technological and territorial unity, which permits a fuller and more efficient utilisation of raw stuffs and intermediate materials. There are three basic kinds of integration:

(1) Integration by combining consecutive production process stages; for example, integrated chemical-and-metallurgical plants

in which mining of ore, and production of pig-iron, steel and rolled steels are combined; or textile plants which combine the spinning, weaving and finishing of fabrics.

(2) Integration based on the utilisation of waste materials. This form of integration is extensively employed in metallurgy (for instance, the use of slag for producing cement), in the wood-working industry, etc.

(3) Integration based on all-round utilisation of raw materials. Thus from one raw material it is possible to produce, by various processing methods, a wide range of products. Such integration has been broadly used in the chemical industry and in non-ferrous metallurgy.

## 4. DEVELOPMENT PLAN FOR AGRICULTURE

Agriculture is closely linked both with industry manufacturing means of production and with that manufacturing consumer goods. It plays an extremely important part in the U.S.S.R.'s economy. Including forestry, it employs one-third of all workers in the country, accounts for more than one-fifth of all fixed productive assets, and produces more than one-fifth of the gross national income.

In the period from 1913 to 1964 gross agricultural output increased by 150 per cent, while the number of workers engaged in agriculture diminished to less than a half. However, the level of development of Soviet agriculture does not meet the country's steadily growing needs. The consumption level of animal proteins and vegetable oils is insufficient. Neither is the output of industrial agriculture raw materials—raw cotton, flax fibre, wool, leather, etc.—adequate. Nor is the steadily growing demand for textiles, hosiery, woollen clothing and leather footwear satisfied in full.

The shortage of agricultural products inhibits the development of the food, meat, dairy, footwear and textile industries.

We have already mentioned that the rate of agricultural development in the U.S.S.R. has declined in recent years. This was chiefly caused by violations of the economic laws which govern production, disregard of the principles of material incentive, and failure to effect the harmonious combination of public and personal interests. There were also shortcomings in organising the procurement and purchase of agricultural products and an underestimation of the role of science and of practical experience.

Following a comprehensive and sober analysis of shortcomings and their causes, some important economic measures were introduced, aimed at boosting the efficiency in all branches of agricultural production. After the March (1965) plenary session of the C.P.S.U. Central Committee, measures for improving both planning and economic incentives were carried out to boost agricultural production.

A basically new method of purchases of farm produce was established. Collective and state farms were notified of stable realistic plans of produce purchases for five years to come. State purchase prices on many products of arable farming and livestock breeding were raised, and higher prices for above-plan sales of staple grain crops to the state were introduced. At the same time, the prices of many producers' goods were reduced, as well as of electrical power supplied to collective and state farms. Rural prices of manufactured consumer goods and foodstuffs were reduced, and levelled out with those in the towns.

These measures produced positive results. Despite the fact that in 1965 there was a severe drought in many areas of the country, especially in the zones which produce marketable grain, the gross output of agriculture amounted to 55,300 million roubles (in comparable prices), which was more than had been produced in any of the preceding years.

Agriculture receives a great deal of attention in the Directives of the 23rd C.P.S.U. Congress on the 1966–70 five-year plan. The central target for the coming five years in agriculture is to achieve a considerable increase in the output of farm and animal produce with the object of satisfying more fully the population's growing demand for foodstuffs and industry's demand for agricultural raw materials.

The planning of agriculture has a number of specific features.

Prior to 1955 state plans fixed rigidly detailed indices for the development of agriculture (size of sown areas, yields, head of livestock, etc.). At present only a few indices are set by the state plans. Collective and state farms exercise a broad initiative in planning agricultural production.

The following assignments for agriculture are set in the state plan:

(1) state purchases from collective farms and delivery of staple farm products by state farms;

(2) irrigation and land reclamation, watering of pastures;

(3) electrification of agriculture.

Prior to 1965 the purchase plan was fixed annually and the assignments were frequently changed in the course of state purchases. This had an adverse effect. In 1965, purchase plans for all staple farm products were fixed for 1966 and through to 1970. The purchase plans acquired the force of law and cannot be altered.

The Directives provide that between 1966–70 agricultural output must increase annually by 25 per cent as compared with the annual average output during the preceding five years. The purchase plan for the five years was already fixed and that is why the Directives deal only with above-plan purchases of grain and other farm produce at higher prices. They pay much attention to the technical equipment of agriculture—capital investments are to be doubled, as compared with the preceding five years. In the course of 1966–70 collective and state farms will be supplied with 1,970,000 tractors, 1,100,000 lorries, 550,000 grain combines; work on farm electrification is to be extended considerably, repair facilities are to be developed, and mineral fertiliser supplies will reach 55 million tons in 1970.

To work out the centralised plan of agricultural production, use is made of the following indices submitted by Union Republics: total output of staple crop and animal products, as well as output per 100 hectares of farm land and *per capita*; sown areas and the pattern of cultivation; yield of agricultural crops; head of livestock by species; livestock productivity, etc.

On the basis of produce purchase assignments collective and state farms themselves determine in their economic plans the size and pattern of sown areas, yield of crops, and head of livestock and its productivity. In determining state purchases for the individual Republics, territories, regions and districts, their production level, marketed output and possibilities of expanding output in the plan period are taken into consideration.

In order to co-ordinate the production and consumption of agricultural products, balance calculations are made for the staple products in the plan period for all categories of farms, distinguishing collective farms and state farms.

Annual production is a most important item of the resource section of these balances. The potential output of produce is calculated separately for arable farming and livestock breeding.

The output of arable farming is determined on the basis of the balance of farm land, balance of crop areas and yield.

The balance of farm land takes into account all the land available, including arable land and pasture, as well as that under structures, felling areas, burned-out plots, water reservoirs, gullies, ravines, etc. The estimate of farm land available is the basis for estimating the opportunities for agricultural production and determining output per 100 hectares of land. The extent and pattern of the sown areas are determined by the collective and state farms so as to guarantee intensive utilisation of land, fulfilment of state purchase assignments, and satisfaction of the collective and state farms' requirements with the least possible input of labour.

Assignments for crop yields are substantiated by draft balances of mineral and chemical fertilisers, the balance of mechanical and animal traction, and the balance of farm machinery.

Livestock breeding is the other main branch of agriculture. The output of livestock produce is determined on the basis of an estimation of the head of livestock and its productivity. These calculations are supported by balances of cattle, balances of fodder, as well as by zootechnical measures.

The substantiation of assignments for the head of livestock and productivity serves as the basis for planning the gross yield of animal produce, which is calculated separately for products not dependent on slaughter (milk, wool, eggs) and for those dependent on slaughter (meat, hides, horns, etc.).

Among the most important problems of agricultural planning is that of the distribution of purchase plan assignments throughout the areas of the country, for this predetermines to a considerable extent the line of agricultural development. The settlement of the purchase plan with reference to the country's areas involves all-round consideration of agricultural production specialisation and of the level of its marketable output, as well as of the efficiency of the production of various kinds of produce in different agricultural zones.

The specialisation of agriculture presupposes rational siting of agricultural production in the country's zones, the establishment of correct crop rotation, an efficient sown area pattern and an adequate combination of different kinds of agricultural production in accordance with the specific features of each zone.

Specialisation and siting of agriculture are carried out by agricultural zones which have similar production conditions and common agronomic and economic factors. In conformity with scientific recommendations, the U.S.S.R. is divided into 40 agricultural zones which, in turn, are divided into 100 subzones. Each Republic includes, as a rule, several agricultural zones and a large number of subzones, covering the territories of a number of administrative regions and districts having uniform natural and economic conditions. If these conditions in a region or district are not uniform, it may come under several subzones, which makes for a more ramified specialisation, this being quite important for bringing out latent reserves.

In defining agricultural zones and determining their specialisation, their natural, historic and economic conditions are taken into consideration. The natural and historic conditions include: soil composition, flora and fauna, the level of ground water occurrence, direction of predominating winds, degree of soil erosion, mean air temperature, amount of precipitations, duration of vegetation period, etc. The economic factors comprise: the requirement of the natural economy for the given kinds of agricultural products, adequate utilisation of all land and raising soil productivity, the provision of optimum conditions for using farm machinery and equipment, raising crop yields and livestock productivity, the provision of raw materials to manufacturing industry, the setting up of suburban agricultural enterprises around industrial centres and cities, reduction of production costs and raising the efficiency of agricultural production.

A number of criteria are used to determine the efficiency of agricultural production:

(a) yield of produce per 100 hectares of sown land or farm land (this is the criterion most often used);

(b) yield of produce per 1,000 roubles of fixed productive assets;

(c) yield of products per worker engaged in agriculture.

### 5. PLANNING OF TRANSPORT

The plan of production of industrial goods and the plan of agricultural produce purchases serve as the basis for determining the demand for all types of freight transport, while the plans for raising living standards determine the requirements to be met by passenger transport.

The summary plan for the development of transport includes the following chief sections and indicators:

(1) Freight and passenger traffic plan on the whole and for different kinds of transport (rail, sea, river, road and air transport, as well as pipelines).

(2) Plan for the development of the transport network (development of railways and motor roads, waterways, airlines and pipelines and their mileage at the end of the plan period).

(3) Plan for the utilisation of rolling stock.

The following assignments for railway transport are set in the Directives: the goods turnover of railways will be increased by 23 per cent; the change-over from steam to electric and diesel traction will be completed in the main; a total of about 7,000 km of railway lines will be built.

Sea-borne freight is to be increased by about 80 per cent. Merchant marine tonnage will be enlarged by about 50 per cent. The handling capacity of ports will be extended by approximately 40 per cent.

The river fleet must be able to handle in full all freight available in the vicinity of inland waterways.

The amount of crude oil and oil products transported over pipelines will be doubled and about 12,000 km of pipelines will be built.

Freight carried by road transport will be increased by about 70 per cent. In the next five years a total of 63,000 km of motor roads will be built.

About 80 per cent more passengers will be carried by air transport. Some 35 to 40 airports will be built for air services of national importance and 200 airports for local services.

The planning of freight transport begins from the quantity of freight to be handled in the period planned. In drafting long-term plans, calculations are made for eight types of goods which together account for almost 80 per cent of the total freightage (coal, oil products, ore, iron and steel, timber, coke, building materials and grain).

The annual transport plans include assignments for 34 types of freight, ten of them being agricultural goods. For the goods that are not included in the centralised state plan, the scope of transport is fixed by the local transport agencies jointly with the planning and economic agencies of the corresponding Republics.

The establishment of the amount of goods to be handled, both by items and on the whole, involves the drafting of balances of the production and consumption of staple products according to the following approximate scheme:

| Resources | | | | Utilisation | | | |
|---|---|---|---|---|---|---|---|
| Carry-over at beginning of year | Output | Other sources | Total | Local consumption | Carry-over at end of year | Remains on the spot | To be transported |
| | | | | | | | |

Once the total scope of transport is set, goods shipments are distributed among the different kinds of transport with due account for the specific features and potentialities of each of them and on the basis of calculations of the comparative efficiency of using each type of transport (according to transport cost indices, capital investments per unit of freight, fuel consumption, speed of delivery, etc.). This involves also calculations of the development of transport facilities in the various areas and throughout the country as a whole.

Freight turnover is determined not only by the amount of goods handled, but by the average distance of shipments as well. To determine the distance of shipment, rational diagrams of freight shipments and balances of inter-district freightage are drafted. Growth or decrease of shipment distances depends to a considerable extent on changes in economic ties among areas and Republics. Rational freight shipment schemes are based on rational siting of production and on the level of the cost of production and transport of goods, as well as on capital investments essential for the development of production and of transport lines in the given areas.

The basic criterion for rational economic regioning of transport is found in the sum total of current expenditures involved in the production of goods in various areas and their delivery to the site of consumption. These schemes indicate between what points and along what transport lines the given freights are to be shipped. They also prohibit certain routes for the shipment of certain freights.

Freight shipment schemes are not immutable. They change together with changes in the siting of production, with the introduction of more rational methods of obtaining and processing raw materials, and with the development and improvement of the transport network.

It is on the basis of rational freight turnover schemes and of the accepted arrangements for supplying the areas in need of certain goods that the balances of inter-regional exchange are worked out for the staple freights.

## 6. CAPITAL CONSTRUCTION PLAN

The scale of construction in the Soviet Union is steadily increasing. More than 39,000 large and a great number of medium and small state enterprises were built or restored and put into operation in the Soviet Union between 1918 and 1964. Many operating enterprises were reconstructed and expanded. More than 200,000 km of railway track were laid or restored, more than 9,000 state farms were set up and large-scale work was undertaken in building homes, schools and other educational institutions, medical, cultural and scientific centres.

At the beginning of 1966, the total of all fixed assets of the Soviet Union was more than four times that in 1940, while the fixed assets of industrial production increased nearly seven times over the period.

A steady growth of fixed capital and productive capacity is secured by planning capital investment. The capital investment plan solves the following basic problems:

(a) provision for high and stable rates of growth of production and popular welfare, with the corresponding growth of fixed capital,

(b) provision for inter-sectoral proportions of production,

(c) provision for territorial proportions of reproduction in accordance with scientific principles of the distribution of production and the need for levelling out economic and cultural development in different Union Republics and economic areas of the country, and

(d) maximum rise of the effectiveness of capital investment for the national economy.

An important characteristic of the capital investment plan is its long-range projection, since both construction and the utilisation of fixed capital introduced as a result of it are prolonged processes.

An organic part of the plan for the national economy, the capital investment plan is intimately linked with all other sections of the plan for the national economy. These links are above all as follows:

(1) With the finance plan of the national economy, since fixed assets account for the bulk of the accumulation fund and of all national property.

(2) With the plan for the development of heavy industry, since it is heavy industry that furnishes the material basis of construction, including the supply of energy. A major manifestation of the interconnection between the capital investment plan and the heavy industry development plan is the interdependence of the capital investment plan and the plan for the development and introduction of new plant.

(3) The capital investment plan specifies the development and distribution of all sectors of production in terms of industrial capacity growth (this is especially important in long-range plans).

(4) The capital investment plan specifies the development of equipment, materials, etc., for residential and municipal construction and maintenance, education, health, culture, art and other non-productive spheres.

(5) The capital investment plan is closely linked with the plans for manpower and finance. The scale, pattern and distribution of capital construction essentially influence the quantitative and structural indicators of the plans for manpower and finance.

The state capital investment plan is developed for the following interdependent items:

(1) Introduction of units producing major products in the key sectors of the national economy.

(2) Introduction of residential, municipal, cultural and service projects.

(3) Introduction of fixed capital. The final indices of the introduction of fixed capital and production capacity make it possible to co-ordinate the capital investment plan with the national economy's demand for the reproduction of fixed capital. Therefore, the plan for the introduction of fixed capital and major production units is the main part of the capital investment plan.

(4) The volume of capital investment in construction and assembly for the national economy as a whole as well as for each Union Republic and key sector. Distinguished as separate items in the total volume of capital investment are investments in the construction of new productive capacities, residential and municipal construction, and construction in education, science, culture and medicine.

(5) Title lists of capital construction. The total volume of capital investment is distributed over specific projects on the basis of title lists.

The national economic plans also specify targets for prospecting and surveying, and for developing the building industry on which the capital investment plan rests.

The Directives of the 23rd Congress of the C.P.S.U. for the five-year plan for the development of the national economy in 1966–70 define the principal tasks in the sphere of capital construction as: the most effective use of capital investment, the timely completion of new industrial, residential and other projects at lowest costs, and a higher quality of building.

From 1966 to 1970 the total volume of capital investment in the Soviet national economy from all sources (state centralised and non-centralised investment, the investment of collective farms and co-operatives, the privately financed building of homes) is set down at approximately 310,000,000,000 roubles or 47 per cent more than in 1961–65.

The Directives specify the volume of investment for each sector of the economy as well as the major directions of investment. To raise the effectiveness of capital investment (state the Directives) it must be channelled first of all into the technical re-equipment of operating enterprises, the mechanisation and automation of production, its greater specialisation, etc., to ensure a substantial increase of output at the operating enterprises within a shorter period and at less costs than in the case of new construction. According to the Directives, capital investment should first of all be channelled into the completion of projects already started, or scheduled to be soon commissioned, in order to accelerate the introduction of productive capacities and fixed capital into operation.

The Directives provide for a continued effort to raise the level of industrialisation of construction, to make building cheaper and improve the work on designs and estimates.

The central section of the capital investment plan is the plan for introducing into operation fixed capital, productive capacities and housing projects. The key target is to ensure the integrated and proportional introduction into operation of fixed capital and productive capacities.

The targets for putting fixed capital into operation are specified in the state plan for Union Republics and departments, the introduction of productive fixed capital being specified for each major sector. The plan for putting these assets into operation is based on their estimated cost.

The introduction of productive capacities is planned for the major products of the key sectors. Targets are worked out separately for putting productive capacities into operation through new construction, through the expansion and reconstruction of operating enterprises, and through the growth of output owing to organisational or technological measures.

The planning for the introduction of productive capacities and fixed capital is based on the title lists of projects under construction. The compilation and endorsement of these are of primary importance.

The title lists of projects under construction are compiled and endorsed for the entire period of construction, specifying for each year the volume of capital investment and the targets for introducing productive capacities and fixed capital, and taking into account the standard schedule ratings of building endorsed in due procedure.

The title lists of construction projects may include only those projects which were provided, as of September 1 of the year preceding the planned year, by duly endorsed designs, blueprints and estimates for the volume of work to be done in the year planned. To be entered in the title lists of construction projects, a project must be backed by adequate outputs of construction and assembly agencies by the beginning of the construction schedule.

The title lists of each project indicate: the name and location of the project, the period of construction (the year when it starts and the year when it is to be completed) and the total estimated cost and the rated output of the entire project; the volume of capital investment and the introduction of productive capacities into operation in the previous period (for each project the construction of which started before the period planned); the volume of capital investment in the period planned and the scheduled introduction into operation of productive capacities and fixed capital.

The title lists of started and continued projects constitute an important element of the capital construction plan. It is on the basis of these documents that the structure of capital investment, the progress scheduled for the period planned, and the volume of productive capacities and fixed capital to be put into operation are determined. The title lists of construction projects are itemised for each sector.

Three types of construction projects are distinguished: completion projects (production capacities to go into operation within the period planned), start projects (projects newly started and having no productive capacities scheduled to go into operation in the period planned) and transfer projects (started before the period planned and scheduled to be completed after this period expires).

Apart from the title lists of the construction sites endorsed for the entire period of construction, intra-project title lists are endorsed for the current year by clients in agreements with chief contractors.

*The intra-project title lists* include the sections of the project (structures, sections of the structures, highways, etc.) which are to be completed in the period planned. The intra-project title lists indicate the estimated cost of each project, its carry-over as at the beginning of the period, the annual plan of work specifying the cost of equipment as well as construction and assembly, and finally the schedule for commissioning each specific project.

The intra-project title lists are the basic documents for financing construction sites, sub-contraction plans, and construction progress supervision.

The title lists are basic to the development of major account plans, like the capital investment account, the account of fixed capital and the account of productive capacities.

The volume of capital investment in the title lists is indicated in the estimated prices as of July 1, 1955, taking into account piece-rates for building work effective as of January 1, 1956, standard overhead ratings effective as of January 1, 1958, and rates for structural assembly work effective as of January 1, 1959.

The capital investment account has approximately the following pattern:

| | State Construction | | |
| --- | --- | --- | --- |
| | Productive projects | Other than productive projects | Total |
| Carry-over of unfinished construction cost as at the beginning of the year | | | |
| Plan for capital investment, incl. investments increasing value of fixed assets | | | |
| Introduction of fixed assets into operation | | | |
| Carry-over of unfinished construction cost as at the end of the year | | | |

The capital investment account makes it possible to determine the basic targets of the cumulative or summary plan for putting into operation fixed capital and productive capacities as well as to calculate the targets for the cost of unfinished and newly started building.

By "unfinished construction cost" is meant the total cost of all projects unfinished and not yet put into operation. Under this heading comes the value of unfinished buildings and structures, the assembly of equipment, productive plant as well as temporarily discontinued construction, unused work and the carry-over of materials and plant.

The work done in the current period and scheduled to be continued thereafter accounts for the bulk of unfinished construction cost.

In 1961 the State Construction Board of the U.S.S.R. (Gosstroy) endorsed model monthly schedules for the construction of enterprises, complete operational complexes, workshops, buildings and structures as well as various types of special buildings and structures and the model distribution of capital investment over the annual construction schedule (in per cent of the total estimated cost).

Shorter construction schedules constitute one of the most important economic problems at the present stage of development of the Soviet Union, and this problem is intimately linked with the more general problem of raising the effectiveness of capital investment.

The "complete operational complex" for each project is determined as the capital investment plan for this project is developed. The complete operational complex is the set of sub-projects all of which must be completed in order to put into operation the main workshops of an enterprise under construction. For example, the complete operational complex in the construction of a blast furnace consists of: the blast furnace proper, air heaters, ore bunkers, the casting house, dust catchers, throat gas purifiers, the throat platform, hoisting and handling equipment, water supply, sewerage, railway track, etc.

To accelerate construction and raise its effectiveness, standard ratings for transferred-schedule work are developed in some industries and housing construction. By "transferred-schedule work" is meant the work to be done on projects the construction of which is scheduled to continue in the next year planned. The purpose is to ensure the rhythm of construction and the on-schedule introduction into operation of productive capacities and fixed capital.

In industrial construction we have:

(a) *sectoral work cost*, which is the cost of unfinished construction for a sector as a whole in accordance with the long-range plan and standard schedule ratings,

(b) *schedule progress of an enterprise under construction*, which is the ratio of the entire cost of capital investment for both completed and unfinished units to the total estimated cost,

(c) *transferred-schedule work*, which is the ratio of the cost of capital construction for unfinished units to their estimated cost.

While rating the above schedules, several factors are taken into account: the total period of construction, the estimated cost, the structure of investment, the intermediate introduction of some units into operation, and the on-schedule date for the completion of construction. Apart from the rated schedules, the cost of unfinished capital construction includes the investment in all kinds of unfinished work: costs of temporarily discontinued units, costs of the units actually put into operation but not yet duly formalised, etc.

Of major importance for planning the introduction into operation of fixed capital and productive capacities is the development of the account of fixed capital according to the total primary estimates, and according to the same, taking into account plant depreciation. The account of fixed capital according to the total primary estimates (by the "total primary estimates" is meant the total of all expenditures on the production, acquisition and transportation of the fixed capital) describes the variation and absolute magnitude of the entire productive apparatus of all sectors of material production and consumer fixed capital. All calculation of the effectiveness of capital and of the output-capital ratio are based on the account of fixed capital according to the primary estimates. The account of fixed capital taking into account plant depreciation describes the variation and absolute results of the assets in current estimates, which makes it possible to co-ordinate the plans for putting into operation fixed capital with the investment account contained in the national account.

The account of fixed capital according to total primary estimates is developed along these lines:

| Fixed capital at the beginning of the period | Introduction of fixed capital into operation | Depletion of fixed capital as a result of obsolescence and depreciation | Fixed capital at the end of the period |
|---|---|---|---|
|  |  |  |  |

The account of fixed capital according to primary estimates taking into account plant depreciation is worked out according to the pattern shown on the next page.

A project under construction cannot be entered into the title lists unless it has been provided with a proper design and estimate specifications, which must be considered and endorsed before the construction project can begin. Industrial enterprises, dwelling houses and civil projects are designed as a rule in two stages:

I

(1) Development of a project assignment, and estimates and accounts for it, and

(2) development of working drawings.

| Fixed capital at the beginning of the period, taking into account plant depreciation | Introduction of fixed capital into operation | Overhauling and renovation | Amortisation of productive capital and depreciation of non-productive capital | Fixed capital at the end of the period taking into account plant depreciation |
|---|---|---|---|---|
| | | | | |

In the designing of large industrial enterprises three designing stages are allowed in some cases:

(a) development of a project assignment and estimates and accounts,

(b) development of a technological design and estimates for it, and

(c) development of working drawings.

The project assignment includes the following specifications: the site, the products the designed enterprise is to turn out, its capacity, the input-output relations of the enterprise with other enterprises and sectors of the national economy, its sources of raw materials and fuel, supply of water and power, the basic types of buildings and structures, the construction of dwelling houses and the construction schedule.

The design and estimate specifications are endorsed by the corresponding economic agencies and by the Council of Ministers of the Union Republic concerned. An exception is made for very large and especially important projects for which the project assignments as well as many technological designs are endorsed by the Council of Ministers of the U.S.S.R. One of the aims of the Gosstroy of the U.S.S.R. is to provide in due time design and estimate specifications corresponding to the latest thing in science and engineering.

The construction estimates are made on the basis of the project as well as of authorised aggregated standard estimate ratings and certified price books. The project specifies the design and expected technical performance of the construction unit, and on this basis estimates are made of the physical volumes of the building elements or types of work (foundation pits in cubic metres, earth work in cubic metres, plastering in square metres, etc.). The expenditure of materials, working-time and machine-shifts per constructional element unit is calculated by handbooks of aggregated estimate ratings. Unit rates for a given construction project (estimated cost per unit of each constructional element or type of work based on certified standard rates and prices in application to a given project) are established on the basis of the project, aggregated standard ratings and price books.

Whenever possible only working drawings are made (for example, for some agricultural or land-improvement construction projects, service establishments, etc.).

Design organisations receive assignments from their clients on the basis of the plans for designing new construction. The assignments indicate: the area or point of construction, the specialisation and co-operation of the designed enterprise, its capacity, the estimated demand for raw materials, electric power, etc., approximate areas of consumption of the enterprise's output, the construction schedule, and the sequence of introduction of productive capacities into operation.

The introduction into operation of the basic assets and productive capacities is planned comparatively simply for a year. In this case the introduction of fixed capital and productive capacities is completely determined by the units to be commissioned according to the title lists by the beginning of the planned year. However, the total volume of capital investment in the planned year is always larger than the volume of capital investment in completed projects in the same year, since part of the investment is chanelled into transfer projects, i.e. projects scheduled to continue for the next year, and starting projects, i.e. those newly started and not scheduled to be completed in the same year.

The development of a plan for putting fixed capital and productive capacities into operation for a long-range period, i.e. a five-year period, is more complex. The starting projects for a five-year plan will be not only the projects figuring as transfer projects at the beginning of the five-year period but also a considerable number of projects started in the first half of the five-year period (for non-productive projects and some productive projects these may well include also those projects the construction of which started only in the third and fourth year of the five-year period).

Hence the immense importance of determining correctly the pattern and distribution of capital investment between different spheres of production, sectors and areas.

In planning the volume and pattern of capital investment, several consecutive stages must be mentioned:

(1) Determination of the total volume of capital investment possible over the period planned, including capital investment under the state plan.

(2) Justification of the possible volume of state capital investment by the size of financial, material and manpower resources which can be used for capital construction, as well as by the possibilities of the development of the building industry and the provision of design and estimate specifications, with the introduction of readjustments if necessary into the preliminary determined volumes of capital investment.

(3) Determination of the structure of capital investments in material, technological, reproductive, sectoral and territorial terms.

(4) Distribution of capital investment between the sectors of the productive and non-productive spheres as well as between different Union Republics and economic areas.

The calculations of the effectiveness of capital investment in the national economy differ at each of the above stages in the type and number of indicators involved.

*The index of the total amount of capital investment* in the national economy belongs to the indices of the national-economic account. Only part of capital investment in the national economy is reflected in state short-term and current plans. On the whole, the composition of general capital investments in the national economy includes:

(1) Centralised capital investment allocated under the state plan to the state-owned economy.

(2) Capital investments which are not allocated under the state plan:

(a) state capital investment in geological surveying which is not connected with definite projects,

(b) state capital investment in the development of design and estimate specifications,

(c) state capital investment in the formation of the basic livestock of state farms,

(d) capital investment allocated by enterprises from their own funds and from loans of the state bank,

(e) capital investment made by collective farms, and

(f) capital investment on individual holdings.

In accordance with the decisions of the September 1965 plenary meeting of the Central Committee of the C.P.S.U., capital investment in the expansion of operating enterprises has to be made by these enterprises. They are to plan and finance from non-centralised capital investment all the measures necessary to improve production and in particular to replace plant, introduce new technologies, methods and controls, eliminate bottlenecks and carry out other measures raising the effectiveness of production.

The capital investments specified in items (a), (b), (c) and (d) are worked out in the calculations of the summary financial plan and the state budget, those indicated in (e) are worked out in the plans for the capital construction of collective farms and the accounts of the Gosplan (the State Planning Committee of the U.S.S.R.), and those indicated in (f) are determined on the basis of the centralised account calculations performed by Gosplan.

A major and decisive source of capital investment is the accumulated part of the national income.

To determine the total value of capital investment (under the state plan) is to take an important but only an initial step in capital investment planning. It is necessary to check whether a preliminary calculation of the volume of investments is justified in terms of financial, material and manpower resources and the prospects for development of the building industry and designing agencies.

The sources for capital investment under the state plan are: the state budget, the centralised fund of allowances for plant depreciation and capital construction (the renovation fund) and that part of the profit which remains at the disposal of enterprises.

The ratios between different sources for capital investment have been shown to be sufficiently stable.

The proportion of budgetary allocations for capital investment in the grand total of budgetary spending is also sufficiently stable. As the current economic reform is implemented in industry, the importance of capital investment made by enterprises from their development funds and state bank loans is bound to increase.

Capital construction at operating enterprises will be financed almost completely from the development fund and state bank loans. It is only into the construction of new workshops that centralised investment will be siphoned if necessary.

An approximate model method is used for the calculation of long-range plans and at the initial stage of current planning to establish whether the contemplated volume of investment can be financed. At subsequent stages of planning, the volume of capital investment is compared with the volume of the state's financial resources on the basis of a cumulative or summary financial plan.

The volume of capital investment must be justified not only financially but also in terms of material resources, i.e. materials, equipment, etc. The final amount of capital investment for the period planned cannot be determined without this procedure. The need for material resources depends on the volume and structure of capital investment. The portion of capital investment allocated for acquiring equipment gives the total value of machinery necessary for the contemplated construction. The volume of construction and assembly work is the point of departure for calculating the need for building materials of all kinds, including timber and metal as well as prefabricated structural units.

The sectoral structure of construction and the schedule progress of projects under construction at the beginning of the period planned essentially influence the calculation of the materials, plant, etc., needed for capital construction.

The need for equipment for capital construction is determined on the basis of equipment account calculations. Developed and endorsed designs are already being used for determining the need for assembled equipment. For equipment requiring no assembly or installation (motor-cars, locomotives, tractors, etc.), the calculations of the need for equipment are based on the data of the total volume of work for each project and on work quotas. The equipment accounts ensure the co-ordination of the needs of capital construction for equipment with other needs for equipment (e.g. for the replacement and renovation of obsolete stock, replenishing of spare machine parts, replenishing of the machinery of operating enterprises, etc.).

The equipment accounts are drawn up for major groups of equipment (machine tools, forging and pressing equipment, etc.) as well as for separate items (turbines, steam boilers, locomotives, etc.). Apart from these accounts, a cumulative or summary account of equipment is drawn up in terms of cost, which makes it possible to bring the capital investment plan into line with the production programme for machine building. The need for building materials at the beginning of planning and at central planning agencies is determined with the aid of aggregated indices and at building agencies by direct calculations on the basis of the specific construction design. The former method of determining the need for building materials is based on the expenditure of major kinds of building materials per 100,000 roubles worth of construction and assembly work. The national plan establishes quotas for the expenditure of rolled metal, cement, timber, slate, reinforced concrete, iron roofing, glass, etc. The Gosplan of each Union Republic differentiates the quotas by economic areas, taking into account the sectoral composition of construction.

The method of aggregated ratings is simpler than any other, but it has serious defects. First of all, it should be noted that the expenditure of materials largely depends on the sectoral composition of capital construction, and on the relation between newly started and continued construction, and between entirely new building and reconstruction.

The aggregated ratings are therefore worked out or revised every year by the U.S.S.R. Gosstroy, taking into account all possible measures to save materials, substitute more desirable materials, etc., and are then submitted for endorsement to be incorporated in the state plan.

The method of directly calculating the need for building materials by the quotas of expenditure per construction unit and the physical volume of work is used by building agencies. Specified in this way, the the need for building materials is compared with the resources of the national economy as expressed in the accounts of building materials developed for major types of building materials (walling, roofing, etc.).

The calculation is accompanied by the development of measures for saving building materials (the introduction of expenditure quotas, application of cheaper and more effective materials, utilisation of local building materials, etc.).

The capital investment plan must also be justified in terms of manpower resources.

To determine the need for manpower, including highly skilled labour, the method of aggregated ratings is used at the initial stage of planning on the basis of the number of employees per 100,000 roubles worth of construction and assembly work. The latter index is determined from an analysis of the reported data and is corrected to allow for a possible growth of the productivity of labour. At subsequent stages of planning, and especially in the development of construction projects, the number of employees is established by the quotas of expenditure of working time for each specific kind of work.

The capital investment plan must also be carefully co-ordinated with the targets for the development of the building industry. The building industry is the foundation of building. It includes building and assembly agencies working under contracts with their clients. These agencies have everything necessary for construction, including assembly equipment, construction and road-building machinery and designing teams. They account for 87 per cent of all construction and assembly work (in heavy industry as well as civil construction and housing).

The plan for the development of the building industry is developed on the following principles: satisfying the targets for putting fixed capital and productive capacities into operation under the schedule specified by the state plan; concentration of the productive resources (including manpower) of building agencies on a limited number of completion projects, as well as projects simultaneously under construction, laying emphasis on the development and expansion of work under contracts; all-out use of the productive capacity of the building industry, with further specialisation of and co-operation between construction and assembly agencies; consistent industrialisation of construction by extensive use of prefabricated designs, units and parts, buildings and structures manufactured completely at enterprises, integrated automation and mechanisation, and mass line production.

The building industry development plan includes: a programme of construction and assembly work, a plan for technical development and organisational and technological measures, a plan for mechanisation and automation in construction, a plan for the development of specialisation and co-operation, and a plan for providing construction with materials, semi-finished products and prefabricated parts and units.

The planning of the structure of capital investment is an important element of capital investment planning. In this process the technological, productive, sectoral, reproductive and territorial (area) structure or distribution of capital investment is established.

By the "technological structure" is meant the distribution of capital investment between construction and assembly work, equipment and other items. In 1964 this structure was as follows: the proportion of construction and assembly work, 48 per cent, the proportion of equipment, 43 per cent, and the proportion of other costs, 9 per cent. The proportion of equipment in the total of capital investment is still low in the Soviet Union and the problem is to raise it steadily.

Construction work includes the erection, reconstruction and

expansion of permanent or temporary structures; construction of public utilities, including lighting mains; construction of all kinds of bases under heavy equipment, the lining of boilers, furnaces, etc.

Assembly work includes the assembly and installation of equipment for permanent and temporary projects, including the test and trial of the assembly.

Capital investment in equipment is subdivided into investment in technological, power-generating and other equipment requiring assembly, investment in equipment which is put into operation without assembly work (locomotives, railway cars, ships, motor-cars, tractors, field agricultural machinery, lorries, etc.) and finally investment to aquire equipment the value of which is added to the fixed capital.

Other capital costs included in capital investment are the costs involved in construction but not included in the cost of construction and assembly work. These are surveying and prospecting, part of drilling, the allocation of new sites and resettlement as a result of construction, etc. Some of these costs do not increase the value of fixed capital (the costs of training personnel for enterprises under construction, the costs of search drilling, etc.).

The capital investment plan is co-ordinated with the plan for production of building materials and the plan for manpower according to the volume of construction and assembly work with allowances for its specific, physical composition, while the capital investment plan is co-ordinated with the plan for production of equipment according to the volume of contemplated expenditure on equipment.

The general principle of planning the technological structure of capital investment is to try to increase the proportion of capital investment in equipment, since this raises the proportion of the effective part of fixed capital and hence the economic effectiveness of capital investment.

By the "productive structure" is meant the ratio between investment in productive projects (industry, farming, construction and transport) and non-productive projects (the construction of homes, schools, hospitals and other non-productive assets). In the fourth five-year plan period capital investment in the productive sphere accounted for 71 per cent, in the fifth five-year period also for 71 per cent, in 1956 to 1960 for about 65 per cent, and in 1961 to 1965 for about 64 per cent. The proportion between productive and non-productive investment is of major importance for planning the ratio between subdivisions I and II, between the sphere of production and the sphere of consumption, and also directly influences the sectoral structure of industrial production (a higher proportion of non-productive investment raises the demand for building materials, since construction bulks larger in the non-productive sphere).

By the "sectoral structure" is meant the distribution of investment over sectors of the productive and non-productive spheres. The sectoral structure of capital investment shapes the sectoral structure of national production as a whole as well as intersectoral relations. The distribution of capital investment must anticipate desirable trends in the structure of production and ensure the development of these trends in the desired direction.

By the "reproductive structure" is understood the ratio between capital investment in simple and expanded reproduction, and inside the latter between the cost of new construction and the cost of expansion, reconstruction and modernisation. According to tentative estimates, the amortisation fund accounts for 14 to 15 per cent of state capital investment in the Soviet national economy, and the accumulation fund for 85 to 86 per cent. Over the seven-year plan period (1959–65) the cost of reconstruction, modernisation, etc., in mining and extraction accounted for approximately 40 to 50 per cent and in the processing industries for about 60 to 70 per cent. Changes in the reproductive structure have a decisive effect on the rate of economic development and the effectiveness of production. The ratio between new building and reconstruction directly affects the technological structure of construction and hence the sectoral and territorial structure of national production as a whole and in particular of industrial production. A general principle of planning the reproductive structure is to raise steadily the proportion of investment in reconstruction and modernisation. The criterion for the choice between investment in new building and reconstruction must be the calculation of the comparative effectiveness of these investments.

By "territorial structure" is meant the distribution of total investment over the country's territory—its division between Union Republics and large economic areas. The territorial structure of investment shapes the territorial structure of production and is connected with planning for each specific area of the country.

The planning of the distribution of capital investment is determined by the economico-political targets set at a certain stage of development. The basic principles of planning the distribution of capital investment are:

—to prevent the diffusion of resources and concentrate them on completion projects or other key projects;

—to accelerate the introduction of productive capacities and fixed capital into operation;

—to ensure high technical standards for projects under construction and take into account all principles of the scientific distribution of production;

—to keep bringing down construction costs by eliminating architectural extravagance, making extensive use of model designs and intensifying the industrialisation of construction; and

—to determine the amount of investment for each project over the entire period of construction and its distribution over the years.

Capital investment is distributed first of all between all sectors, the key sectors taking priority.

For the sectors of the productive sphere, capital investment is distributed on the basis of the accounts of productive capacities or the accounts of fixed capital by approximately the following procedure. In the sectors with uniform products (coal, oil, cement, etc.) calculations are performed by working out the account of productive capacities by the following scheme:

| Production programme | Productive capacities needed | Productive capacities in operation | Productive capacities to be introduced | | | Specific capital investment | Volume of required capital investment |
| --- | --- | --- | --- | --- | --- | --- | --- |
| | | | For growth of productive capacities | For replenishment of productive capacities | Total | | |
| | | | | | | | |

By "specific capital investment" is meant the capital investment required for creating unit productive capacity or producing unit output.

The account is used to determine the entire additional introduction of productive capacities needed for meeting the production targets. Then the total volume of these productive capacities is calculated proceeding from the standard ratings for specific capital investment. Allowances are made in these calculations for possible measures to improve the exploitation of available productive capacities as well as to expand and renovate currently operating enterprises. The carry-over increments must also be taken into account.

In the sectors with a wide range of products (textiles and other consumer goods, foodstuffs, machine building, etc.) the required capital investment is determined differently, by drawing an account of fixed capital by the following scheme:

| Production programme | Capital: output ratio | Fixed productive capital required | Assets in operation | Required introduction of assets | | | Change of unfinished construction cost | Investment augmenting assets |
| --- | --- | --- | --- | --- | --- | --- | --- | --- |
| | | | | For growth of assets | For replenishment of assets | Total | | |
| | | | | | | | | |

The total demand for fixed capital is calculated proceeding from production targets and the assignments for the capital output ratio of production.

It is highly important to take into account investment not only in the sector under consideration but also in allied sectors. For example, to expand the output of the rolled metal workshop of an iron and steel works provision should be made for investment to increase the output of several allied sectors supplying the sector under study with raw materials, fuel and power, as well as to increase the output of other workshops of the same iron and steel works.

In the sectors of the non-productive sphere the need for capital investment is determined on the basis of the plan for development of network indices (i.e. the indices showing the expansion of a network of public institutions) and standard ratings for specific capital investment per unit area or capacity (for schools these are the indices of the introduction of new schools for so many students proceeding from the plan for school education and the estimated cost per student; for hospitals these are the need for the introduction of so many hospital beds and the estimated value of one bed, etc.).

Capital investment in the construction of productive projects is planned for each Union Republic, and for each ministry or department at the all-Union level, specifying capital investments for the key industries.

Capital investment in residential and municipal building as well as the building of educational, scientific, cultural and medical projects is planned for each Union Republic as a whole for all projects regardless of jurisdiction. An exception is made for the enterprises and organisations of the following ministries: Communications, Sea Transport, Transport Construction, Defence, Medium Machine Building, Electric Power Construction, etc., for which capital investment in the non-productive sphere is specified by the state plan directly.

Territorially, capital investment is distributed according to the general principles of scientific distribution of production.

Capital investment is distributed between Republics and economic areas as well as inside them on the basis of calculating the comparative effectiveness of investment by comparing the technological and economic indices for the key sectors of each Republic or area with the same for other areas and for the Soviet Union as a whole. To justify the construction of projects in a certain area, calculations are made of available raw materials, fuel and power, water supply and manpower, the output and consumption of basic products, the optimum size of the contemplated enterprises, their specialisation, co-operation and integration of production. Calculations are also made of specific capital investment and the prime cost of the products (including transport costs).

The state plan specifies the volume of capital investment for each Republic as a whole as well as for the key sectors. Each Union Republic distributes capital investment over its districts. This makes it possible to co-ordinate the growth of the productive capacities of allied sectors within restricted areas regardless of the subordination of the enterprises concerned. The integrated development of the economy of each area is vital for the most effective development of new residential units.

At all stages of capital investment planning, elaborate calculations are made of the economic effectiveness of measures aimed at introducing new equipment or mechanising and automating certain elements of production. These calculations bring out the most effective trends in the development of industrial production, establish priority in the contemplated measures, give the annual saving from these measures and specify their influence on the other targets of the national economic plan.

An investment is regarded as effective if it ensures an increase in the productivity of social labour for minimum total expenditure (capital investment and operation and maintenance cost) and thus yields the largest saving for the national economy.

The following criteria of higher capital investment effectiveness are especially important: higher productivity of social labour, smaller investment per unit output and quicker returns and, finally, lower production costs. Of decisive importance for raising the effectiveness of capital investment is the correct economically justified choice of proper directions in the development of proper sectors of the national economy.

A major means for raising the effectiveness of capital investment is improvement of the sectoral and technological structure of capital investment.

Calculations of capital investment effectiveness must answer two questions: (1) to what extent a contemplated measure for introducing new equipment is progressive and whether it can be accepted for introduction, and (2) what effect it will have in the national economy. To answer the first question, the parameters of the best types of Soviet or foreign-made equipment are accepted as the reference standard for comparison, and to answer the second question, the parameters of the equipment to be replaced are used for comparison.

If the newly introduced types of equipment are to be used on a wide scale, the parameters of that type of equipment in current use in the sector in question can be used as the base reference for determining the capital investment effectiveness. The parameters of the best types of Soviet or foreign-made equipment are used as the base reference in effectiveness calculations at research institutions and in designing offices concerned in new industrial construction as well as renovation and modernisation.

The main criteria of the effectiveness of introduced equipment are the rates and periods of return on capital investment needed for its introduction, as well as the production cost and labour productivity which could be attained as a result of its introduction. Other criteria are also used to choose the most effective variants of introduction of new equipment, such as specific capital investment per unit of newly introduced productive capacities, change in the rates of expenditure or raw materials, fuel and power, change in the rates of expenditure of manpower, and use of equipment and of productive areas per unit of output or of unfinished work.

In practice the determination of economic effectiveness often involves new equipment introduction variants for different scales of production. In such cases, to make the basic indices of economic effectiveness comparable (investment in fixed and circulating capital and the cost of annual output), these indices are reduced to a common denominator, so to speak. The annual output for that variant which has the largest scale of production is used as the denominator. Accordingly, extra investment into fixed and circulating capital which would be required for bringing the annual output to that of the reference variant without changing the productive equipment is added to the capital investment required for the variant with a smaller scale of production. When output is increased as a direct result of the introduction of new equipment, the calculation of the economic effectiveness includes the saving on a conventionally permanent part of overhead expenses per each unit of product.

If the development, introduction and assimilation of new equipment is planned over several years, the basic economic indices of the base reference (investment into fixed and circulating capital and annual output cost) are corrected taking into account possible changes of these indices by the time the new equipment is actually introduced. This procedure makes it possible to allow for an additional effect due to a better assimilation and use of new equipment.

A condition for well-justified calculations of economic effectiveness is the correct appraisal of the amount of capital investment. It is necessary to take into account for compared (reference and introduced) variants: (a) the cost of the construction and renovation of the structures involved, (b) the cost of the required equipment, including the cost of delivery and installation, (c) the cost of the modernisation of operating equipment (d) the renovation cost of that part of equipment which is contemplated to be used as new plant is introduced, and (e) the cost of the designing involved in the introduction of new equipment.

The cost of new equipment, including means of mechanisation, is determined by official price lists, and in the absence of such, by price books compiled on the strength of revaluation of fixed capital on January 1, 1960, or by the prices specified in the contracts for the delivery of equipment. The costs of special equipment manufactured by an enterprise for its own use as well as of modernisation of operating machines and mechanisms are determined by corresponding estimates. If there are no estimates (there may be none at the pre-design stage), the cost of new machines and mechanisms is determined in tentative terms by aggregated standard ratings for weight, labour per unit output and the average cost of 1 kg of similar equipment. The data on the average sectoral level of overheads and planned accumulations are also used in these calculations.

Investments in both design projects and allied sectors are taken into account when economic effectiveness is calculated. However, the procedure is confined to relations of the first and second degree, otherwise the calculations become too involved.

A serious drawback of the period-of-return-upon-investment method is the fact that standard return periods are based on the periods reported in the past rather than those which follow from projections for the future.

The comparison of several capital investment variants by their return-periods (or effectiveness factors) initiates rather than culminates the analysis of the effectiveness of capital investments. Before the preferable variant of capital construction is determined, a study should be made of the effect of each variant on the schedule for the introduction of productive capacities, on the development of allied sectors, on the range and quality of output in the particular sector concerned and allied sectors, on the social factors of production (such as working conditions, safety measures, living conditions, etc.) and on the country's defences. This specific and all-round analysis of the prospects for economic development can lead to different conclusions from those of a mere comparative study of capital investment variants by their return periods.

It is only in the total system of input-output relations in the national economy and in a perspective of several years that we can reliably solve the problem of the effectiveness of capital investment planned for a certain period as a whole or for each specific project.

At the first stage of the development of a long-range plan only key trends are established and the effectiveness of capital investment is calculated by aggregated indices only for large economic areas, sectors and the national economy as a whole. At the second stage the principal and auxiliary effectiveness indicators are determined for all levels of planning.

The effectiveness indices are calculated differently in planning and designing. In planning, groups of enterprises at different stages of construction are considered, whereas in designing complete projects fully constructed and operating at capacity are visualised. In designing, the effectiveness of investment is determined for any arbitrary year, while in planning it is determined for a specific planned period, and not only for individual enterprises but also for groups of them, sectors and the national economy as a whole.

The indices of total capital investment take into account allied sectors as well as total economic results (for both producers and consumers) in terms of cost, growth of (gross and net) product, profit, etc. In contrast to designing, the planning of economic effectiveness does not involve extensively the application of the indices of additional capital investment and of additional results from measures to lower costs, etc.

The indices accepted as the base indices in planning are those for the preceding period or consist of currently reported data, whereas conventional standards or the best projects of a similar type, are accepted in designing. Indices calculated for an increment of output and capacity over a period planned and not only for total rated capacity (as is done in designing) are used extensively in planning.

One item of essential importance for planning the economic effectiveness of capital investment is to take into account a certain lag of its yield behind the period of its realisation.

Capital outlays per unit output (including the standard ratings of these outlays as well as the standard ratings of the duration of construction, of required schedules, and of periods of assimilation of productive capacities) and the plan indices for the growth of productivity of labour, cost reduction and the yield of profit are all extensively used in calculating the planned economic effectiveness of capital investment. The standard ratings can be used as the base references when working out targets for designing, or for supervising the financing of construction projects and mapping out a draft plan for capital investment when there are as yet no design and estimate specifications. The standard ratings for capital investment are especially important in long-range planning.

All comparisons of investment and effect are made according to a uniform scheme: the total of productive capital investment for the period planned is compared with the economic result attained in the last year of the period (e.g. in 1970).

The total or summary effect for the entire period, obtained by adding up the effects of the years, is calculated in planning as an additional index. Indices of this type apply to the calculation of the return of resources to the budget or the reserve of the national economy.

The calculations of the economic effectiveness of capital investment culminate in the calculation of the following two coefficients or rates:

(a) national income increment per rouble of capital investment, and

(b) national product increment per rouble of capital investment.

The effectiveness of shorter construction schedules, a quicker introduction of projects into operation, a higher productivity of labour, a better structure of capital investment, etc., are also used as additional indices.

## 7. PLAN FOR RAISING MATERIAL AND CULTURAL STANDARDS

The ultimate purpose of all national economic plans in the Soviet Union is to meet as fully as possible the people's demand for the means to a full life. Proceeding from this proposition, it is necessary, as is stated in the Directives, to continue in the current five-year plan period (1966 to 1970) to raise living standards by stepping up the productivity of labour, increasing the production of material values and accelerating the rate of growth of the national income.

By "living standards" is meant all material and cultural values which are used or may be used (in the period planned) by the population of the country as a whole or some social group of it. "Living standards" is a complex socio-economic concept which can only be expressed by an inter-related system of indices. These can be reduced to the following three groups: (a) indices of living conditions (b) indices of cultural or spiritual conditions, and (c) indices of working conditions and social opportunities.

The principal indices of the first group are:

—summary index of *per capita* consumption of material values, measured as the ratio of the total fund of consumption in the national income to the total numbers of population;

—summary index of incomes, measured as the total of final (really used) incomes *per capita*;

—summary index of the *per capita* consumption of goods other than foodstuffs (measured as the ratio of the value of all goods other then foodstuffs in trade to the total numbers of population);

—summary index of the *per capita* consumption of foodstuffs;

—indices of consumption of some selected major goods;

—summary index of the *per capita* level of consumers' property, calculated as the ratio of the total fund of consumers' property (non-productive fixed assets) to the total numbers of population;

—summary index of the *per capita* level of consumption of consumers' services calculated as the ratio of the total valuation of these services (health, transport, housing, municipal services) to the total numbers of population;

—indices of the level of housing, medical services and various kinds of utilities and services.

The second group of indices includes:

—summary index of the *per capita* consumption of the services rendered by cultural institutions, calculated as the ratio of the total of the maintenance cost of these institutions (including education and art) to the total numbers of population;

—indices of the extent to which the spiritual requirements of the population are being met: literacy, the proportions of the secondary, specialised-secondary and higher education groups, the number of students at general-education schools, specialised secondary schools and higher schools per 10,000, the number of libraries, the number of books available, the number of theatres and cinemas and the number of attendances, the circulation of periodicals per 1,000,000, etc.

The third group of indices includes:

—summary index of life expectation;

—indices of the relative employment of able-bodied population, pension standards, the length of the working day, working week and paid leave, the relative level of industrial accidents, etc.

Planning for higher living standards involves many complex problems, including the following:

(a) projection of incomes and their distribution over sources, including the public funds of consumption;

(b) projection of the level and pattern of the demand for goods and services;

(c) projection of the level and pattern of the demand for goods and services taking into account possible outputs of goods and services;

(d) co-ordination of consumer demand and the practicable volume of goods and services; and

(e) planning of the development of services and the production of the goods necessary for the process.

A special section of the Directives provides for the following targets for the growth of living standards:

(1) To raise the wages and salaries of employees in 1966–70 by no less than 20 per cent on the average, and the collective farmers' incomes in cash and kind from collectively-owned farms by 35 to 40 per cent on the average.

(2) To increase the consumption of foodstuffs.

(3) To improve consumption patterns. The intention is to raise the *per capita* consumption of meat and meat products by 20 to 25 per cent on the average, of milk and dairy products by 15 to 18 per cent, of sugar by approximately 25 per cent, of vegetables by 35 to

40 per cent, of vegetable oils by 40 to 46 per cent, of fruit by 45 to 50 per cent, of fish and fish products by 50 to 60 per cent. It is also intended to increase the sale of fabrics, clothes and knitted goods by 40 per cent, including that of knitted goods by 90 per cent.

(4) To increase the sale of goods through retail trade by 40 per cent and through restaurants and other catering establishments by 45 per cent.

(5) To increase by no less than 40 per cent grants in cash and free services financed from the public funds of consumption.

(6) To expand housing construction by 30 per cent and raise its quality.

(7) To increase by 1970 the volume of services by approximately 2·5 times on the average and more than 3 times in rural localities.

(8) To complete in the main the introduction of universal secondary education. To increase the number of children maintained at pre-school establishments by 60 per cent. To increase the output of higher-school and specialised-secondary school-trained specialists by 65 per cent (7,000,000 persons instead of 4,300,000).

(9) To improve the medical services.

(10) To develop extensively the network of cultural institutions (including the arts) and expand publishing and printing.

There can be no doubt that living standards in the Soviet Union will increase substantially. The primary factor is the growth of wages and salaries. The average pay of employees in the new five-year plan period will increase from 95·3 roubles a month to 115 roubles. It is intended to increase wages and salaries in two directions: to increase the pay of low-paid and medium-paid employees and to increase the remuneration of all employees from the incentive funds set up at enterprises in accordance with the economic reform in industrial production. The minimum pay was raised in the years 1959 to 1965 by from 27 to 40 roubles a month. In 1966 to 1970 it will go up by from 40 to 60 roubles a month. Apart from direct increases in the pay of low-paid employees, the Directives provide for raising earnings by raising the skills of employees, and by consistent mechanisation and automation. Of essential importance will be the higher rates of wages projected in the Directives for those engaged in arduous or dangerous work, underground work and work of a higher than normal intensity, as well as work in the Far East, Siberia, the North and similar areas. It is intended to abolish or reduce direct taxation for some income-brackets of employees in the five-year plan period.

An important feature of the period is that the incomes of collective farmers will increase twice as quickly as the average pay of employees, which will narrow the gap between the living standards of the rural and urban population. For this purpose a monthly guranteed minimum will be introduced for collective farmers comparable with the wages of state-farm workers, the pension scheme for collective farmers will be brought closer to that enjoyed by employees, and the investment in building houses, schools, hospitals, nursery schools, clubs, libraries, etc., will be greater in rural than in urban localities.

In the new five-year period public funds are to be increased by 40 per cent while real incomes *per capita* are to increase by approximately 30 per cent.

Owing to the growth of public funds, maximum increases of old-age pensions will exceed 30 per cent, and the collective farmers will be ranked with employees as regards old-age pensions and the age at which these are granted. At present the pension age in the Soviet Union is lower than in most countries, including the U.S.A., the Federal Republic of Germany, Sweden, Norway and Canada.

Another important item in the plan is to increase by 1·6 times the number of children at pre-school establishments, and to increase the number of school pupils in after-class groups by more than twice. Considerable emphasis is laid on culture, and science in particular, in the new five-year plan period.

The Soviet Union is already leading the developed capitalist countries in general medical, educational and cultural standards. Universal complete secondary education will be introduced under the new five-year plan (universal eight-year, or incomplete secondary education is in force at present). Today there are three times as many higher-school students in the Soviet Union as in Britain, France, Italy or West Germany. Under the five-year plan their number is to increase from 3,800,000 to 5,000,000. The number of pupils graduating from higher- and secondary-specialised schools will be 65 per cent greater than in the period 1961–65. At present the Soviet Union has the world's lowest death rate and the largest number of medical personnel per 1,000 of the population. The Soviet Union accounts for 7 per cent of the world's population, engages one quarter of the world's research personnel and publishes more than one quarter of the world's books.

The growth of living standards under the new five-year plan relies on a considerable increase in the production of consumer goods, a growth of trade, an immense growth of residential and municipal building, and the conversion of the social services into a large-scale well-equipped sector of the national economy.

The state plan for raising living standards usually includes the following sections:

(1) Summary of living standards, specifying national income, real private incomes, real wages, the length of the working week, the length of the paid leave, the social funds of consumption, pensions, retail price and service rate indices, collective farmers' incomes, the total consumption of goods and services, etc.

(2) Development of retail trade and growth of the total volume of consumption of goods (retail trade, public catering turnover, network of trade establishments, *per capita* consumption of major foodstuffs and other consumer goods, cultural and recreational goods per family, etc.).

(3) Development of housing and municipal construction (the building of homes, the housing level, investment into municipal establishments, consumption of municipal services, etc.).

(4) Development of services (the volume of services rendered by service establishments and the development of the network of these enterprises).

(5) Development of passenger transport and communications.

(6) Development of public education and other cultural activity.

(7) Development of the health service.

All the above indices are specified in absolute values as well as *per capita* (or per 100, 1,000 or 10,000), the computation of many indices in relative terms being related to those population groups to which these indices directly belong.

The list of indices for the development of trade, municipal construction, education, health and culture is enlarged considerably when plans are developed for Union Republics, territories, regions, cities and districts.

The target assignments for living standards must rely on a corresponding increase of incomes.

Real incomes are computed by the following approximate scheme:

I. Nominal incomes: total.

II. Minus:

(a) taxes and other obligatory payments,

(b) payments for services.

III. Real incomes (I minus II).

The payment for services is subtracted from nominal incomes to avoid double counting, since the total of incomes includes the incomes of the service personnel whose remuneration is contained in the payment for services.

Analysis of incomes makes it possible to establish the rate of growth of incomes for various population groups, the composition of incomes, the relative importance of different sources of income for different groups and in particular the relation between the incomes from collective farms and those from personal farms. Besides, the data of the analysis can be used to determine the structure of taxes and other obligatory payments in cash, and to analyse the level and rate of growth of the welfare of the population as a whole as well as of separate social groups.

Incomes are computed for different social groups to establish the correct relation between the level and rate of growth of the incomes of employees and those of collective farmers, as well as the correct relation between different sources of incomes and between private incomes, and expenses to stimulate the development of the socialist economy, including rise of the productivity of labour and growth of welfare.

The real income of a population group includes: (a) actually used incomes, (b) savings (as an increment of savings-bank deposits, insurance fees, shares of co-operative members and state loans), and (c) private contributions to public organisations.

Private savings are taken into account in the description of real incomes. However, in the description of the real living standards as of a certain date, all forms of savings and contributions to public organisations must be subtracted from the real incomes, since savings and contributions mean that the population partially relinquishes for a certain period its right to the national product.

If private savings decrease in the period planned, the really used incomes will prove to be larger than the real incomes obtained in the period.

The really used (final) incomes turned to buying goods and services are computed by the following scheme:

(1) Real incomes: total.
(2) Minus:
    (a) Savings,
    (b) contributions to public organisations.
(3) Really used incomes: total.

Of special importance for the computation of the real incomes of

employees and collective farmers is the account of private incomes
and expenses drawn for different social groups and the account of
agricultural products specified for farms.

In planning private incomes it is important to determine correctly
the volume, proportion and rate of growth of incomes derived from
the public funds of consumption.

By "public funds of consumption" is meant the total of all incomes
used by the state, co-operatives, collective farms and public organisations for meeting specific collective or individual demands. Most of
these services are enjoyed regardless of the different amounts of labour
each citizen contributes to the wealth of society.

The public funds of consumption are at present used to finance
free education, the maintenance of children in pre-school establishments free of charge or at a small charge, free medical care, pensions,
allowances for large families and unmarried mothers, temporary
disablement grants, paid holidays, free libraries and clubs, discounts
in rent, including municipal services, etc.

Allowances and discounts from the public funds (including the state
budget and the funds of enterprises) keep growing, as the following
table shows (in 1,000 million roubles):

|       | 1940 | 1960 | 1965 | 1970 |
|-------|------|------|------|------|
| Total | 4·6  | 27·3 | 41·5 | 57·0 |

At present allowances and discounts from the public funds account
for about one quarter of the real incomes of employees.

The importance of the public funds will steadily increase as a form
of distributing the national product and as a method of raising the
living standards of working people.

## 8. PLAN FOR DISTRIBUTION OF PRODUCTIVE FORCES AND ECONOMIC DEVELOPMENT OF UNION REPUBLICS

Production always involves the territorial distribution of the forces of
production. The distribution of production has been a necessary
element in all societies. Wherever there is production, the problem of
its distribution arises simultaneously.

When society owns the principal means of production and organises
the latter for the benefit of all members of society, it is possible to

distribute production over the entire territory of the country according to a single plan.

The integrated treatment of the rational distribution of productive forces over the country's territory is a major problem of planning the national economy at the present-day stage.

To raise the effectiveness of production, the Directives call for a better distribution of productive forces, the complex development and specialisation of the economy of the Union Republics and economic areas, attraction of a larger part of the able-bodied population to production and a correct combination of territorial planning with the sectoral principle of control of the national economy.

The territorial aspect of the economic development plan is based on the plans for the economies of the Union Republics. The U.S.S.R. national plan contains a special section specifying the principal projections of development of all the 15 Republics: the Russian Federation, the Ukrainian Republic, the Byelorussian Republic, the Kazakh Republic, the Moldavian Republic, the Georgian Republic, the Azerbaijanian Republic, the Armenian Republic, the Uzbek Republic, the Kirghiz Republic, the Tadjik Republic, the Turkmen Republic, the Lithuanian Republic, the Latvian Republic and the Estonian Republic.

A special section of the Directives is concerned with the assignments for economic and cultural development of the Republics and indicates major construction projects in industry, farming and transport. Under the five-year plan the total industrial output is to increase 1·5 times in the Russian Federation, 1·5 times in the Ukraine, 1·7 times in Byelorussia, 1·6 times in Uzbekistan, 1·7 times in Kazakhstan, 1·6 times in Georgia, 1·6 times in Azerbaijan, 1·7 times in Lithuania, 1·7 times in Moldavia, 1·5 times in Latvia, 1·6 times in Kirghizia, 1·8 times in Tadjikistan, 1·8 times in Armenia, 1·6 times in Turkmenia and 1·5 times in Estonia. Clearly, higher rates are envisaged for those republics which are less developed industrially (Byelorussia, Kazakhstan, Moldavia, Tadjikistan and Armenia).

The indices of the district-level section of the national plan describe the integrated plan for the economic development of the corresponding republic. These indices show the production and use of national product and national income, the industrial outputs specified over the key sectors, purchases of farm products and their delivery to the public funds. The section contains also the following indices: state capital investment, the introduction into operation of fixed capital and major productive capacities, manpower, the wages fund, the reduction of production and circulation costs, the profit and the rate of profit for the republic's economy, construction and assembly work under contracts, surveying and prospecting, and trade. In the economic plans endorsed by the governments of Union Republics the plan indices are specified much more elaborately over the range of products and are itemised for republican ministries, autonomous republics, territories, regions and republican-level cities (also over areas in the Republics which are not divided into regions). Besides, the republican plans contain sections which are absent in the U.S.S.R. plan and which are specified by a comprehensive system of indices. These sections include the plans for development of inland waterways and automobile transport, education, culture, medicine, housing and municipal construction as well as more elaborate plans for retail trade and public catering.

The point of departure for the territorial planning of the national economy is a real distribution or allocation.

The latter originated as an element of planned economic development in the first years of Soviet power.

The net of large economic areas is an important tool in the treatment of problems involved in the distribution of productive forces and the territorial planning of production. The net of economic areas now in force was endorsed in 1961 and divides the entire territory into 18 large economic and geographic areas.

Some of them comprise the territory of several Union Republics with a similar pattern and direction of economic development. Thus, the Trans-Caucasus area includes three Union Republics: Armenia, Azerbaijan and Georgia; the Central Asian area comprises the territory of Turkmenia, Kirghizia, Tadjikistan and Uzbekistan; and the Baltic area the territory of Estonia, Latvia, Lithuania and the Kaliningrad Region.

Each of these areas is an economic unit based on the specialisation of industrial and agricultural production.

The section of the national economic plan for a large economic area includes the indices describing gross industrial output, the principal items of industrial output, the purchases of agricultural products, capital investment, the introduction of productive capacities into operation, the number of employees, the productivity of labour, and initiation and development of new industrial centres.

The Directives provide for the following projections to improve the distribution of productive forces:

(a) To avoid the construction of new power-intensive manufactures and restrict the development of operating manufactures of this kind in the economic areas of the European part of the U.S.S.R. and the Ukraine, and to develop the productive forces in these areas mainly by the renovation and better use of the productive capacities already in operation.

(b) To develop at a high rate the output of fuel, the generation of electric power, the power-intensive types of the production of non-ferrous metals and chemicals as well as wood processing in the Eastern areas of the country where cheap fuel, power and raw materials are available, and

(c) To advance inter-area and inter-Republic economic relations, especially between the Western and Eastern areas of the country.

The economic effectiveness of an economy largely depends on the concentration of production. Progress in science and engineering concentrates industrial production at large enterprises, which essentially changes the system of their organisation. Socialism opens wide prospects for the rational combination of production and in particular the establishment of large industrial complexes.

The major Soviet economico-geographic areas contain several production complexes. By "territorial production complex" is meant an economically justified and co-ordinated set of enterprises and manufactures ensuring the highest possible economic effect by making an all-round use of the natural and economic conditions of the area. As a rule, a production complex comprises the territory of several areas.

Large territorial production complexes are now developing in Siberia on the basis of the cheap electric power of the Siberian rivers and the rich deposits of East and West Siberia.

The plan for initiating and developing new industrial centres (by an "industrial centre" is meant a set of enterprises having common sources of raw materials, fuel and power plus a residential area with municipal and other services, cultural institutions, etc.) is an important section of the plan for developing a large economic area.

The territorial planning of economic development must always take into account the inter-relation of many factors often operating in opposite directions.

A thorough analysis of the current distribution of production is first of all necessary. The current distribution of production reflects the entire previous economic activity of society. A concentration of operating productive capacities is always accompanied by a concentration of highly-skilled manpower. Hence the objective trend towards the further territorial concentration of productive forces, since their distribution over settled economic areas yields a considerable saving in both capital and current outlays.

At all stages of social development the territorial distribution of production depends on the distribution of natural sources of power and raw materials. The dependence is the greater the lower the level of productive development and the smaller the scale of using the progress of science and engineering in production. More advanced means of transporting raw materials, power and finished products inevitably lead to a trend towards uniform economic distribution territorially. The progress of physics and chemistry, diminishing the dependence of manufacturing processes on natural sources of power and objects of labour, intensifies this trend.

These contradictory trends can only be combined optimally for each planning period with respect to the plans of sectoral and area development on the basis of a thorough analysis of all natural, technological, economic, social and political factors. The main principles of planning the territorial proportions of production can be summed up as follows:

(1) The planned development of production of all areas by drawing on all possible resources, including manpower.

(2) Maximum proximity of production to sources of raw materials, fuel and power to minimise outlays of all kinds.

(3) Raising of the national defence potential.

(4) Planned steady rise of the level of material production and civilisation in general of all Union Republics and all nationalities of the Soviet Union; elimination of still lingering elements of uneven economic development of different national areas.

(5) All-round specialisation of areas in combination with integrated economic development.

(6) Sensitivity to the requirements of the socialist division of labour between socialist countries.

Such are the major principles of the territorial planning of the national economy. Apart from them, planning must take into account the specific pattern in the distribution of each individual sector of production as well as the historic and national antecedents of each area. The Soviet Union is a multi-national country, and naturally the correct development of national relations is of major importance for economic and cultural planning.

Specialisation in, and integrated development of, the economy of an economic area are two major principles of the socialist distribution of production.

Each economic area and each Union Republic must specialise in the production of certain manufactured and farm products. By "specialisation" is here meant a form of the social division of labour over different sectors of production as expressed in the identification of areas or sectors (industries, farming, construction) with the output of definite products. Specialisation implies not only the output of specialised finished products, but also the use of specialized implements of labour, specialised methods of economic organisation and special techniques. Specialisation is the most salient expression of the social division of labour and at the same time a major factor in the productivity of labour and the efficiency of production.

The specialisation of an economic area is determined by the requirements of a proper geographic division of labour conducive to a higher rate of reproduction on an expanded scale.

Of decisive importance in the appraisal of the conditions for the specialisation of a given area is the determination and comparison of the economic effectiveness of the output of certain products in different areas and the evaluation of the effect of the production of these items on productivity and the saving of labour.

Factors accelerating and decelerating the specialisation of areas under study must be taken into account.

To work out the specialisation of a Union Republic or a large economic area, a system of dependent indicators is used, including: (a) the specific weight of a sector under study in the economy of a given Republic (or area), (b) the proportion of the area in the total output of the sector for the Soviet Union as a whole, and (c) the proportion of the sector's output consumed in other Republics (or areas). The computation of the indices should take into account the data on the area's outputs, fixed assets and the number of employees.

Sectors such as timber, oil (extraction), gas, coal, iron and steel, non-ferrous metals, many branches of machine building, some branches of food processing (sugar, fish, wines, etc.) and some branches of farming (grain, cotton, southern crops, sheep, etc.) may be specialised sectors in the economy of a Union Republic or economic area. Electrical power, oil (processing), some chemicals, some building materials, many branches of food-processing and consumer production, some branches of farming, etc., are auxiliary or servicing sectors.

The specialised and integrated development of an economic area or Republic is incompatible both with excessive lop-sided specialisation and with parochial autarchy and resulting lag of the Republic or area in the development of its productive forces.

The specialisation of an area must be combined with the integrated development of its economy, by which is meant an economically expedient and mutually co-ordinated development of all the sectors, meeting the area's demand for all producers' and consumer goods and services, the all-out development of the key sectors and their co-operation inside the area as well as the proportional development of each sector of the area's economy.

The integrated development of an area must ensure the production within the area of sufficient quantities of major kinds of raw materials, fuel and power, consumer goods, foodstuffs, etc., as well as the development of transport, services and cultural institutions.

Excessive specialisation of an area may entail very large in-flows of raw materials and consumer goods from other areas of the Republic and will increase the transport range with resulting increases in transport costs. Excessive integration of the economic development of an area will shut in its economy, with resulting low levels of productivity.

A major peculiarity of the distribution of farming is its direct dependence on natural conditions. The distribution of farming depends indeed on the climate, soil, local skills, productive levels of different branches of arable farming and livestock breeding within the different natural and economic zones, and finally on the assignments made in each area for the specialisation of its farming. Zonal farming specialisation makes it possible to use land and skills in the most effective way and, in particular, with the lowest expenditure of all resources, including manpower.

The point of departure for planning the distribution of farming is the premise that each area should concentrate on those crops and kinds of livestock which are most economic under the specific natural and economic conditions. At the same time the distribution of farming must take into account the objective need for combining different branches of farming in one zone so as to keep busy in all seasons, and raise the economic effectiveness of arable farming and livestock breeding.

Special problems confront the planning of the distribution of horticultural and dairy farming zones around industrial centres and large cities to meet the urban population's demand for fresh vegetables and dairy products.

## 9. PLAN FOR SCIENTIFIC AND TECHNICAL PROGRESS AND FOR UTILISATION OF PRODUCTION RESERVES

Planning for technical progress and the use of production reserves bulks large in national economic plans. This section of long-range and current plans comprises the plan for the development and introduction of new plant, the plan for labour and manpower, the plan for reducing production and circulation costs, and the financial plan.

In the Directives the assignments for technical progress, growth of the productivity of labour, reduction of costs, and a higher yield of profit are included in the sections concerned with individual sectors of the national economy.

In specific projections and current (annual) plans all the plans listed above are made as special parts of a single national economic plan.

The state plan for the development and introduction of new plant includes the following sections:

(a) targets for major research, experiment and designing;

(b) targets for the development and manufacture of new types of machines, mechanisms, equipment, instrumentation, materials and products;

(c) production of new industrial products (first consignments of new products in high-volume production);

(d) targets for the mechanisation and automation of manufacturing processes and the introduction of advanced manufacturing methods; and

(e) termination of the production of obsolete machines, equipment, mechanisms, devices and instruments.

The above sections provide for measures conducive to the basic directions of technical progress: electrification, chemicalisation or extensive introduction of chemicals and chemical processes, mechanisation and automation.

Since 1960 the working out of planned technical measures has been undertaken before the development of the plan for production, so as to improve the technical aspect of the plan and co-ordinate effectively the targets for the development of new equipment with the other sections of the plan. The relevant research and design agencies function under the auspices of the ministries responsible for the introduction of new equipment and manufacturing processes into production, and for the technical standards of the corresponding sectors and the specialisation of industrial production.

The Directives provide for:

—acceleration of scientific and technical progress on the basis of extensive research, and a prompt use of its results, as well as of inventions, in production;

—priority growth of electrical power, machinery and chemicals compared with overall industrial growth;

—output of products with technically advanced high-quality parameters;

—introduction of highly effective manufacturing processes such as physico-chemical, electro-physical, power-intensive, etc.; and

—development of specialisation of and co-operation between enterprises.

Planning for technical progress proceeds from the following premises:

(1) Thorough analysis of the development of science and engineering abroad and working out measures aimed at introducing the best results of science and engineering in the national economy.

(2) Establishment of the sequence and priority in the introduction of the above measures, taking into account the current level of technical development of a given sector.

(3) Isolation of the crucial factors (sectors, manufacturing methods, technical devices, etc.) in the technical re-equipment of a sector.

(4) Selection of those measures which are dictated by the requirements of the national economy, expedient, technically possible and economically effective.

The targets of the plan for the development and introduction of new equipment take into account the required allocation of plant, materials, financial resources and manpower, including specialists.

A decisive factor in technical progress today is the development of science and the introduction of scientific discoveries into production. The advance of manufacturing processes depends more and more not on the quantity but rather the quality of introduced plant. And this depends largely on the progress of science.

In the planning of scientific development it is more important than in any other type of planning to determine the level of development in different directions and the trends in the development of each field, to determine what is really progressive and should receive a maximum impetus and what has ceased to be progressive, and simultaneously to ensure adequate theoretical margins in science, i.e. the development of those fields which cannot be expected to yield tangible practical results within the next few years.

A major principle for planning research and planning the introduction of scientific and technical discoveries is a uniform national policy in technical progress, and in particular a wide dissemination of scientific and technical knowledge and advanced economic experience in all sectors of the national economy.

The plans for research and for the introduction of scientific and technical discoveries into the national economy are drawn up directly at enterprises, and at building agencies, research institutions, designing offices and higher- and specialised-secondary schools, on the basis of plans for the technical development of enterprises.

The more important measures specified by plans for the technical development of enterprises are transferred to the plans for research and and introduction of scientific and technical discoveries into the national economy worked out by the ministries and departments of Union Republics. The plan also includes all assignments of importance to industrial development as a whole.

On the basis of draft plans submitted by the ministries and departments, the Republican Gosplans (the state planning committees of Union Republics) develop Republican plans for research and the introduction of scientific and technical discoveries into the economy.

The state plan for research and the introduction of scientific and technical discoveries incorporates the more important investigations and designs dealing with integrated, intersectoral and crucial sectoral scientific and technical problems, theoretical problems of the natural and social sciences, advanced manufacturing processes, mechanisation and automation, and the manufacture of new machinery, equipment instruments and materials decisive for the technical development of various sectors of production.

The annual economic effect, saving or reduction of costs, capital investment per unit output or expenditure of labour are computed for all equipment-introduction measures for each year of a period planned.

The effectiveness of the introduction of technical measures as well as of inventions, improvements and rationalisation proposals is determined on the basis of the following principal indices:

(a) capital investment per unit of annual productive capacity introduced;

(b) cost of output and the reduction of production cost per annum (after the introduction of a measure has been completed);

(c) growth of labour productivity; and

(d) periods of return on the outlays invested in technical measures under consideration.

As additional indices for describing economic effectiveness recourse is often made to indices describing:

(a) length of production cycle (e.g. the speed of drilling, the speed of railway traffic, etc.);

(b) level of yield of productive capacities (e.g. daily output of steel per square metre of open-hearth effective area),

(c) expenditure of raw materials, construction materials, fuel, power, tools and finished products per unit output.

These indices are differentiated for each manufacture, taking into account its specific features.

The productivity of labour and the saving of manpower are among the most general indices of the economic effect attained by the introduction of programming techniques.

To determine the effectiveness of the application of advanced equipment at new enterprises, the projected indices of cost, the labour output ratio and capital investment per unit output should be compared with the actual results attained at the best Soviet and foreign enterprises.

Planning for the development of science and engineering is vital for steadily raising the productivity of labour, bringing down production costs and increasing the rate of accumulation.

The most important indices of the plan for labour are:

(1) Productivity of labour per employee for each section, Union Republic and department.

(2) Number of employees for each section, Republic and ministry.

(3) Average wages and the wages fund for each sector, Union Republic and ministry.

All indices of the plan for labour are co-ordinated to ensure proper relations between increases in the number of employees and the productivity of their labour, between the wages fund and the number of employees, between an increase in the productivity of labour and an increase in average wages.

The productivity of labour for 1966 to 1970 is to grow, according to the Directives, as follows: 33 to 35 per cent for industries, 40 to 45 per cent for state farms and collective farms, 23 to 25 per cent for railway transport and 35 to 50 per cent for construction.

The growth of labour productivity is the most important index of the effectiveness of the use of manpower and means of production, and is decisive in the plans for production and the target assignments for reducing production costs and increasing the profit of enterprises.

The projected rate of growth of labour productivity is used for setting targets for the growth of the number of employees for each sector and the increase of wages and salaries and of rural incomes. The relation between the growth of labour productivity and wages constitutes a major factor for reducing production costs and increasing accumulation.

At enterprises turning out heterogeneous products recourse is had to value indices of labour productivity. The most important of them is gross output per worker per time unit. The application of this index makes it possible to calculate the productivity of labour on the scale of a sector or a Republic as well as of production as a whole, and to compare the labour productivity curves for different sectors.

Physical indices, i.e. indices in terms of actual products, are extensively used in sectors and manufactures turning out homogeneous products (electric power, metal, timber) or in manufactures where different products are reducible to a conventional unit (e.g. fuels).

Since 1959 the productivity of labour is planned per employee, counting all employees engaged in manufacture (in industry), all employees engaged in construction and assembly (in building), and all personnel engaged in farming (in state farms). The ministries and Republican Gosplans (the state planning committees of Union Republics) also submit data on the growth of labour productivity per employee for major sections of the national economy.

The principal method of planning the productivity of labour is that of computation by productivity factors, which makes it possible to take into account the effect of all measures for raising the productivity of labour projected for a planned period.

The factors responsible for the growth of the productivity of labour are grouped as follows:

(1) Factors responsible for a higher technical level of production and equipment per employee (the introduction of new equipment and manufacturing processes, integrated mechanisation and automation, modernisation and renovation of equipment, specialisation and co-operation, improvement of the designs of products, introduction of more economical raw materials and construction materials).

(2) Factors responsible for the improvement of the organisation of production and labour (elimination of idle time, reduction of the

number of employees engaged in auxiliary operations, better job rating, higher skills, dissemination of advanced experience, improvement of the organisation of production control, rationalisation of the structure of administrative personnel, etc.).

(3) Factors responsible for changes in the sectoral structure and the distribution of production (increase of the proportion of open work in coal and ore mining, change of the quality of raw materials, reclamation of new mineral deposits, advance of crops to new areas as well as other factors influencing the labour-output ratio of products but independent of the operation of individual enterprises).

The establishment of targets for labour productivity must include their comparison with targets for the volume of production and the number of employees. The relation between these targets must ensure the growth of output mainly due to the growth of labour productivity at relatively lower rates of increase of the number of employees.

Planning for manpower is based on the determination of its total size in a period planned and the possibilities for its absolute and relative growth, as well as its proportional distribution between spheres of society, sectors, areas, etc.

The planned organisation of the Soviet economy makes it possible to use labour to the best advantage for the benefit of society as a whole, to predict the demand of the national economy (individual sectors, enterprises, areas) for manpower, and take measures to meet this demand.

A rational distribution and effective use of resources of manpower is a major aim of planning.

Planning of the demand for manpower is based on the development of manpower input-output tables.

Among many manpower input-output tables of special importance in national economic planning are:

(a) the manpower input-output table for industry, construction and transport specified for each Republic and basic to the planning for an additional demand for manpower in the key sectors of the national economy;

(b) the manpower input-output table for collective farms, specified for each economic area, Republic and region; this input-output table is basic to the planning of the redistribution of manpower between farming and industry (through organised engagement and enrolment at vocational schools) as well as the territorial distribution of manpower within farming by the resettlement from little-land areas to much-land areas and newly reclaimed lands;

(c) the skilled manpower input-output table specified for each Republic; this input-output table estimates the total demand and supply, including skilled manpower, specified over occupations and skills; it is basic to the plan for training highly skilled manpower and the plan for raising skills; and

(d) the input-output table for specialists, which is basic to planning for meeting the demand of each Republic for specialists trained at higher schools and specialised-secondary schools; without this table it is impossible to draw up an adequate plan for the enrolment at higher and specialised-secondary schools.

Under the new five-year plan (1966–70) much attention is paid to rational employment of manpower. The Directives provide for an increase in the number of employees in the national economy by 15 million (from 76 million to 91–92 million). To make a better use of manpower, new enterprises will be chiefly built in medium and small cities, taking into account the need for employment of men and women. Higher rates of housing and municipal construction are planned for the country's Eastern areas than the average for the country as a whole.

Economic development in accordance with the targets of the national plan requires immense resources. What resources are used for capital construction and for the improvement of material and cultural standards? They are provided from regular savings of production costs and steady growth of accumulations. Indeed, the aim of the planning of costs, prices and finances is to solve the problem of resources.

The Directives set the following targets for industry: to reduce industrial production costs, make all enterprises operate with a margin of profit, increase the yield of profit in industry twice over by the close of the five-year plan period; and for construction, to decrease the estimated cost of industrial construction and the cost of construction and assembly. By the "cost of output" is meant the total of the enterprise's outlays on the manufacture and sale of the output.

The aim of planning costs is to ensure the maximum decrease of costs and to raise the profit in all sections and units of the national economy so as to obtain the best results at the lowest cost.

The cost plan comprises the targets for minimum outlays in all sectors of the national economy and in particular in industrial production costs, costs of the output of state farms, costs of construction and assembly work, costs of transportation (specified for each type of transport), as well as the outlays of procurement, supply and sale agencies, and of public catering enterprises.

The current system of cost plan indices includes:

(a) the targets for the total sum, structure and level of outlays, with the aid of which the cost plan is co-ordinated with the other sections of the national economic plan;

(b) the targets for bringing down the level of outlays, which indicates the effectiveness of measures aimed at saving resources and reflects the dynamics of production and circulation costs; and

(c) the targets for lowering the costs of individual kinds of output or work.

In accordance with the current economic reform, the targets for lowering production costs will be estimates rather than obligatory assignments for enterprises. However, this does not detract from the importance of such estimates in indicating possible savings from lowering production and circulation costs. The cost indices will continue to figure in the plans of enterprises and will remain as estimates in the plans of ministries, departments and Republics.

It is important in planning to take into account the differences in the structure of costs due to the specific conditions of production of each sector and to its technical equipment. The cost structure differs especially markedly in extraction and processing sectors. Since the object of labour in extraction sectors is a natural product, the outlays in wages predominate in the total volume of outlays in output in these sectors. Thus, in coal mining the proportion of wages accounts for 68 per cent of the costs, in the production of peat for 51 per cent and in timbering for 50 per cent. We say that *these are labour-intensive sectors*. These also include construction, farming and transport.

In some processing sectors raw materials and construction materials account for the bulk of costs. For example, in the chemical industry raw materials and construction materials account for 69 per cent of total costs, in garments for 87 per cent and in food processing for 89 per cent. These are *materials-intensive sectors*. In the production of aluminium and some other sectors of non-ferrous metallurgy as well as many chemical manufactures the expenditure of electric power accounts for a large part of total costs. These are *power-intensive manufactures*.

Finally, we have *capital-intensive sectors* in which the amortisation of fixed assets accounts for a large portion of total costs. Under this heading come the hydro-generation of power, oil extraction, etc.

The cost structure reflects the specific formation of cost in each sector and the extent of the influence of various factors on the level of costs and its decrease compared with the base period. In materials-intensive and power-intensive sectors the main factor for lowering costs is the saving of raw materials, construction materials, fuel and power. In labour-intensive sectors, costs are lowered above all by raising the productivity of labour, and introducing new manufacturing means and methods, which decrease the payment for labour per unit output or work.

In capital-intensive sectors costs are reduced above all by introducing more efficient equipment and making a better use of fixed capital.

Forms and methods of lowering production costs are many and varied. Production and circulation costs depend on a multitude of factors. Some of these are directly connected with the quality of operation of a given enterprise, while others depend on the performance of the national economy as a whole. However, this division is conventional since the two groups of factors are closely inter-related, which must be taken into account in the practice of planning.

The general national economic factors include:

(a) the introduction of new advanced equipment and technology;

(b) improvement of the distribution of productive forces;

(c) organisation of rational specialisation and co-operation on the scale of the national economy as well as for individual sectors;

(d) rise of technical as well as general cultural standards of working people; and

(e) transition to new economical raw materials, construction materials, fuels and types of power.

The cost factors independent of the operation of an enterprise include, besides, changes in the wholesale prices of means of production or producers' goods, transport costs, rates of interest on loan, pay rates and salaries.

The factors directly connected with the performance of an individual enterprise include:

(a) improvement of the use of fixed capital;

(b) improvement of the use of raw materials, construction materials, fuel and power;

(c) mechanisation and automation of production and the improvement of manufacturing processes;

(d) rhythmic organisation of work;

(e) improvement of the organisation of labour (the organisation of the workbench, improvement of labour discipline, etc.);

(f) improvement of the skills of employees engaged at the enterprise; and

(g) improvement of management.

The above factors influence either individual cost elements or several cost elements simultaneously. The importance of each group of factors depends on the length of the planned period. In annual plans priority goes to the first group of factors which ensure savings mainly at operating enterprises, while a long-range plan gives precedence to general national economic factors responsible for essential changes in the level of production.

The average cost for a sector is influenced, especially in mining and agriculture, by the distribution of production over the territory of the country depending on natural conditions (the extent of seams and their depth under the surface of the ground, metal content of ferrous and non-ferrous ores, soil, type of terrain, climate, etc.). Territorial changes in the distribution of sectors scheduled for a period planned may lead to changes in average sectoral costs without any significant decrease at separate enterprises.

The influence of the above factors on average sectoral costs can be determined by weighting the outlays for each area (methods of mining, productivity of land, etc.) by the outputs or their proportions in the base and planned periods. The difference will show the size of saving and the decrease of costs owing to structural changes.

The influence of structural changes in the national economy is also calculated by weighting the costs of output for the base and planned structure of consumption of different raw materials, construction materials and fuels. A comparison of these data indicates the saving obtained for the entire volume of production per unit output.

A major factor for bringing down costs is the improvement of the organisation of production by specialisation, co-operation and integration. The effect of specialisation and the saving of resources as a result of it are computed by comparing costs per unit output under the former and planned conditions.

Average sectoral costs are also directly influenced by national economic factors such as improvement in the apparatus of production as a whole. The influence of this factor is determined by the size of cost at new enterprises and the proportion of their output in the total output of a sector.

The establishment of the national economic cost factors and the calculation of their influence on the level of outlays makes it possible to plan average sectoral costs for each major product. At enterprises the cost targets are determined in accordance with the operation of intra-enterprise cost factors, which makes it possible to establish the costs for a given enterprise and calculate the saving from its reduction as well as the size of profit under the plan.

The principal aim of the cost planning of industrial production is the detection and use of reserves for lowering production costs at enterprises so as to obtain higher output at lowest costs.

Prior to 1958 targets for lowering the costs of comparable products were planned and assigned to enterprises. In view of certain defects of the comparable product cost index, another index came into use in 1958 for planning and estimating the progress of plans: cost per rouble's worth of commodity output. The earlier use of a single index in the plans for all enterprises, without taking into account the individual character of production in each enterprise caused difficulties in working out plans and estimating the progress at many enterprises and in some cases gave rise to misleading conclusions about reductions in production costs.

Since 1963 cost targets have been established in terms of costs (in kopecks) per rouble of commodity output in the annual plans for each industry as a whole and in the plans of Union Republics, ministries and departments. On the other hand, in the plans of enterprises the following differentiated indicators are used:

(a) the cost of unit output for enterprises putting out one principal product;

(b) the cost of electrical power and heat unit for power stations generating electrical power and providing heat; and

(c) different indices, depending on the cost of products compared or cost per rouble of commodity output, for the enterprises of all the other industries putting out different products. If comparable products predominate in the total output, enterprises plan a reduction of the cost of comparable products. Those enterprises whose total output contains mainly incomparable products plan their production costs per rouble's worth of commodity output.

Apart from the above indices, all enterprises plan the costs of their entire commodity outputs in absolute value terms.

The output cost plans are drawn up for industrial production as a whole as well as being specified for each sector.

A very important section of the output cost plan is that containing the estimate of production outlays. This makes it possible to co-ordinate the cost plan with other sections of the national economic plan and thus to determine justified targets for the cost level of industrial production.

The cost index for the operation of transport and the cost of a unit of haulage, measured in ton kilometres (or ton-miles for sea transport), are used in the planning of transport costs. The targets for reducing costs of railway, sea and air haulage are therefore specified in the national economic plan, and those for road and inland water haulage in the plans of Union Republics.

Construction, on the other hand, consists as a rule of individual projects, and it is rather difficult to determine the cost structure over years for the same building agency. Therefore, reduction of costs in construction and assembly work is planned, not with respect to the actual cost of the previous period, but with respect to the estimated cost of a given construction project.

Another special feature of construction costs is that planning for reduction of costs is done not for the entire volume of capital outlays but only for the volume of construction and assembly work, i.e. without taking into account the cost of equipment. The reason is that the quality of construction does not influence the cost of equipment. Therefore, the plan specifies an assignment for lowering the cost of construction and assembly work as against their estimated value.

## 10. PLANNING OF PRICES

The planning of the costs of output and work is a major premise for the planning of prices.

The *price* is the expression of value in terms of money, and originates as an economic category at a certain stage of development of commodity production. In the Soviet economy the existence of *price* as an economic category is due to the presence of commodity production and hence to the operation of the law of value connected with the production and circulation of goods.

The state fixes wholesale prices, estimate-prices of construction and price-rates charged for the economic circulation of the means of production, and procurement prices for the output of collective farms, as well as the retail prices of state and co-operative trade in consumer goods. The planning of prices is directly connected with the planning of costs, of circulation expenses and of net income in all its forms.

The Soviet State uses the pricing mechanism as an economic lever in the planned control of the country's economy. The output of economically important products is stimulated and a more rational use of the means of production is encouraged through a system of wholesale prices (by establishing price rates leading to reduction in the consumption of scarce products and increase in the consumption of effective substitutes, local raw materials, by-products, etc.). Through a system of freight charges, which constitute a major element of pricing, the Soviet government stimulates a more rational distribution of production as well as a better co-ordination of the operation of different transport facilities (railways, ships, automobiles, etc.).

By establishing the retail prices of individual goods and differentials between the prices of several groups of goods (meat and fish, vegetables and groats, fabrics and garments, fabrics made of natural and synthetic fibre, etc.), the state controls consumption patterns, and by establishing charges for the services of municipal or cultural institutions as well as the level of rent, it controls the effective demand for services. Using the lever of pricing, the state contributes to the welfare of the working people, introduces higher material and cultural standards, and provides personal incentives to contribute to the growth of material production and of accumulation.

The state, the co-operatives and the collective farms use pricing for planning and accounting of all aspects of economic activity.

The Council of Ministers of the U.S.S.R. directly authorises only the purchase and delivery prices for raw materials and farm and timber products, but it also deals with problems of changes in the general level of wholesale and retail prices and rates for haulage, power and services.

The U.S.S.R. Gosplan (the State Planning Committee of the U.S.S.R.) in co-operation with the State Committee for Prices functioning under its jurisdiction:

(a) issues general obligatory instructions for the calculation of costs and prices;

(b) submits to the Council of Ministers of the U.S.S.R. recommendations on changes in the general level of wholesale prices and rates as well as advice on the problems of purchase and delivery prices for farm products;

(c) endorses wholesale prices for major industrial products as well as foodstuffs and other goods;

(d) endorses the rates for haulage, electric power, thermal energy and services; and

(e) endorses retail prices for major foodstuffs and other goods and submits to the Council of Ministers of the U.S.S.R. recommendations on general changes in the level of retail prices.

Many prices (approximately about one-quarter of all prices in heavy industry and more than one-third of retail prices) are endorsed by the Councils of Ministers of Union Republics, or on their behalf, by the Regional (Territorial) Executive Committees of the Soviets of Working People's Deputies. Thus, they endorse wholesale prices for construction materials, parts and constructional units, peat, wood, equipment for consumer production including food processing and many consumer goods (furniture, sports facilities, haberdashery, felt footwear, garments, confectionery, wines, beer, etc.).

The Councils of Ministers of Union Republics and the Regional (Territorial) Executive Committees are entitled to endorse the wholesale prices of manufactured goods consumed locally or within one Union Republic.

The ministries are entitled to endorse the wholesale prices of goods in individual or small-scale production in the absence of prices already duly established.

Industrial enterprises establish wholesale prices for products and services intended for their own capital construction and internal needs, as well as for equipment and devices manufactured as part of rationalisation proposals financed from State Bank loans.

The following prices are used in the Soviet national economy:

(a) wholesale prices for means of production and objects of consumption (i.e. capital and consumer goods), special varieties of which are the estimate-prices for construction work and the rates for haulage and power;

(b) retail prices for objects of consumption (i.e. consumer goods) sold to private persons, state organisations, co-operatives and collective farms;

(c) purchase prices for agricultural raw materials and products turned out by collective farms (and delivery prices for similar products of state farms); and

(d) collective-farm market prices of products turned out by collective farms and personal subsidiary farms and sold on the market to private persons.

The wholesale prices of most manufactured goods include:

(a) average sectoral actual and planned production costs;

(b) a special element—turnover tax—for some consumer goods (sugar, alcoholic drinks, tobacco, matches, fabrics, flour products and oil products); this element is also contained in the rates for electric power.

In place of the average sectoral cost and profits of enterprises, the wholesale prices of farm products and raw materials include the average price of state-purchased farm products.

Profit constitutes an important element in the wholesale prices of the means of production. And another major constituent of prices is the turnover tax.

Part of society's net income goes as a turnover tax directly under the control of the state, forming society's centralised net income. The existence of these two basic forms of society's net income—the net income of an enterprise (profit) and the centralised net income of the state (turnover tax)—is due to the cost-accounting organisation of socialist enterprises and the need for stimulating the personnel of each enterprise to work for a larger quantity and a better quality of output.

A turnover tax on oil products is necessitated by proper cost relations between different fuels. The entire system of fuel prices in the Soviet Union is based on the wholesale price of coal, central to the fuel balance. However, the calorific value of oil is much higher than that of coal, while the cost of a ton of oil is only two-thirds that of a ton of coal. Therefore, the price of oil, taking into account the difference in the calorific value of oil and coal, is an excess yield of profit, the excess being taken off as a turnover tax. The rates for electric power are established taking into account the fact that along with large district power stations there are small municipal power stations as well as power stations of industrial enterprises which also supply energy to outside consumers. The rates must ensure a positive yield of profit for all these power stations. However, such rates provide an additional rate of profit for the larger stations, and this excess profit is removed as a turnover tax.

The wholesale prices of farm products are used in the accounts between state procurement bodies and industrial enterprises, trade agencies and the departments concerned with export. The wholesale prices of farm products are differentiated as

(a) prices minus turnover tax (used for accounts with export organisations and industrial enterprises); and

(b) prices including turnover tax (used for accounts with trade agencies for products transferred to retail trade without processing).

In its general form the wholesale price of a farm product includes the purchase price of the product, the surcharge of procurement agencies incorporating the expenses of the procurement of the product, profit and turnover tax.

The economic exchange of construction work between state enterprises and organisations is served by special wholesale prices or *estimate prices*. Since construction projects, including even those using model designs, differ among themselves in several ways connected with the conditions under which construction is organised, available constructional elements and building materials, location, etc., the application of uniform state wholesale prices listed by official price-lists for instruction, is difficult and undesirable. The prices of construction are determined according to the estimates for each specific project.

The economic exchange of services furnished by transport and communications is served by special price-rates. The system of rates includes:

(a) rates for passenger traffic;
(b) rates for the haulage of products turned out by heavy industry;
(c) rates for the haulage of consumer goods and
(d) rates for communications services.

The system of rates at present in force was established as a result of the reform of rates in 1949 and subsequent reductions in 1950–55.

The structure of a rate for a transport or communications service is identical with that of a wholesale price for an enterprise. Just like the latter, the rate includes not the entire product for society put out by a transport or communications unit, but only part of it in the form of the net income of this unit. The rate includes:

(1) total cost of haulage (or communications work); and
(2) profit of transport and communications units.

The planning of wholesale prices must be based on correct relations between cost and profit in the price of each product or service responsible for the growth of production, a range of products specified by planning and a better quality of products. To meet these requirements, the system of wholesale prices must ensure:

*uniform prices* for similar products, without which prices cannot function as standard measures of production costs and outputs;

*a positive yield of profit* of all or most enterprises of each sector as a major condition of socialist cost accounting; and

*a positive yield of profit for various products* within each sector, ensuring a larger range and a higher quality (for example, the establishment of a relatively high rate of profit for products the output of which is required sharply to increase, or the application of discounts for lower-grade products).

The key problem of wholesale pricing—uniform prices for enterprises run under uniform operating conditions—is solved in planning by different methods for taking into account the common conditions of each sector and discounting the conditions of operation of individual enterprises.

The above principle of uniform wholesale prices is observed by establishing, along with general or national prices, uniform zonal prices for areas with conditions that sharply differ from average national conditions in the level of required outlays on the production and transportation of a product. For example, uniform national prices are accepted for producers' and construction goods the transportation cost of which accounts for only a small fraction of their wholesale price (rubber products for industrial use, ferrous metals, etc.) as well as products put out by processing industries provided they are consumed where they are turned out. Uniform zonal prices are established for each area of consumption for the products whose transport involves relatively high costs (oil products, cement, etc.) and for each area of production for mining products if there are sharp natural differences in their production costs (coal, timber, ore).

But differences in cost levels cannot, of course, be reduced to zonal differences. Costs are affected by transport factors, the technical equipment of enterprises, differences in capital outlays as well as defects in the planning and organisation of production. In some cases where deviations of individual costs from average sectoral costs are insignificant, the operation at a profit or at least without loss of the bulk of enterprises using uniform prices can be ensured by raising the level of profit for the entire sector. If there are considerable deviations of individual costs, the establishment of prices must be preceded by calculations redistributing the accumulations inside the sector. Thus, a system of special accounts at the State Bank is used to eliminate in meat packing and dairy production the effect of different pricings of raw materials coming from different sources. The difference between the actual prices at which an enterprise buys raw materials and general uniform prices is charged to this account. This difference is finally adjusted at the close of a year.

The elimination of the effect of natural and transportation differences on the level of costs is effected in two ways. One method is to determine a wholesale price on the basis of the average sectoral cost for all enterprises not run under especially favourable conditions. The additional income of the latter enterprises is then channelled into the state budget in the form of rent payments. This procedure is applied in timbering, for example. The other method is to establish a wholesale price on the basis of an average sectoral cost, the formation of which involves all enterprises. To ensure the operation of enterprises without loss recourse is made to differentiated accounting prices at which sale agencies settle accounts with each producer. Accumulations inside a sector are thus redistributed and the unity of prices is observed. Accounting prices are extensively used in mining and extraction, and in particular in oil extraction and coal mining.

Another major problem of pricing is that of planned reduction of wholesale prices. Wholesale prices are reduced, in accordance with the requirements of the national economy, owing to lower production costs for individual enterprises as well as for a given sector as a whole.

Therefore, planning for lower wholesale prices is based on a chess-board input-output table describing the inter-dependence of these changes in separate industries.

The chessboard input-output table of price changes consists of two input-output tables: the table of profit-and-loss changes of the national economy and the input-output table of changes in the relations of enterprises with the budget. The first table takes into account a decrease of the profit of producers as a result of lower prices and the distribution of the difference over consumers. The effect of the lower prices on pricing in consumer sectors is first calculated without taking into account the mutual advantages from price cuts; then the effect of these advantages is determined for the sectors providing raw materials and fuel, and then for the allied and manufacturing industries. This procedure makes it possible to determine the total sum of cuts, distri-buted over consumers, and plan on this basis decreases in wholesale prices which would correspond to the interests of the national economy.

The second input-output table describes the losses and income increment due to a planned decrease of prices (e.g. a decrease of the profit from the sale of goods at reduced prices, increase of profit as a result of lower costs, etc.). Comparing losses and additional profits due to lower prices, the planning agencies readjust the latter's level to prevent unwarranted deviations in sectoral yields of profits as well as to ensure a continued accumulation of funds and their delivery to the budget.

Thus, the chessboard table makes it possible to revise the prices of manufactured goods and plan their reduction corresponding to proper input-output relations emerging in the national economy.

Wholesale prices in industries are planned separately for the means of production (capital goods) and objects of consumption (consumer goods) because of special features of pricing for the sectors of group I (i.e. producing capital goods) and group II (i.e. producing consumer goods). The prices of capital goods are established by a single price-list and those of consumer goods by two price-lists: one for the wholesale prices of enterprises and the other for retail prices. The system of two price-lists makes it possible to differentiate prices, which is especially important for the group II sectors, in which production is distributed over a large number of enterprises sharply differing in operational conditions.

Wholesale prices of capital goods also differ from those of consumer goods in the procedure of compensation of transport costs. The wholesale prices of consumer goods are established mainly as prices f.o.b., plus haulage when the transport cost is charged to the supplier. This system of pricing ensures uniform transport costs which are incorporated into prices according to uniform national or zonal ratings, and the unity of prices in different areas is attained. The prices of capital goods are determined mainly as f.o.b. prices, which must stimulate rational consumer-supplier ties. As more direct economic ties spring up, there is a growing transfer to prices f.o.b. plus haulage, for they ensure uniform input-output accounts for individual enterprises regardless of their location.

The planning of wholesale prices assumes a certain procedure for their endorsement, which is to combine a centralised pricing policy with extensive rights for Republican and local bodies; the endorsement of wholesale prices for most products is the competence of central planning agencies and republican-level bodies. Wholesale prices can only be endorsed by the State Principal Standards, technical specifications, standard procedures and model calculations necessary to justify the prices to be endorsed. The endorsed prices must be entered into official price-lists and brought to the knowledge of producers.

To strengthen the role of prices in economic development, and in particular production effectiveness in accordance with the aims of the economic reform, the Council of Ministers of the U.S.S.R. has instructed the State Committee of Prices under the U.S.S.R. Gosplan to work out recommendations for the key directions to be followed in the new wholesale pricing of manufactured goods. The basic principles must be: (a) to bring prices as close as possible to the level of socially necessary expenditures of labour, taking into account compensation of

M

the production costs for all normally operating (normally efficient) enterprises and a yield of profit for them ensuring as a minimum the payment for productive assets and the establishment of an enterprise fund; and (b) the establishment of proper price relations for interchangeable products ensuring the stimulation of technical progress and the attainment of adequate proportions in the development of individual sectors of production. It is recommended to make the new prices effective in 1967.

The following measures to improve the current wholesale prices have been recognised as deserving priority:

(a) Revision of the wholesale prices of products simultaneously with introduction of new standards and technical requirements, to make prices take into account additional outlays and the economic benefit to consumers from the better quality, reliability and durability of a product; surcharges for prices if the products priced show better qualities as compared with standards and prescribed technical requirements.

(b) Establishment of wholesale prices for new products at a level to ensure economic benefit to the consumer from the better quality of a new product and to allow the producer a higher profit.

(c) Uniformity of the profits of equally efficient enterprises in each sector, achieved by taxation, readjustment of official price-lists and the application of accounting prices.

(d) Extension of the practice of endorsement, for products subject to turnover taxation, of the wholesale price-lists of enterprises minus turnover tax.

(e) Timely revision of outdated wholesale prices for separate groups of products.

The necessity has been recognised of doing away, so far as possible, with temporary or provisional prices. Instead, the practice is being extended of establishing limiting group prices, as well as model computing ratings, for products priced by agreement of the parties concerned.

The planning of transport rates is based on transport costs. However, the rates cannot be directly derived from the level of operational costs since the latter are strongly affected by the extent to which available transport facilities are used. Hence the need for differentiating the rates depending on the conditions of transport operation and in particular on the type of cargo, speeds, ranges, directions and scales of haulage.

Recourse is also made in planning to a system of exceptional rates (higher or lower than the standard rates) stimulating the exploitation of insufficiently dense traffic routes, restricting traffic on congested routes and discouraging unjustifiably long haulages. For example, the rates for the carriage of grain to Central Asia from the Ukraine and the North Caucasus have been raised, since there are less congested routes from Siberia. Higher rates are charged for the carriage of coke from the Ukraine to the East, since the latter has a sufficient supply of local coke. Lower rates (lower than the costs in some cases) have been established for the haulage of large cargoes over short distances.

The system of transport charges should ensure proper relations between the rates for different types of transport. These relations are aimed at a rational combination of the operation of all types of transport and the best use of available rolling stock, taking into account the effectiveness of each type of transport in a given area, over different distances and for each type of cargo. Thus, if there are parallel railway and inland water routes, the railway rates are increased when the inland water routes become navigable, which stimulates the use of the latter. The rates for road haulage over short distances deviate more from the average (they are lower than the average rates) than railway rates, so as to stimulate the best use of automobiles.

The *state-purchase prices of farm products* express the economic relations between the state-owned sectors and the collective farms. They must ensure the compensation of socially necessary costs of farm output and the accumulation of funds for expanded reproduction on collective farms.

The state-purchase prices are differentiated for agricultural zones to take into account different production and sale conditions, the quality and importance of some types and grades of goods, and seasonal fluctuations in the production and sale of certain products.

To make state-purchase prices an economic tool for increasing farm output, many factors are taken into account in this kind of pricing, and in particular, the demand for farm products, the need to reclaim new areas, the quality of products, their potential uses, etc.

State-purchase prices are planned to ensure an all-out effort to raise the quality of output. For farm products intended for processing, state-purchase prices are differentiated according to the content of the main substance used, in particular the content of starch in potatoes, the content of fat in milk, and the content of sugar in grapes.

The state-purchase prices of staple farm products (cereals, oil-bearing plants, potatoes, cotton, sugar-beet, beef, milk, eggs and wool) are endorsed by the Council of Ministers of the U.S.S.R. for each Union Republic. It is left to the Council of Ministers of each Republic to differentiate these prices by zones, grades and times of purchase; the Council of Ministers of each republic also endorses the prices of those products which are not included in the competence of the U.S.S.R. Government (vegetables including melons and water-melons, hay, straw, etc.).

The *state retail price* of a consumer product is the final price at which it is sold to private persons and collective farms through state and co-operative retail trade.

The retail price structure has the following form:

(1) the wholesale price (after turnover tax—see above) of a manufactured product or the wholesale price of a farm product; plus

(2) trade surcharge including:

(a) the circulation costs of trade agencies plus

(b) the net income (profit) of trade agencies.

The retail state price is a uniform price. Its uniformity applies either to the entire territory of the country (such are the prices for all principal manufactured products and some foodstuffs) or to a certain territory or zone (the prices for all principal foodstuffs are established for two or three zones). The uniformity of retail prices is of immense importance for planning the growth of employees' and collective farmers' incomes.

Retail prices are formed on the basis of wholesale or (in the case of farm products entering trade without processing) state-purchase prices, and differ from the latter by the amount of trade surcharge compensating the circulation costs and forming the profit of the trade agencies. Trade surcharges are determined in percentage of retail prices or as differences between wholesale and retail prices (for petrol, kerosene and other goods). They are differentiated for different goods depending on the conditions of their storage, as well as additional expenses on processing and transport.

The planning of state retail prices establishes uniform national and uniform zonal prices for key products accounting for more than half of the country's retail trade value. This in turn furnishes conditions for unifying wages, facilitates the planning of trade and currency circulation and simplifies the turnover tax revenues from enterprises.

*Uniform all-Union (national) prices* are established for those goods the production cost of which does not differ appreciably from area to area and the transport of which does not involve heavy expenses (clocks and watches, bicycles, fabrics, footwear, tobacco, etc.). If differences in production and transport costs are appreciable, *zonal prices* are fixed (at present there are three zones, except for fish and timber products the prices of which are differentiated for two and seven zones respectively). These prices are uniform within one zone. Zonal prices are applied mainly to foodstuffs and certain other poorly transportable goods (such as furniture or timber products) produced in areas totally differing in the level of costs and/or requiring heavy transport expenses. The lowest prices are established for the first zone comprising the areas where a commodity is produced on a mass scale. In some cases the first zone may include areas buying a commodity elsewhere. The purpose is to stimulate specialisation. Thus, in Central Asia the grain prices are comparatively low, as a result of which the development of cotton growing becomes comparatively more profitable. For the other zones (the second and third zones) prices are established depending on the transport costs of the goods concerned.

Thus, the national price of a commodity is determined on the basis of its average national cost and the national transport cost rate, while the zonal price of a commodity is based on the average production and transport costs within each specific zone. Zonal differences must strictly correspond to actual differences in costs and be readjusted as the production and sale conditions of goods change.

The most important document used in pricing is the official pricelist, specifying the main properties and qualities of goods, retail prices and trade surcharges.

A special economic type of prices serving the circulation of products put out by collective farms and personal subsidiary farms are the *collective-farm-market prices*. These are based on the value of farm products influenced by supply-demand relations. The collective-farm market therefore implies the possibility of a spontaneous redistribution of private incomes in favour of the sellers. The registration of collective-farm-market prices and their variations is of immense importance, since a considerable part of the commodity output of collective farms and individual smallholdings is sold on the collective-farm markets.

Collective-farm-market prices depend not only on supply versus demand but also on the controlling influence of state prices in retail state and co-operative trade, as well as the state-purchase prices of farm products. The price curves of collective-farm-market trade reproduce sufficiently accurately the dynamics of state and co-operative trade.

Linked intimately with the planning of costs and prices is the planning of the yield of profit.

The role of profit in planning the national economy is being emphasised at present. Prior to the economic reform, profit was not included as a target in national economic plans. Now the necessity has been recognised of bringing to the fore the role of profit in the economic stimulation of enterprises, as well as that of employees' remuneration as an incentive for better results. Under the new system the profit left at the disposal of an enterprise depends on its economic and financial performance.

Profit is derived from the difference between the price of a product (without the turnover tax) and its cost to the enterprise. Thus, at a fixed price profit directly reflects the variation of the cost of output. It is a major economic indicator of the efficiency of an enterprise's economic performance. Together with the turnover tax, profit is the main source for financing capital investment and raising the living standards of all the people. Two types of profit are distinguished: profit from sales and balance-sheet profit. *Profit from sales* is the difference between the receipts from sales (without the turnover tax) and the cost to the enterprise of the goods sold. By *balance-sheet profit* is meant the total sum of profit on the enterprises' balance sheet, i.e. the algebraic sum of the profit from sales plus other-than-sale receipts and minus other-than-sale expenses.

Along with the sum of profit an important plan index is *the rate of profit*. In contrast to the earlier procedure, when the rate of profit was determined as the ratio of balance-sheet profit to the total cost of output, the rate of profit is now measured as the ratio of profit to the total value of productive assets.

This difference is highly important, since the new practice will stimulate a more thrifty use of productive assets. If an enterprise yields a higher rate of profit than the target, it will have additional funds at its own disposal. And the enterprise can attain a higher rate of profit not only by increasing the mass of profit but also by decreasing the productive assets it uses.

Under present-day conditions profit is a source for forming the enterprise's own funds, financing its own capital investment, increasing circulating assets, etc.

## II. FINANCIAL PLANNING

The planning of finances is a vital element in national economic planning. The state budget, loan plans and the cash plan of the State Bank are worked out and endorsed along with the national economic plan. The system of financial planning is the basis for the fiscal plans of sectors and enterprises, and culminates in the summary fiscal plan comprising all national revenues and expenditures.

Financial planning aims at determining the volume of currency resources necessary to meet the national economic plan, the distribution of currency resources over economic sectors and cultural activities in accordance with the plan targets, and the saving of material and financial resources.

The state budget is the pivot of the entire financial system of the U.S.S.R. Its object is the planned formation of a national fund of currency resources for meeting the targets of the national economic plan. The state budget functions as the principal state fiscal plan, connecting all fiscal plans into a single system of financial planning; and the finances of sectors and enterprises are connected with the budget through payments in the form of turnover tax, deductions from profit, the financing of capital construction and the replenishment of circulating capital. The budget's currency resources are used to finance the loan plan. The cash plan is connected with the state budget through the payment of wages and salaries to personnel engaged in the non-productive sphere, pensions, allowances and grants, tax revenues and some other payments. The state budget comprises about three quarters of all national financial resources.

The principal sources of state budget revenues are: revenues from enterprises (turnover tax and deductions from profit), tax revenues (personal income tax, tax on the incomes of collective farms and co-operatives, and tax on non-commercial operations) and funds of state social insurance.

The revenues from the socialist economy account for more than 90 per cent of all budgetary revenues. They enter the budget (as indicated above) in the form of turnover tax and deductions from the profit of state enterprises and organisations.

The turnover tax is the state's centralised net revenue channelled entirely into the state budget to be used for national needs. By its socio-economic nature, the turnover tax is not a tax in the proper sense of the word. Its size is determined by the state by planning economically justified prices, as well as the costs of output and the rate of profit of enterprises.

In contrast to the profit of enterprises, the size of which depends on the fulfilment of the production cost plan and part of which remains at the disposal of an enterprise, the turnover tax does not depend on the fulfilment of the production cost plan and constitutes a fixed system of deductions channelled into the state budget.

Part of the profit of state enterprises is also converted into the state's centralised net revenue in the form of deductions from profits. This form of profit distribution makes it possible to combine the formation of national financial resources with a material stimulus to sectors and enterprises to decrease the production costs of their output and raise their rates of profit.

The planning of budgetary revenues in the form of the turnover tax, deductions from profit and other incomes of the socialist economy is based on the production programme, on plans for raising the productivity of labour and decreasing the cost of output and, finally, on measures aimed at a higher rate of saving and more rational use of physical and financial resources.

The turnover tax revenues which constitute part of the net profit of the socialist economy are derived from the output and sales specified by the national economic plan, mainly for the sectors producing consumer goods.

Deductions from the state enterprises and organisations are planned for each sector of the national economy, taking into account its specific forms of operation. Thus, for heavy industries profit is determined as a difference between the volume of commodity output in current wholesale prices and its planned cost. In food-processing and other sectors producing consumer goods the size of profit is established in accordance with the previous year's rate of profit, the planned volume of production and sales, and the targets for lowering production costs and changing the prices of products in the year planned.

To meet national targets, the state budget absorbs personal means (personal income tax, loans and deposits at the savings-banks). The proportion of personal tax payments in the budget has been steadily decreasing. During the seven-year period (1959–65) income tax was abolished for some sections of employees. Under the current five-year plan (1966–70) the reduction and abolition of personal tax payments will continue.

The point of departure in planning the expenditures of the state budget are the targets for the development of production and construction, and for social and cultural measures, as well as the costs of administration and defence.

The state budget of the U.S.S.R. incorporates the all-Union budget and the budgets of the Union Republics. The latter incorporate

Republican budgets, budgets of autonomous republics and local budgets, i.e. the budgets of territories, regions, districts, cities, settlements and villages.

The sizes of the Republican budgets and their importance in the national economy increased very much as a result of the reorganisation of the control of industries and construction and the extension of the rights of Union Republics. The proportion of the Republican budgets in the state budget of the U.S.S.R. increased from 28 per cent in 1955 to 60 per cent in 1966.

The relations between state budget and economic organisations are regulated on the basis of the business budgets of organisations, departments, ministries or individual enterprises. At the same time, its business budget is of independent importance as the principal financial document of an enterprise or economic group.

In so far as an enterprise's financial resources are to be used up or replenished, its business budget must be thoroughly co-ordinated with the plan of a higher-level agency and, through it, with the state budget. Thus, the financial plan of an enterprise is the primary cell of the financial plan of the entire socialist state.

The business budget of an enterprise finishes with a special section showing the relations of the enterprise and sector with the state budget. This section ensures the close co-ordination of the financial plans of enterprises and sectors with the state budget.

Under the current economic reform the financial plan of an enterprise as a whole does not have to be endorsed by a higher-level agency. Only the total sum of profit, the rate of profit, payments to the budget and allocations therefrom have to be endorsed.

Of major importance in the organisation of national economic activity is the State Bank of the U.S.S.R., granting short-term credits to the national economy and functioning as a single accounting and currency-issuing centre of the country. The State Bank functions in accordance with the national economic plan. All current financial operations of enterprises and organisations are carried out through the departments and offices of the State Bank. This makes it possible to control financially the progress of the entire national economic plan, since these financial operations reflect the planned input-output relations in the national economy.

Bank crediting is the state's important tool for controlling the progress of the plan and influencing the process of reproduction. The activity of the State Bank is planned on the basis of the credit plan, directly connected with planning production, supply and trade. The credit plan of the State Bank is endorsed every quarter of a year as a business budget. The revenue section includes the State Bank's own funds, the carry-over of the funds of enterprises and other economic units on their current and deposit accounts, the carry-over of budgetary funds on their current accounts, and other resources of the State Bank. The expenditure part of the credit plan specifies credits to Union Republics, ministries, and kinds of credit (for seasonal stocks of assets, accounts payable, etc.). The credit plan contributes to balancing the cash receipts and outlays of economic organisations.

The cash plan of the State Bank, directly connected with the plan of personal cash incomes and expenses, is basic to the regulation of currency circulation. In accordance with the indices of the national economic plan and the state budget, the cash plan of the Soviet Bank specifies the receipts of cash from various sources, their issue for specified purposes and if necessary the emission or withdrawal of currency.

To co-ordinate the entire system of financial plans and verify more reliably the provision of the national economic plan with financial resources, a summary financial plan is drawn up to reflect all national receipts and expenses over a period planned. This plan is not endorsed directly by the government and is an account document used for the development of the state plan and financial planning.

The resources of the summary financial plan comprise the following basic receipt items: the turnover tax, profit, depreciation deductions, revenues from collective farms and co-operatives, state social insurance funds, revenues from private persons to the budget and their deposits at savings-banks, foreign-trade earnings and other revenues. The expenditure part of the summary financial plan includes expenses on capital work, including capital repairs, increase of the circulating assets of state enterprises and organisations, socio-cultural measures, increase of state stocks, defence, administration, replenishment of the resources of banks, etc.

Insufficient financial resources registered in the calculations of the summary financial plan indicate that the targets for production, consumption and accumulation, the quantitative and qualitative indices, have not been adequately co-ordinated in the national economic plan. Additional possibilities for increasing output or saving in state expenditures must in that case be found to make good the deficiency of financial resources. An excess of financial expenditures over receipts revealed by the summary financial plan makes it possible to provide in advance for the required replenishment of financial resources.

## 12. CO-OPERATION WITH OTHER COUNTRIES

Expanding economic co-operation with all countries, on the basis of reciprocity, is an important premise for an important development of the Soviet national economy.

Soviet commercial and economic relations with other countries have been developing especially vigorously in the post-war period. In 1964 Soviet foreign trade reached 13,900 million roubles. This was 12 times more than in 1938, while world trade had expanded only 2·5 times over the same period.

Today the Soviet Union is one of the largest suppliers and buyers of goods, trading with nearly 100 countries, under government-level agreements with 70 of them.

The socialist countries naturally bulk large in the Soviet Union's foreign economic relations.

Economic co-operation with other socialist countries takes many forms: foreign trade, which has led to a world socialist market; co-ordination of economic plans; scientific and technical co-operation, which has provided an important stimulus to technical progress; specialisation of and co-operation between national economies; and joint construction projects.

An organisation known as the COMECON, or the Council for Mutual Economic Aid, was set up in January 1949 to plan the economic co-operation of the socialist countries, make the most rational use of their natural resources and accelerate the development of their productive forces. COMECON was founded at the Moscow Economic Conference of representatives of Bulgaria, Hungary, Poland, Rumania, the Soviet Union and Czechoslovakia. Albania joined in February 1949 (late in 1961 it ceased to participate in COMECON activities). The German Democratic Republic joined the organisation in September 1950 and the Mongolian People's Republic in June 1962.

An agreement was signed in September 1964 between COMECON and Yugoslavia, whereby Yugoslavia participated in the work of some of the COMECON agencies, namely, these concerned with problems of foreign trade, currency and finance, metallurgy, machine building, chemicals, and scientific and technical research.

The principal COMECON agencies are: the COMECON Session, the Executive Committee, the standing committees and the COMECON Secretariat.

The International Bank for Economic Co-operation functions under COMECON auspices. Apart from the Council for Mutual Economic Aid, the socialist countries co-operate through their international agencies in railway and automobile transport, electrical power and the postal service. The Soviet Union and the Danubian socialist countries also co-operate in using the Danube.

The first principle of COMECON activity is strict equality of rights and respect for the state sovereignty and national interests of each COMECON country, as a stable and sound basis for their reciprocal economic co-operation and mutual aid.

After sixteen years, COMECON agencies have accumulated considerable experience in the development of multilateral economic co-operation. Their main purpose is to contribute, by combining and co-ordinating the efforts of COMECON countries, to the planned development of their national economies, accelerating their economic progress, raising the level of industrialisation, increasing output and establishing higher living standards.

The principal method of COMECON activity is the co-ordination of the plans of economic development of the member countries.

By co-ordination of economic plans is meant voluntary joint planning activity of the member-states for maximum use of all the advantages of a socialist economy.

Economic plans are co-ordinated on the following principles: an appraisal of objectively necessary proportions in the economic development of each country; advances in the economic effectiveness of social production; combination of international specialisation of production with the integrated diversified (multi-sectoral) economic development of each socialist country, so that each country shall use its domestic resources in the most thorough and expedient way and eliminate gradually the historically evolved gaps in the levels of economic development of different socialist countries.

Of essential importance for the co-ordination of national economic plans is the fact that each country works out its draft plan for economic development independently, proceeding from its specific domestic conditions. Each country determines independently the indices of distribution of its national income between consumption and investment, the rates of growth of sectors, the methods of improvement of the national economic structure, distribution of the productive forces, etc.

The economic plans of the COMECON countries are co-ordinated by their own state planning committees as well as by COMECON agencies. The co-ordination usually begins with bilateral consultations of the central planning agencies of the countries concerned, to discuss jointly the key trends of economic development and to determine tentatively reciprocal deliveries. Then the development of the sectors covered by COMECON international specialisation is considered on a multilateral basis. Finally, long-term agreements are signed between the countries concerned on reciprocal deliveries or other economic measures.

It should be emphasised that the plans are co-ordinated on the basis of strictly observed national sovereignty, non-interference in domestic affairs, reciprocity, mutual aid, etc., and both bilaterally and multi-laterally, these two forms complementing each other.

Recommendations are worked out by the COMECON countries on problems requiring joint consideration. These recommendations are presented at annual sessions in standing committee reports. Recommendations for co-ordination are conditional on agreement of all sides concerned.

Prior to 1960 the plans of COMECON members were co-ordinated by nationally endorsed long-range plans and not by their drafts. That meant that each member country first worked out and endorsed its plan, and this was co-ordinated with its counterparts in other socialist countries only after it had been legislated. The co-ordination comprised a limited number of items and its effect on the development of the socialist division of labour, specialisation and co-ordination was correspondingly restricted. For the member-countries proceeded to the co-ordination of their national economic plans when they still lacked data on the long-term prospects of economic development of other COMECON countries.

At the June 1962 and July 1963 conferences of the leaders of the COMECON countries it was decided to co-ordinate henceforth the *drafts* of economic plans. Only after the drafts have been co-ordinated are they endorsed by the national legislatures.

Since 1960 the COMECON countries have had exchanges of opinion on the prospects for the development of their national economies and economic relations for the next twenty years, up to 1980.

Formerly the use of investments was not practically discussed. At present the COMECON agencies consider the title lists of the principal national projects, and work out jointly estimates of their productive capacity and schedules for the construction of those enterprises whose prospective products are in demand in several COMECON countries.

Work has been completed on the co-ordination of plans for 1966 to 1970, tentative input-output tables have been co-ordinated for the key sectors, bilateral agreements have been concluded between COMECON countries on reciprocal deliveries in 1966 to 1970, and recommendations have been adopted for the development of specialisation and co-operation in machine building, metallurgy, chemistry and other fields.

This extensive economic co-operation between COMECON countries has undoubtedly contributed to the economic progress of the Soviet Union and other socialist countries.

In the first years of COMECON activity there was a trend in some countries towards the development of the total complex of industrial production. Comparatively small enterprises were often built as a result. This led not only to unjustified overlapping in the development of some sectors but also to the establishment in some cases of economically unsound enterprises and manufactures lacking adequate raw materials and skilled manpower. To a certain extent this was explained by the fact that the trend of economically unjustified universalisation based on low-volume production had existed in some of the countries previously.

The development of the complete complex of industrial production is justifiable only for countries possessing considerable natural resources and manpower, together with a high-capacity domestic market whose demand for goods and services is so considerable that it can only be satisfied by high-volume production, extensive specialisation and effective economic co-operation inside the country.

A premise for making the international socialist division of labour economically effective is the attainment of rational proportions of production. Concentration of the production of similar parts, units or products at large enterprises ensures a higher level of efficiency and lower costs than at small enterprises.

The international socialist division of labour does not interfere with the integrity of each national economy. It merely implies a certain specialisation, taking into account the new possibilities furnished by large-scale production. This specialisation rests on a strict observance of national interests, equal rights and economic expediency. Naturally, no country relinquishes any of its rights of ownership of the natural wealth and products it possesses.

Of major importance in the co-ordination of the socialist countries' planning is a wide exchange of experience in science and engineering, which saves material resources, labour and time. For example, Czechoslovakia has a high scientific and technical potential in machine-building and the production of consumer goods, the German Democratic Republic in machine-building and chemicals, Hungary in electrical communications and electronics, Rumania in oil, Bulgaria in food processing, etc.

Between 1950 and 1962 the COMECON countries exchanged more than 38,000 sets of technical specifications: capital projects, machine drawings, manufacturing specifications, etc.

An important form of economic co-operation is the training of personnel and raising its skills in all economic, scientific and cultural fields.

Between 1950 and 1962, 30,000 specialists from COMECON countries studied at first hand the progress of science, engineering and production in other COMECON countries.

Other international socialist agencies set up for economic co-operation are also important. These include the Common Rolling Stock of 100,000 goods wagons aimed at rationalising the traffic between COMECON countries, the International Economic Co-operation Bank, etc.

The Soviet Union is likewise engaged in vigorous economic co-operation with all countries which have embarked on independent development. These economic relations are based on equality, reciprocity, respect for territorial integrity and sovereignty, and non-interference in domestic affairs.

The co-operation takes various forms:
   (a) reciprocal trade,
   (b) granting of loans and credits,
   (c) technical aid.

The Soviet credits and other allocations for the economic development of the developing countries totalled by mid-1965 3,500 million roubles (nearly 4,000 million dollars.)

Especially large credits were granted in Asia to India, Indonesia, Afghanistan, Ceylon, etc., and in Africa to the United Arab Republic, Ethiopia, Ghana and Guinea. Soviet credits met about 5 per cent of India's foreign currency needs (under its second five-year plan) and almost 70 per cent of Afghanistan's foreign currency needs.

Apart from granting loans, the Soviet Union extends credits charging no interest. These include the Soviet construction of educational, cultural and medical institutions, and the supply of literature and equipment to educational establishments.

The less economically developed countries are also aided by the Soviet Union through the United Nations, above all under the expanded programme of technical assistance and through special funds.

The Soviet Union attaches great importance to economic co-operation with less developed countries on a bilateral basis. Between 1958 and 1965 the annual growth of Soviet trade with these countries exceeded 20 per cent, i.e. was twice the rate of growth of Soviet foreign trade as a whole. And according to Soviet economists, Soviet foreign trade with less developed countries should increase by 1980 roughly 7 times compared with 1965, and exceed 10,000 million roubles (11,000 million dollars).

The Soviet Union has no excess capital which must be invested abroad. This practice does not correspond to the nature of the Soviet system. Nor does the Soviet Union recognise the policy of capturing foreign markets and exploiting other countries. At the same time the Soviet Union finds it possible to allocate some funds, which could otherwise be effectively used inside the country, to aid the developing nations in the development of their national economies. All enterprises and structures built with Soviet aid in these countries remain the national property of the countries in which they are built.

Soviet technical co-operation now covers more than twenty developing countries, including the United Arab Republic, Afghanistan, India, the Republic of Guinea, Burma, the Republic of Ghana, Indonesia, Cambodia, the Republic of Somali, Ceylon, Nepal, Sudan, Syria, Pakistan, and Iraq. The Soviet Union is aiding them technically and economically in 600 industrial and other construction projects of vital importance for the development of their national industries, farming, transport, medicine, science and culture.

Construction and other economic activity aided by the Soviet Union in the developing countries comprises practically all sectors of their economy. However, most of the Soviet technical assistance commitments under the agreements signed with these countries aim at their industrial development.

For example, the key trend of Soviet–Indian technical and economic co-operation is towards the development in India of heavy industry: iron and steel, heavy machinery including power generators, instruments, oil, as well as coal, chemicals and pharmaceutics and some other industries.

Metallurgical works are being built in Indonesia and Ceylon with Soviet assistance for the first time in the history of these countries. Of special importance to Ceylon is an automobile tyre works now under construction, where raw rubber will for the first time be processed locally instead of being exported.

The Aswan complex as well as many enterprises to produce oil products, machinery, electric equipment, ships, metals, chemicals and medicines, textiles and food products are being built with Soviet aid in the United Arab Republic.

The Soviet Union transfers free of charge all the drawings and specifications necessary to the recipient countries for production. Only the costs of the actual manufacture and transfer of these drawings and specifications are chargeable. The gratuitous transfer of patents is stipulated in the Soviet agreements with India, Ceylon, Indonesia, etc. The only reservation made is the recipient country's obligation to use the specifications within the country at the enterprises built with Soviet aid and not to transfer them to foreign physical or juridical persons.

Of substantial economic importance to several developing countries is Soviet aid in surveying and prospecting. This work has yielded good results. For example, several commercial-scale oil-fields were promptly discovered in India, which started India's national oil industry. Two oil refineries built with Soviet aid in India will be able to process 6,000,000 tons of oil annually, which accounts for about 70 per cent of the oil processed in India at present.

Versatile technical aid is rendered by the Soviet Union to the developing countries in transport and communications. It is intended to build or improve more than 50 projects of this kind with Soviet aid, and many of these are already functioning.

For its part, the Soviet Union buys in Asia, Africa and Latin America goods which are staple exports of the countries concerned: natural rubber, jute, cotton, raw leather, coffee, cacao beans, tea, sugar, etc. This improves the currency position of the countries concerned, contributes to the sale of their staple products and helps to establish stable trade relations.

The Directives provide for a considerable increase of Soviet foreign trade. Special emphasis is laid on the development of all-round economic association among socialist countries. This is regarded as a priority target, since it corresponds to the vital interests of each socialist country and the community of socialist countries as a whole. In the report of the Head of the Soviet Government, A. N. Kosygin, at the 23rd Congress of the C.P.S.U. it was stated that under the five-year plan the Soviet Union would buy in socialist countries more than a thousand sets of equipment for enterprises and workshops producing chemicals, consumer goods, foodstuffs and other goods, and the deliveries from these countries would meet 48 per cent of the Soviet demand for sea transport ships, 40 per cent of the demand for electric locomotives for goods transport and industrial purposes, 36 per cent of the demand for passenger railways cars, etc. Under the agreements signed, the Soviet Union will buy large quantities of various consumer goods and will for its part meet the demand of other socialist countries for many types of equipment and machinery, fuel, metal and metal ore, cotton, timber, pulp and paper and other products.

The Directives stress the need for expanding Soviet economic association with the independent countries of Asia, Africa and Latin America. Co-operation with the developing countries concentrates on the establishment in these countries of key industries, training of scientific and technical personnel, and larger foreign trade. The Soviet Union contemplates considerable increases in the import of staple goods of the developing countries: cotton, wool, raw leather, ore concentrates, non-ferrous metals, fruit, coffee, cacao beans, tea as well as some manufactured products.

Simultaneously the Directives provide for a continued growth of Soviet trade with capitalist countries.

# 5

# The Realisation of Plan Targets

## 1. PLANS MUST BE FULFILLED

From the previous chapters it is clear that to draw up an economically and technically justified plan is by no means simple. The process involves a great amount of work, including painstaking research. Yet drawing up a plan is only the first step in planning. The hardest part begins after the plan has been worked out, considered and endorsed —at the second stage, i.e. the realisation of the plan. What has been thought out, computed and expressed in specific targets must be converted into tons of metal or coal, metres of fabrics, new enterprises, residential areas, schools, etc.

Only practice can demonstrate beyond doubt whether the targets of an economic plan are realistic and whether the planners took into account the actual possibilities of production in the light of society's demand. The progress of an economic plan may reveal the planners' misconceptions or miscalculations as well as discrepancies between the targets for the development of different sectors, areas or enterprises. On the other hand, reserves which were overlooked as the plan was worked out or which have been detected as it is fulfilled may accelerate the development of production in all sectors and hence raise higher the material and cultural standards.

Targets cannot be met spontaneously and automatically. The progress of a plan has to be organised.

—Every enterprise must be provided with adequate plant, raw materials, fuel, electrical power, etc., in accordance with the output targets.

—The output of an enterprise must have a steady market.

—Every enterprise must have an adequate number of employees of adequate skills.

—Every employee and the entire personnel of an enterprise must be encouraged materially and morally to work for the best results possible.

—The progress of the plan must be supervised thoroughly and

constantly by higher-level state bodies as well as by workers, engineers, office employees, collective farmers, agronomists, etc.

The experience of capitalist economies indicates that it is impossible to ensure the fulfilment of a plan if the basic means of production are privately owned. Volumes of tables, calculations and graphs can be compiled and these volumes can be called the "plans" for the development or reconstruction of a country's economy. It is impossible, however, in a capitalist economy to ensure the fulfilment of what has been specified by the plan.

In socialist countries the drafting and fulfilment of a plan are inseparable constituents of a single whole known as the planning of the national economy. How is the fulfilment of the national economic plan ensured? By way of illustration we can draw the following analogy.

"To cook a ragout of hare, one must have at least a rabbit." This French proverb does not indicate (probably, taking it for granted) that the ragout cannot be cooked either without implements of labour (an oven, a knife, etc.) and, of course, without cooks. The same applies to the process of production. To make it possible, we must combine the means of labour (structures, machinery, measuring and controlling instruments, transport facilities, tools, etc.), objects of labour (raw materials, principal and auxiliary construction materials, fuel, package, spare parts, etc.) and manpower.

Every enterprise can be provided with a necessary and sufficient quantity of satisfactory means and objects of labour as well as skilled workers, specialists and managers by a society able to plan the production of output as an integrated whole as well as to create adequate means and objects of labour and train sufficiently competent manpower.

This is the case in the Soviet Union. Every enterprise is provided by the state with adequate means and objects of labour which form its fixed and circulating capital. The enterprise uses them on the basis of the socialist cost accounting system.

The means of labour are kept efficient by planning renovation, overhaul and maintenance repair, and they are expanded by planning capital investment in the construction of new enterprises and workshops as well as in the technical reconstruction, expansion and modernisation of operating enterprises.

To ensure a steady supply of raw materials, construction materials, fuel, equipment, etc., is the aim of planning what is known as "material-technical supply".

To supply enterprises with adequate manpower including specialists and managers is the aim of planning labour and wages. Various forms of stimulation are also planned to encourage individual employees or the personnel of an enterprise as a whole to work more effectively.

It has been mentioned above that every enterprise is provided by the state with definite funds or assets which it uses under the Soviet cost accounting system. In some respects the latter is similar to the costing systems extensively used in capitalist economies, while in others it is different from any of them.

## 2. COSTING IN SOCIALIST ENTERPRISES

Any capitalist costing system implies an economy run privately for private interests. To get more profit is the only motivation underlying capitalist cost accounting. For the entrepreneur the interests of society at large are superfluous sentiments. In contrast with all capitalist systems of cost accounting, the Soviet system is used as a method of planned production and is based on a proper combination of the interests of society at large and those of each economic unit.

Planned economic development assumes both a rigorous system of costing (and thus controlling) inputs and a no less precise system of evaluating outputs.

Economic controls are organised in such a way as to make inputs and outputs correspond to the targets planned. Enterprises have a large leeway for manœuvre to increase output at their own initiative.

The values an enterprise receives from the state as assets or funds, and the values it gives society as goods and services, are properly aligned and balanced.

A strict and regular account of input costs and output values and their correspondence to the rates specified by the plan is not the only requirement of the Soviet cost accounting system. A method of economic control, it is co-ordinated all along with other active controls of economic performance. Under the Soviet cost accounting system all aspects of the operation of an enterprise are considered, planned and controlled as costs, i.e. in terms of money used as a vital instrument for steering the economic activity of enterprises.

Apart from costs, outputs, i.e. the qualitative results of production, are also checked by evaluating them in terms of money.

Thus, the Soviet cost accounting system is, essentially and basically, the control of inputs and outputs by the rouble. This control is exercised not only by the relevant state agencies, like the Ministry of

Finance or the banks, but also by all enterprises reciprocally as they meet their contracts (payments or delivered products, allowing for on-schedule delivery, the quality and range of the products delivered, etc., discounts, fines, etc.).

Consequently, we can consider Soviet cost accounting in two aspects:

(1) as a method of organising and controlling the economic activity of enterprises; and

(2) as a method of organising the input-output relations of enterprises and their reciprocal control of their performances.

A major condition for Soviet cost accounting is the availability of adequate assets or funds at each enterprise to enable it to meet its targets. These funds, supplied by the state, make up its productive capital. Means of labour form its fixed productive capital, on which output directly depends, and objects of labour its circulating capital.

Fixed capital constitutes the bulk of the national wealth of the Soviet Union. The state is steadily augmenting it, expanding thereby the productive capacity of enterprises by capital investment.

We discussed the reproduction of fixed capital in a special section of chapter 4. There we also outlined the changes introduced by the current economic reform in the planning of capital construction at operating enterprises.

To ensure a continuous process of production as well as to keep various financial accounts, each enterprise covered by the cost accounting system is provided by the state with circulating capital. These assets are used to form adequate stocks of raw materials, construction materials, fuel, packing materials, spare parts, and also a required margin of products in process.

Another part of the circulating capital allocated for the enterprise is engaged in the circulation of finished but not yet sold products, the sums on account, etc. This part is known as current assets.

A major principle (having the force of a law) basic to the organisation of circulating capital, is the fixing of a norm, by which is meant the establishment of the minimum size of enterprises.

Each enterprise obtains circulating capital strictly in accordance with its needs under the plan. Minimum standard rates are established for an enterprise's stocks of raw materials, construction materials, fuel, packing materials, tools and spare parts, finished but as yet unsold products, etc., these minimum rates ensuring a continuous process of production and sale. They are usually expressed in days, i.e. they indicate the number of days of an enterprise's operation that a given stock of material values, including inventories or products in process and finished products, should last.

Circulating capital is divided into own and loaned circulating capital. An enterprise's own assets are assigned permanently. Loaned assets are assigned for an enterprise's temporary use in the form of State Bank credits. This division of circulating assets ensures the most rational use of them and prevents excessive inventories.

Enterprises are provided with resources by planning material and technical supply. By "material and technical supply" is meant the state-planned distribution of plant, raw materials, construction materials, semi-finished products, etc., as well as the organisation of timely deliveries of sets of these products from producer to consumer to ensure an uninterrupted development of production.

The sale of a product is at the same time the supply of it to another economic unit. However, the functions of supply and sale are differentiated on the scale of enterprises or groups of enterprises for the sake of efficiency.

Supply agencies detect and estimate the need of enterprises for resources, work out supply plans, distribute funds, organise direct supplies for each consumer down to the workshop level, and supervise the consumption of material resources.

Sale agencies determine the demand of the national economy and each sector of it for specific products, supervise the full-capacity operation of enterprises in accordance with orders filed, and organise the delivery of goods from producers to consumers.

Uninterrupted and integrated material and technical supplies are of exceptional importance in the rhythmic operation of enterprises and the progress of the technical level of production.

The demand for resources is calculated by enterprises themselves, which draw up orders or applications for required raw materials, construction materials and equipment. These calculations are sent to the sectoral boards of the relevant ministry and the latter forward summary applications to the Gosplan of the corresponding Republic.

Summary calculations of the demand for the Republic are submitted, depending on the range of required products, either to the U.S.S.R. Gosplan or to the State Committee for Material and Technical Supply of the Council of Ministers of the U.S.S.R.

The planning of supply for the entire national economy is the concern of the U.S.S.R. Gosplan and the State Committee for Material and Technical Supply, both of which are Union-Republican agencies (i.e. function at two levels: the national, all-Union or U.S.S.R. level, and the republican level). Besides, the plans for distribution of resources as well as the plans of inter-republican deliveries and the plans for the delivery of products classed under the specialised range are developed by the chief boards for inter-republican deliveries under the State Committee for Material and Technical Supply.

Soviet cost accounting requires the estimation of inputs and outputs. However, this does not imply its indifference to the physical form of products (this indifference being characteristic of capitalist economic activity). The Soviet cost accounting system demands that the plan targets be met not only in terms of money but also in physical terms: in physical outputs and the range of products.

Soviet cost accounting is closely linked with the principle of a single integrated system of control. Its most important feature is a proper combination of centralisation in planning and management in the pivotal problems, on the one hand, and independence in the performance of current economic functions, on the other.

As we have said above, Soviet cost accounting is essentially registration and control of production in terms of money on the basis of planning the cost of output. Besides, Soviet cost accounting implies compensation of expenses from receipts specified by the plan, i.e. non-deficit or profitable economic operation of an enterprise.

The development of the cost plan at an enterprise begins by costing all products. The cost plan is based on cost calculations. It is on the level of cost calculations at an enterprise that the correctness of the targets for lowering the cost of output depends.

Four basic types of cost calculation are used in practice: account-report, planned, standard and estimate cost calculations.

*Account-report calculations* make it possible to establish the factual costs of individual products. This type of costing is used to control the progress of a plan, analyse the cost level and trend, and work out the plan cost of output.

*Planned cost calculations* establish the cost targets for all products. Therefore, the planned cost of all commodity or marketable products is calculated as the total cost of all the costs of plan products and all work done for other organisations or for the enterprise's own capital construction.

In contrast to planned cost calculations, *standard cost calculations* determine the costs for products proceeding from the rates or standards in force at a given enterprise for a certain period.

Finally, a possible level of output costs is determined from *estimate cost calculations* when new enterprises or new products are designed.

However, the use of cost calculations for costing marketable products is restricted to enterprises at which these cost calculations comprise all products. At higher levels, plan cost calculations are developed only for major mass products and uniform outputs (coal, oil, cement, timber, etc.), and the cost of marketable products is determined from the estimate of expenditures.

In contrast to the estimate of expenditures, cost calculations are based on the principle of the production assignments of costs, i.e. the place of production where certain expenses are made. Therefore, along with economically uniform elements (wages, raw materials and construction materials, fuel) cost calculations include integrated costs, e.g. costs for a workshop or an enterprise as a whole. At the same time some items of cost calculations do not cover all costs for a given element. For example, the expenses on fuel are reflected not only under the corresponding heading of direct expenses but also in integrated items of expenses (workshop and enterprise costs). The difference in the costing by (a) economic elements of costs and (b) by cost calculation items are of essential importance in planning.

*Output Cost Structure*

| By economic cost elements | By cost calculation items |
|---|---|
| Raw materials and basic construction materials (minus waste products) | Raw materials and construction materials (retrieved waste products are subtracted) |
| including: bought products and semi-finished products | including: bought products and semi-finished products |
| Fuel and power of all types obtained from outside sources | Fuel and power of all types on technical purposes |
| Wages and bonuses, etc. | Wages and bonuses, etc. for employees engaged in production proper |
| Deductions for social insurance | Plant maintenance costs |
| Depreciation of fixed assets | Workshop costs |
| Other cash expenses | General enterprise costs |
| | Non-productive expenses |

The cost elements in the estimate of expenditures are classified by the principle of uniformity regardless of where, in what part of production, the expenses are incurred. Thus, under the heading "raw materials and construction materials" come all expenses on raw materials and construction materials used in production as, for example, lubricants, etc. The item "fuel and power of all types obtained from outside sources" takes into account all types of fuel and power used for production proper as well as for other economic needs. The item "wages" indicates all kinds of payments to employees regardless of their specific employment at an enterprise.

The cost element grouping makes it possible to determine which products are used at an enterprise and which expenses are made for each output. It also makes it possible to establish the need for and expenditure of each cost element at an enterprise. Therefore, on the basis of this grouping we can supervise the cost plan and co-ordinate it with the plan for labour, the plan for material and technical supply, and the plan for capital investment and the introduction of assets into operation. The cost element grouping is also necessary for calculating the national income created in industries and mining.

However, the cost element grouping does not as a rule make it possible to cost separate products. Therefore, the cost calculation grouping is used to cost them. In this grouping, cost is distributed over groups indicating the origin of the costs.

The item "raw materials and construction materials" indicates the expenditure of raw materials and construction materials which go directly into the output of products. Under the same heading come semi-finished products obtained through co-operating deliveries. The costs of raw materials, construction materials and semi-finished products are entered minus the costs of retrieved waste products at their sale prices.

When the proportion of the cost of fuel and energy is large, it is entered under separate items: "fuel" and "power". Under these headings come the fuel and power the enterprise has obtained from outside sources or has produced and is expending only on manufacturing processes.

The items "workshop costs" and "general enterprise costs" are complex groups including the expenditure of resources servicing production, depreciation, and wages and salaries.

Apart from the costs involved in the production of output, the enterprise makes non-production expenses, including the expenses involved in the sale of finished products as well as those needed for the training of personnel.

Three types of cost are distinguished depending on the level at which the expenses are incurred:

*Workshop cost* includes all expenses made by a given workshop on the production of its output. It describes in general terms the results of the workshop's performance.

*Enterprise cost* indicates all expenses made by an enterprise on the production of its output. It outlines the performance of the enterprise as a whole.

*Total cost* includes all expenses on both production and sale.

In costing a unit output, all expenses are divided into direct and indirect.

The expenses on raw materials and basic construction materials, the fuel consumed in manufacturing processes and the wages of productive employees are called *direct expenses*.

*Indirect expenses* are the expenses on the maintenance of equipment, workshop costs, general enterprise costs, non-production expenses, etc. These expenses are called "indirect" because they do not influence directly the cost of individual finished products.

Soviet cost accounting stimulates the saving of expenses and the detection of new sources of socialist accumulation.

The enterprise must earn the bulk of funds necessary for its expansion by saving its expenses. Consequently, in order to meet the targets for output, the enterprise must meet its targets for the reduction of costs and accumulation. It is from its saving on expenses that the enterprise pays various bonuses; for the fulfilment of quotas, and saving of fuel, electric power, metal, etc. Employees are personally interested in a larger saving.

Under the Soviet cost accounting system the enterprise is an independent economic unit controlling cash resources assigned to it and having its own business budget.

The enterprise is also independent in meeting its plan targets provided it strictly observes prescribed economic and financial rules. What is meant is independence in the choice of specific means for meeting plan targets. The enterprise-state relations vividly demonstrate the principle of combining centralised leadership with local initiative: on the one hand, the strict fulfilment of the state plan, and on the other, initiative, research for the ways and means of the most rational use of resources.

The enterprise is responsible materially and legally for the results of its economic activity. This responsibility is not restricted to the fulfilment of its commitments under contracts but embraces all plan targets for output and saving.

Thus, Soviet cost accounting covers every enterprise paying for its expenses out of the sales of its output. In this respect the enterprises operating under the Soviet cost accounting system differ from those which are financed from the budget according to estimates.

An enterprise operating under the Soviet state accounting system is interested in the successful fulfilment of its targets for the size and quality of output. The more an enterprise exceeds its targets by saving funds, the better will be its financial position and the higher will be the remuneration of the personnel in the form of bonuses, etc.

Cost accounting helps financial agencies to supervise the progress of plans. It encourages the initiative of personnel in the detection and use of latent reserves, contributes to the growth of accumulation and the successful fulfilment of the plan, and implies the need for a system of contract relations between enterprises. These contract relations make the plan more specific and also constitute a means of checking its progress. Contracts stipulate the volume, range and quality of products to be delivered, the time of delivery, the form of settling accounts and the responsibility of suppliers and clients for violating a contract (penalties for overrunning the time limit, indemnities, damages, fines).

One of the basic propositions of the current economic reform is a further development of Soviet cost accounting and a wider range of the independence of enterprises in current economic activity.

The rules of the socialist state enterprise endorsed by the Council of Ministers of the U.S.S.R. on October 4, 1965, extend considerably the jurisdiction of enterprises in economic activity. According to these rules, the enterprise is obliged (i.e. is not simply entitled but obliged) to submit recommendations to relevant agencies for stopping production of products no longer in demand. The enterprise is obliged independently, without any sanction from higher-level bodies, to take out of production obsolete products and replace them with new products in high demand, provided trading organisations have filed orders to this effect. The enterprise is also entitled to put out products over and above the target specified by the plan, provided there is an ensured market for these products.

The enterprise's jurisdiction has been extended in the use of circulating capital, in the use of depreciation deductions intended for capital repairs (overhaul) and the replacement of obsolete productive assets.

Enterprises are entitled to decide independently how they will dispose of excess material resources. They also independently decide matters like the building of houses for employees, service establishments, cultural institutions, kindergartens, nurseries, children's summer camps, etc. Within the limits of its wages fund the enterprise is entitled to apply any system of pay, use any system of bonuses and endorse independently its personnel structure and estimate of expenses of management.

Enterprises acting as producers must enter in advance into agreements with enterprises acting as consumers, sales agencies and trading establishments, concerning the quantity, range and quality of products as well as the delivery schedule.

The economic reform draws special attention to the development of cost accounting. At some enterprises cost accounting had become largely a formality, since the independence of enterprises was much too restricted. The entire activity of an enterprise must be aimed at searching for ways and means of improving production, raising the rate of profit and hence increasing the amount of national income.

Henceforth enterprises will solve independently the key problems of production improvement. Enterprises retain a larger part of their profit to develop production, improve equipment, provide material incentives for their personnel and improve the working and living conditions of their employees. The amount of profit an enterprise retains is made directly dependent on the enterprise's effective use of the productive assets at its disposal, on increase of its output and improvement of its quality. The system of material stimulation is organised so as to make enterprises interested in setting and meeting higher plan targets and using their own resources to the best advantage.

The Soviet cost accounting system is coming into its own in relations between enterprises. As a rule, enterprises and organisations must make good to each other damage resulting from a failure to comply with commitments under delivery contracts.

An important requirement is a positive rate of profit for each enterprise. Every enterprise has to work persistently to bring down the costs of output.

The principle of the positive rate of profit for the national economy as a whole applies in socialist society. This means that a higher rate of profit of some enterprises should not be detrimental to the interests of other enterprises but should furnish conditions for a growing rate of profit of the entire national economy.

The bulk of the socialist economy's accumulations is channelled into the state budget by turnover tax and deductions from profit. This makes it possible to solve the problems of the national fund of accumulation simultaneously with the material stimulation of enterprises. The turnover tax goes wholly to the budget as a revenue, while part of profit remains at the disposal of enterprises, so that their financial position is made dependent on the fulfilment of their plan for accumulation.

The rate of profit is planned for all sectors and enterprises to ensure as a rule their normal economic activity, expansion of production and the formation of incentive funds.

To stimulate the expansion of production, deductions out of the profit of enterprises to the budget are introduced as payments for productive assets.

The enterprise transfers to the budget first of all (a) payment for the fixed and circulating assets at its disposal, and (b) fixed payments, and also pays (c) interest on bank loans.

*Payment for fixed and circulating assets* is established as a certain percentage of the total value of the assets at the enterprise's disposal.

*Fixed (rent) payments* to the budget are established for those enterprises which obtain an excess rate of profit owing to their operation under especially favourable natural or transportation conditions.

After the enterprise has paid for its fixed and circulating assets, made fixed payments and paid interest on bank loans, it creates its own funds by long-term standard ratings for deductions from profit minus the payments indicated above.

The remaining part of profit is used to pay back the loans granted for capital investment (except the credit extinguished from the development fund), finance centralised capital investments, increase the enterprise's circulating capital, meet other expenses within the limits specified by the plan, increase the reserve for financial assistance, and other purposes. The balance remaining after all these operations is transferred to the budget.

Every enterprise sets up three funds: (a) the production development fund, (b) the incentive fund and (c) the fund of social and cultural measures and residential building. The development fund is formed from deductions from the profit of the enterprise. Besides, from 30 to 50 per cent of depreciation deductions intended for the complete renovation of fixed capital will in future accrue to this fund. At present this part of depreciation deductions is channelled completely into the centralised financing of capital construction.

The production development fund which enterprises will be able to use independently for the technical development of production is estimated to amount to approximately 4,000 million roubles in 1967, including 2,700 million roubles from depreciation deductions.

In 1964 the expenses from the fund of enterprises on the introduction of new equipment and the development of industrial production amounted to 120 million roubles plus 600 million roubles obtained as bank loans, a total of 720 million roubles.

Effective operation under the Soviet cost accounting system essentially depends on credit. A considerable portion of the circulating capital of enterprises is formed by drawing on credit. The State Bank's credit is strictly purposive and is granted as a rule for a short term. This is conducive to effective supervision of the progress of plans for output, sales and trade turnover.

The credit system provides not only additional cash resources for the expansion and development of manufacturing processes, bonuses, improvement of cultural and living conditions of employees, etc. but also certain sanctions for failing to meet the assigned targets. For example, those enterprises which fail to meet their targets for lowering costs and increasing accumulations, permitting heavier expenses than those specified by the plan and decreasing unjustifiably their circulation capital, are transferred by the State Bank on to a special credit and accounting basis. In this case, short-term credits may be granted only if a higher-level body offers adequate guarantees. In the absence of guarantees the Bank stops credit and demands the recovery of earlier loans ahead of the specified date of payment.

Those enterprises which improve their performance within two or three months of transfer on to this special basis, and in particular meet their targets for accumulation, keep their expenses down to the level specified in the plan and restore their circulating capital as specified by the plan, are restored to the general system of credit. But enterprises which fail to improve their economic performance within six months are declared insolvent. Additional sanctions are established for them: their credit stops altogether and their accounts are settled only by the State Bank's permission: these are first of all accounts involved in the payment of wages, return of loans, etc.

On the other hand, efficient enterprises meeting on schedule the targets for accumulation, incurring no expenses in excess of the plan and preserving a due level of their circulating capital, receive a number of credit privileges.

Apart from this differentiated approach to credit, the State Bank grants loans to pay for expenses of mechanisation, modernisation and improvement of manufacturing processes to stimulate efficiency, higher output and lower costs.

Thus, credit ensures the use to the best advantage of the assets of enterprises, the growth of output and a higher yield of profit.

The economic reform provides for a much more active role of credit in the activity of enterprises. Special emphasis is laid on the gradual transition of all capital construction from financing from the budget to financing by credits granted by the State Bank and the Construction Bank.

### 3. MATERIAL INCENTIVES

The use to the utmost of material incentive is an important means for meeting production targets and developing effectively the national economy. Meeting the targets for the range of products, quality, the productivity of labour, costs, the yield of profit, etc., is stimulated by higher wages and, in particular, the issue of bonuses. This stimulation takes into account the actual growth of output compared with the previous period, the actual size of saving from lower costs, etc.

The state stimulates the personnel of enterprises in two forms: in the form of wages constituting the main form of remuneration, and in the form of bonuses for attaining a certain level of production, a better quality of output, etc. Besides, bonuses can be paid to the personnel of an enterprise for the introduction of especially advanced and effective equipment.

In accordance with the economic reform each enterprise creates a special incentive fund from which its personnel will be stimulated in the form of deductions from the enterprise's profit (according to the scale of long-term standard ratings) and to the amount of a certain percentage of the wages fund. The incentive fund also includes the sum of bonuses to employees, currently paid from the wages fund and savings on it. Until recently, however, about half of industrial enterprises had no incentive funds formed out of profit deductions, and even where an enterprise had such a fund, its size was small and the sums paid out insignificant. Nearly all kinds of bonuses and other stimulating payments are derived not from profit but from the wages fund.

According to preliminary estimates, the incentive fund for employees will amount to 3,500 million roubles in 1967. In addition, approximately 500 million roubles more will be allocated for bonuses in 1967 compared with 1965.

The incentive fund will now be the chief source for paying bonuses and grants to employees. From the same fund they will obtain at the close of the year remuneration for the overall results of the performance of their enterprises depending on the size of their wages and their seniority or length of service. Enterprises are now entitled to determine at their own discretion what they believe to be the most rational form of material stimulation, including the terms and sizes of bonuses, on the basis of sectoral model rules. The size of additional payments will depend not only on the amount of output but also on its quality. If the quality of output rises, the remuneration of personnel will increase and if it deteriorates (and if, in particular, the proportion of rejects is too high) it will be lower.

The new system makes the remuneration of personnel conditional not only on the results of the individual labour of each employee but also on the total performance of their enterprise.

Every enterprise also sets up a fund of cultural measures and house building. The fund is intended to finance the building and repair of homes (over and above the centralised resources allocated for these purposes) and the maintenance of service establishments and cultural institutions from deductions from the profit of the enterprise as well as the sums currently deducted for residential building from the above-plan yield of profit. By "service establishments and cultural institutions" are meant all organisations improving cultural, housing or service standards (the construction and maintenance of children's establishments, rest homes, sanatoria, etc.). The fund is also intended to finance co-operatives for the joint building of homes, service establishments and cultural institutions. This fund will amount to 1,200 million roubles in 1967 (in 1965 the allocations for these purposes amounted to 850 million roubles).

The entire residential area built drawing on this fund is used for meeting the needs of personnel and is distributed by the enterprise itself, which has merely to notify subsequently the local Soviet of Working People's Deputies.

Enterprises are entitled to redistribute between the incentive fund and the fund of cultural measures and house building up to 20 per cent of each fund's total.

Emphasis on the incentives to employees for improving the performance of their enterprises is of immense importance, since it is a sound economic basis for stimulating the initiative of the masses in economic activity, their active participation in management and the cultivation of each employee's awareness that he is the part-owner of his enterprise.

Moral stimulation is extensively used along with material stimulation. Moral stimulation includes extensive publicity given to the good work of an enterprise or of an individual employee in the press, radio and television, at the cinema, and at meetings of employees and conferences of state agencies, together with the award of orders, medals and other signs of distinction to the best employees, etc.

## 7. WHY AND HOW IS THE PROGRESS OF PLANS CHECKED?

The national economic plan specifies society's economic activity for a certain period of time. However, no plan can predict all possibilities latent in the economy or all difficulties which may arise in the progress of the plan.

It is only on the basis of plans regularly checked against current realities that economic activity can be managed and controlled. The checking of plans detects the causes of difficulties and helps the managers to eliminate them.

In Soviet planning the checking of the progress of plans is regarded as a first-priority problem. Where supervision is good there are fewer mistakes and defects, the rates of economic development improve, and plans are successfully implemented.

The regular checking of the progress of the national economic plan has three basic aims:

(1) to prevent disproportions in the national economy;

(2) to detect new latent reserves; and

(3) to introduce adjustments in the plans for sectors and areas in accordance with the results of the actual progress of the plan.

Economic plans reflect in general terms the requirements of the objective economic laws of socialism. A regular check of their progress should reveal those requirements which have not been adequately reflected in the plans. This is the meaning of the first aim of the supervision of the progress of plans: to prevent disproportions in economic activity. Proper proportions between different aspects of the process of reproduction and sectors of material production require the detection of new resources and potentialities emerging during the progress of a plan. New resources emerge as a result of advanced economic experience, progressive technical and economic standard rates and more effective manufacturing processes.

Here is an example with conventional figures. Let us assume that the plan provides for the output of 60 million tons of rolled metal with an average expenditure of fuel equal to 160 kilograms of conventional fuel per ton. During the progress of the plan, the introduction of a new manufacturing process reduces the expenditure of fuel to 155 kilograms per ton. This means that 300,000 tons of conventional fuel can be saved under the plan and the relation between steel-making and coal-mining will change. A check on the progress of the plan will detect additional resources of 300,000 tons owing to the saving of fuel, so that these resources can be directed either to the production of an additional quantity of rolled metal or to meeting other needs of the national economy.

The elimination of disproportions in the development of sectors and the detection of new resources emerging during the progress of the plan are major conditions for introducing readjustments in the targets for sectors and areas, including additional targets for output, redistribution of material and financial resources, etc.

The possibility of readjusting plans in progress by no means implies that planning agencies should not take the utmost care to draw up well-justified plans at the outset. Readjustment is legitimate only if the planning agencies could not, for reasons beyond their control, determine in advance a certain element with sufficient accuracy, or if new possibilities are brought into being by technological innovations or newly detected reserves.

Like planning proper, the check on the progress of plans is organised by Communist Party and state organisations.

The Supreme Soviet of the U.S.S.R. and the Supreme Soviets of the Union Republics audit annually the reports on the execution of the last year's state budget before the approval of the budget for the next year. The Council of Ministers of the U.S.S.R. discusses the progress of the national economic plan, and audits the reports of ministries and central departments on the progress of the plan for each specific economic sector and cultural field. On the basis of the data furnished by the central planning agencies, state committees and ministries, the Council of Ministers decides, if necessary, to change the plan for a sector or department, or establishes additional targets for output in excess of the originally established volume. The same functions are exercised by the Council of Ministers of Union Republics and the local executive committees of the Soviets of Working People's Deputies, taking into account specific local conditions.

Public supervision organisations and financial agencies play an important role in the check of the progress of plans. They supervise the payment of turnover tax and deductions from profit and the use of assets and funds, detect breakdowns in the progress of the plans for output and cost, track down excessive personnel, violations of the estimate standards, etc., and finally take measures for saving on material resources, manpower and cash.

Workers, engineers, office employees and collective farmers take part personally in the check of the progress of plans. Through Communist Party, trade union and Young Communist League organisations, as well as through standing production conferences or general meetings of collective-farm members, they spot defects in the work of managers or personnel and suggest methods for eliminating these defects.

The checkup begins with establishing how, to what extent and within what period the state plan was brought to the knowledge of the producers. Timely information on plan targets is of immense importance, since the enterprise's preparations for meeting targets take much time and effort, especially if the range of products is to be changed considerably or the production programme is to be expanded compared with last year's.

A properly organised check of the progress of plans is exercised regularly and under a carefully worked out programme. It covers not only the enterprises which lag behind in the progress of the plan but also the advanced sectors and enterprises successfully coping with their targets. This is especially vital for investigating and propagating advanced experience. A systematic check of the progress of plans ensures the rhythmic operation of enterprises.

The check must be detailed. Hence the need to analyse the progress of plans not only for sectors but also for individual enterprises and for individual workshops and manufactures inside enterprises. The concreteness of the check also implies an analysis of the progress of plans not only for total or summary indices but also for individual items like the range of products, the quality of output, etc.

The check of the progress of a plan is based on a thorough analysis of plan and account data. The basic materials for this analysis are:

(1) The state plan for the development of the national economy, the plans for supplies and haulage, and the plans drawn up under the state plan.

(2) The government's decisions concerning the development of an economic sector or a cultural field.

(3) Materials of the Soviet press.

(4) Data of the Central Statistical Board of the U.S.S.R. and its branches.

(5) Reports of Republican Gosplans.

(6) Reports of ministries and departments on the progress of the plan.

(7) Data furnished by a direct check of the progress of the plan for a given unit (an enterprise, construction site, state farm, machine and tractor station, collective farm, etc.).

The check on the progress of the plan must first of all be *directional*, i.e. be directed at that organisation or other specific producer responsible for the relevant targets. Second, it must be *sectoral*, i.e. comprise the output of the sector as a whole. Third, it must be directed to each *area*. It is only by checking the progress of the plan for each economic area and Union Republic (and in some cases for each territory and district inside a Union Republic) that partial discrepancies can be detected in due time in the development of individual areas, and measures be taken to eliminate them.

The check must be integrated. This means that it must consider not only quantitative but also qualitative (technical and economic, economic and financial) indices. Besides, it must comprise the entire set of sectoral input-output relations.

*The basic practical technique for checking the progress of a plan is the comparison of the data specified by the plan and those actually reported.* In the analysis of the operation of enterprises or ministries the actual showings are usually compared with the corresponding average indices for the sector as a whole and the reported data of advanced enterprises. Reported and statistical data are also analysed when the local situation is inspected. The two types of supervision complement each other.

The principal tool for checking and analysing the progress of economic plans in the Soviet Union is provided by state statistics investigating all the more important processes of economic activity covered by the national economic planning. Statistical data are organically linked with economic plan indices. It is on the basis of the latter that a system of account indices and statistical investigations is organised by statistical agencies.

In the development and the supervision of progress of plans with the aid of statistical data, concrete forms of the operation of economic laws are revealed and computed: objective economic processes are expressed in quantitative terms.

In the Soviet Union state statistical activity is subdivided organisationally into departmental statistics (the statistics of ministries and departments) and national statistics in charge of the Central Statistical Board.

The basis of departmental statistics is made up of the reports submitted by enterprises and organisations and compiled according to model forms by definite dates. The forms and dates of these reports are endorsed by the Government of the U.S.S.R. or, on its behalf, by the Central Statistical Board (C.S.B.).

The C.S.B. and its local branches form a centralised system organising all statistical studies in the country on the basis of uniform principles and techniques of national statistics. The centralisation of statistics is one of the most important economic tools for combating local-separatist plans, i.e. the trends towards closed economic activity, as well as enforcing state economic discipline and in particular the timely progress of plans.

The apparatus of the C.S.B. includes: the statistical boards of Union and Autonomous Republics, territories, regions, Moscow, Leningrad, the capitals of Republics, and also district and city inspection offices. It is entrusted with the entire system of statistical activity and in particular the regular supervision of the progress of national economic plans as well as the state plans for integrated supplies to major construction sites and projects to be soon completed. Its various statistical agencies ensure the collection, treatment and analysis of reliable data. They are obliged to collect and study data relative to the development of each manufacture in each particular area.

The C.S.B. submits the results of its economic analysis of statistics to the government and state planning agencies, and guides the statistical activity of ministries, departments, offices and enterprises as well as checks their account reports and the measures taken to improve them.

All enterprises and other economic organisations without exception must submit to statistical agencies accounts of their activity according to certified forms. The district and city statistical agencies pass on summary statistical information to higher-level statistical bodies and simultaneously report on the progress of plans for enterprises to the relevant ministries and the regional (territorial) planning committees of the executive committees of the Soviets of Working People's Deputies. This ensures a monthly supervision of the progress of plans.

Account reports constitute in the socialist economy the main form for collecting statistical information. It is on them that the bulk of current statistical work relies, the main aim of this work being to check the progress of the state plan for the development of the national economy.

Another form of collecting statistics relies on special censuses and inventories (population census, inventories in industries, construction, transport, trade, etc.).

Finally, there are special inquiries into sales and prices on collective-farm markets, living standards (family budget statistics, for example), etc. Special statistical inquiries elucidate the factors which are not reflected in statistical reporting, serve for verifying the latter and provide additional data for planning the national economy as well as for individual current measures and establishing the regularities underlying the development of the socialist economy.

# 6

## Economic Planning versus Economic Programming

In the last two decades most West European countries as well as Japan and many developing countries have begun systematically to use long-range economic programmes. The programming of capitalist production started in France (the Monnet Plan, 1947 to 1952/53), and was then applied in the Netherlands ("The First Memorandum on the Industrialisation of the Netherlands", 1948 to 1952), in Norway (the "Economic Development Programme", 1949 to 1952) and in Sweden. Programming was later used in Belgium (the plan for 1962 to 1965) and Great Britain (the plan for 1962 to 1966). In Italy programming agencies have been set up and a new national programme has been worked out (much greater attention is being paid to it than to the recently ended Vanoni programme).

Some Western experts call the practice of economic programming "indicative planning" and contend that this is the only rational method of running the national economy. It is certainly not ineffectual; but at the same time it differs in principle from socialist planning both in the problems it sets and the means it chooses to solve them. To outline the gap which exists between programming and planning, it is worth while comparing present-day methods of programming with previous forms of state interference in capitalist production.

### I. THE DIFFERENCE BETWEEN PROGRAMMING AND PLANNING

Present-day programming is by no means the first attempt to introduce an element of planning into the capitalist economy. At the close of the last century Lenin wrote: "The socialisation of labour by capitalism has advanced so far that even bourgeois literature loudly proclaims the necessity of the 'planned organisation' of the national economy." A little more than sixty years have since passed and today the capitalist world is full of plans for "planning". Something similar was in evidence following the economic crisis of 1929–33: the idea of planning acquired numerous advocates in the capitalist world even at that time. This was reflected in the establishment of various organisations for studying planning, various congresses on planning, etc. Some of these organisations which sprang up in the 'thirties are still functioning, in particular, the National Planning Association in the U.S.A., PEP in Great Britain, etc.

However, the end of the world economic crisis and the outbreak of the Second World War left planning in the 'thirties at the level of theoretical discussion.

The Second World War witnessed a gigantic acceleration of the development of monopoly capitalism into state-monopoly capitalism. State interferences in economic activity became more intense and varied. The state and monopoly sector grew considerably. This process continued after the war and was reflected in particular in a wide wave of nationalisation of industries and services which swept most countries of Western Europe. The emergence of numerous state enterprises and even sectors led the West European countries to the problem of long-term planning.

It should be noted that Keynesian forms of state stabilisation of the economy, like changes in the bank rate and other mainly *current and indirect* measures of regulating capitalist economies, predominated in the developed English-speaking countries up to the '50's. As for France, Belgium, the Netherlands, Sweden, Japan, etc., immediately after the war emphasis was laid on economic programming aimed at a co-ordinated *long-range and preferably direct influence* on capitalist economies by selective investments.

For example, in France, the country with the richest and longest experience of economic programming, the theoretical Keynesian scheme was rejected (though the general idea of state interference was preserved) in the late '40's. In the early '50's France discarded the Keynesian recipes in practice as well.

Industrial growth in the Soviet Union and other socialist countries was a major cause responsible for the shift of emphasis from current regulation to long-term programming of capitalist economies. The struggle of the two systems confronted capitalism with a number of acute global problems of cardinal importance to the entire ruling class and in some cases transcending the framework of interests of even the largest industrial monopolies. Such problems are, for example, a higher rate of industrial growth, a more rational structure of capital investment (more rational from the point of view of the ruling class as a whole), elimination of bottlenecks in the sectoral structure and stimulation of the most dynamic sectors or the "key sectors of growth". Apart from these, there are other important auxiliary problems: smoothing out regional differences in economic development, aiding the process of the capitalist rationalisation of economic activity (i.e. concentration of production and the elimination of inefficient enterprises), etc.

The problem of priority in economic activities confronts all capitalist countries including the U.S.A. However, the U.S. economy remained relatively more stable than in France, Italy, the Netherlands or Britain, which experienced the powerful impact of the national-liberation movement in their colonies and found themselves in an extremely unfavourable economic position in the first post-war years for a variety of reasons. Economic programming found favour in direct ratio to the acuteness of socio-economic problems. However, the introduction of programming has recently been studied in the U.S.A. too, and in other capitalist countries which still refrain from indulgence in long-term programmes as an official and extensive practice.

A peculiar political climate was also a vital factor conducive to the advent of programming after the war. Of interest in this respect is an appraisal of the situation in France given by Pierre Massé, general secretary of the Equipment and Productivity Plan: "In 1945 various circles tended to favour economic planning. The wind of reform which swept over France brought the idea of nationalising the key sectors of the economy and replacing the market mechanism, unable to overcome the social and economic consequences of the great depression of 1930, by planning. In those days the political mood of the cabinet reflected that dominating trend" (Political and Economic Planning, 1961).

Characteristically, having restored their domestic positions, the ruling circles of those countries where programming had emerged in 1946 to 1951 (France, the Netherlands, Norway and Sweden) did not abandon programming but, on the contrary, extended its range of application. Moreover, nearly all countries of Western Europe (with the exception of West Germany, Switzerland and Austria) adopted some form or other of state programming.

Programming has received a new impetus in the last decade from the vigorous reconstruction of the economy of the developed countries of Western Europe as a result of stiffer trade competition due to the functioning of the Common Market and because these countries aim more and more at attaining American industrial standards. Immense changes occurred in the fuel and power structure. Many sectors went over to new kinds of raw materials, and new sectors of material production sprang up. It is no exaggeration to say that the scale of economic renovation had had no precedent in the history of West European countries. A natural consequence of this explosive and contradictory process was the growth of inter-sectoral disproportionality which demanded vigorous measures by the state and the big corporations to adjust capitalism to a changing economic structure. On the other hand, a high level of primary capital investment increased the entrepreneur's risk to such an extent that it necessitated detailed and reliable information on general prospects of economic development. Under these conditions, the methods of current state regulation, the purpose of which was restricted mainly to "stimulating business activity", were insufficient to meet the interests of individual corporations, and still less their common interests. There was a need for a new form of state economic policy which would concentrate private enterprise on the key problems of capitalist production as a whole; and economic programming filled this need.

In contrast to the policy of current Keynesian measures aimed at eliminating those contradictions of capitalism which are evident on the surface, economic programming involves going deeper and, in particular, dealing with such an essential aspect of production as long-term investment policy. Programming creates a certain framework within which all other forms of state interference function, i.e. it plays a co-ordinating role as well. Thus, economic programming combines long-term forecasts with a system of co-ordinated state interference effected mainly in the form of financing selected industries to solve the most essential problems facing the monopoly bourgeoisie as a whole. This means that, first, functioning economic programmes comprise not one aspect of the national economy or two (e.g. war production or the generation of power) nor even the development of a whole area, but the total complex of the most important aspects of the process of production; functioning economic programmes aim, moreover, not at short-term but at long-term results. Second, and this is the main peculiarity of programming, it lays emphasis not so much on the interests of individual monopolies as on the solution of general problems of capitalism as a whole confronted with the need for competing with the world system of socialism.

Programming has a purely superficial similarity to planning in the form practised in the Soviet Union. Essentially, programming does not transcend the framework of regulation of capitalist production, leaving economic development largely to the play of market fluctuations.

On the other hand, capitalist programming has its own scientific basis relying on objective economic laws. It is wrong to assume that there is no element of planning inherent in capitalist production. However, there has never been, nor can there be, planned economic development under capitalism.

In contrast to planning, economic programming can be described as the policy, based on private-capitalist relations, of *state stimulation*, co-ordinated on a global scale, of certain aspects of national production to contribute to the solution of the priority problems facing the dominating capitalist groups. It should be emphasised that programming aims not at the control of all elements of the national economy in accordance with the objective possibilities for harmonious economic development but only at stimulating the growth of the "dynamic" sectors of production of special commercial or strategic importance.

In contrast to socialist planning, economic programming is mainly *advisory*: programmes adopted are not, with rare exceptions, accompanied by any administrative or legal guarantees. In programming countries (which exclude today the U.S.A., Canada, Switzerland and Austria) the state compiles, legislates and promulgates a long-term plan specifying the key trends of prospective economic development by sectors or areas of national production. The plan indicates approximately calculated data on the expected growth of investments, personal consumption, export, etc. There is direct administrative-economic connection as a rule between this plan and the activity of individual enterprises (with the exception of isolated cases of signing "quasi-contracts" in the programming of France and Spain). Economic programmes are to a certain extent binding only for nationalised enterprises which account for a mere fraction of economic activity and cannot escape the influence of the spontaneous market mechanism.

It is no discovery to say that the problem of planning confronts today the programming countries of the West as well as the socialist countries. What are the ways for solving this crucial problem opened by the system of socialist planning, on the one hand, and the Western practice of programming, on the other? Where do they touch, affording possibilities for business co-operation, and where do they differ in principle?

Let us begin with the principle of centralisation, one of the first principles of socialist planning. The development of the national economic plan begins "at the top". Not only are the main reference points of economic development projected in a centralised way (which is characteristic of the Western practice of programming as well); the means for meeting the scheduled targets are specified for all enterprises in a centralised way too. Some Western economists interpret the principle of centralisation as meaning over-detailed instructions for the activity of each enterprise. This interpretation does not correspond to a scientific approach to planning (incorporating the principle of operational independence or self-enterprise, which follows from the objective requirement that every enterprise must be self-supporting) or with the Soviet system of cost accounting in general.

Contemporary rates of scientific and technical progress make it necessary to aggregate national plans for production and resources and impel enterprises to increase not so much the volume of production as its efficiency. At present it is generally recognised that central planning agencies (the U.S.S.R. Gosplan and the national and Republican ministries) should specify the key targets of contemplated production at a sufficiently aggregated level—national and sectoral—and intrude into the sphere of activity of enterprises themselves only as far as there is a reasonable need for it. Now, where does the limit of this "reasonable need" lie? This is perhaps one of the crucial problems of the theory of socialist planning.

The range of problems that the Central planning agencies must deal with at the macro-level is delineated quite definitely. It includes the entire complex of problems involved in determining plan targets for nation-wide quantities like consumption, saving, national output and national income. Formally, the problems of planning in this sphere of activity are similar to those of programming. They are to determine, on the basis of constructing an aggregated optimum inter-sectoral structure (of several dozen sectors), the optimum relation between consumption and investment in terms of a given criterion (which differs, of course, in different social systems). However, in contrast to capitalist programming, dependent on "final demand" and therefore unable to go beyond the development and stimulation of general trends of sectoral production, socialist planning, taking advantage of state-run production, can be based on a scientific analysis of economic inter-relations *inside* each sector. Without this it would be impossible to solve sufficiently accurately the problem of determining the coefficients of industrial consumption of the inter-sectoral input-output tables.

The possibilities for raising the effectiveness of national production grow accordingly. A road opens towards a thorough and versatile control of the national economy depending on a deliberately selected criterion, which is expressed by the choice of the best input-output variant. This criterion may be a maximum of consumption *per capita* (national scale) or a maximum of the productivity of labour (sectoral scale) or a full load of productive capacity or finally a maximum rate of profit (enterprise level), etc.

It is in the latter case that we run into the problem of the limit of penetration of directive planning into the sphere of activity on an enterprise. The development of the productive forces makes it imperative to furnish a material basis for economic initiative. This is ensured by decreasing the centralised part of the national income and increasing that part which remains at the disposal of enterprises as their individual funds.

Now, what is the limit of the extension of the independence of enterprises inevitably involved in this approach? Should this limit be the same for all enterprises, or should it be differentiated according to the range of products and economic capacity of each enterprise?

This question has still to be answered. However, it is already clear that most of the planning of the range of goods, especially for the sectors producing goods not in excess demand, is to be shifted to the system of contracts between enterprises, so that the corresponding item in the plan is an estimate, not a directive.

For example, it appears inexpedient to include in the competence of high-level planning the determination of the total range of products (down to grades and sizes), the rules of organisation of production inside the enterprises, or the concrete forms of inter-enterprise relations. These aspects of production can be best determined by enterprises themselves, aided by the stimuli furnished for them by the central planning agencies.

Such is one of the aspects of the problem of centralised planning in the Soviet Union. Inquiry in this direction is in progress in the programming countries of the West as well, but the impossibility of a centralised controlling influence on private enterprise bars the road to the effective organising activity of the state (let alone private organisations) aimed at the most productive structures and proportions in national production. It is true that an extensive system of state stimulants (tax relief, privileged loan terms, preferential rates for state services, etc.) act in capitalist countries as very active catalysts. However, these "flexible" controls are very rigid in other respects: having given an impetus to the development of some sectors, they cannot later check the inertia of unpredictable processes, the "braking distance" proves to be too prolonged, and losses from resulting accidents known as "recessions" are still considerable. Hence the tactics of "intermediate plans" to which some programming countries (France, Japan) resort during depressions, and hence the failures of the economic "stop-go" policy (in Britain), etc.

The spontaneity of technical development and the alternation of favourable and unfavourable market situations impel the managers of private enterprises to be guided as a rule by nothing except a local optimum of production based on the rate of profit, which rules out any plan in a strictly assigned direction. Indeed, is any effective planning of production possible without specific targets? Without any sanctions which would secure the attainment of these targets? Without any obligation on the part of enterprises to meet these targets? And finally without any real possibility for enterprises to co-ordinate their operations? Such is the situation in the West European countries. Neither the General Secretariat of the Equipment and Production Plan (France), nor the Central Planning Office (the Netherlands), nor the Department of the Plan (Norway) can enforce an economic programme.

In contrast to socialist planning, the Western programmes do not take the form of specific economic assignments for specific enterprises. Finally, the over-all projections of programmes cannot be identified with the targets of socialist plans, the correlation of which depends mainly on the aims set and not on the market situation, and which have the validity of production assignments for definite enterprises. On the other hand, it would be wrong to equate the programmes of capitalist production with mere passive forecasts. The projections of West European programmes combine forecasts and expert estimates (the passive element) with indices computed as indicative prescripts of the monopoly bourgeoisie (the active element). For example, the programming of the growth of exports represents a passive forecast based on abstract analysis and expert estimates. On the other hand, the programming of an annual 10 per cent growth of machine-building (France, 1954 to 1957) is an active projection. This does not mean that capitalist programming was able actually to secure this 10 per cent rate of growth; but without the orientation on this rate, it would have been unrealistic even to pose the problem of French industrial modernisation.

Let us see what is being done in the capitalist countries to secure compliance with economic programmes.

Programming is purely advisory, and this is its basic characteristic. In the West European countries there are no special agencies which could secure the fulfilment of adopted economic programmes. Characteristically, in no country except France are the programming agencies incorporated into the state machinery: elsewhere they remain semi-official advisory agencies. This status can probably be traced to the desire of ruling circles to have a larger leeway for manœuvre in their domestic policies. It is true that in some capitalist countries (for example, France, Great Britain, Italy) there exist administrative forms of influencing private enterprises through legislation (licences for industrial construction in some areas, or supervision over the issue of securities). Nationalised enterprises, with respect to which state programmes are obligatory, also constitute an exception in a sense. However, the mainspring of the programming mechanism is the use of the economic law of capitalist profit, and not of the objective conditions of planned and proportional economic development.

An indispensable tool for influencing the private sector via programming is the state-controlled part of the national income. This part has increased greatly in the post-war period and reaches 30 to 45 per cent in West European countries. Using these funds, the state launches extensive economic activity in new sectors and areas, incurring all the expenses involved in a pioneer effort of this kind and blazing the trail for quicker and higher returns on private investments. On the other hand, by offering opportunities for profit, the state stimulates the development of certain capitalist groups in a desired direction. Apart from programming recommendations, the state creates for the private entrepreneur a system of financial privileges granted in the form of loans, subsidies, tax relief, cheaper state services, etc., to which he is entitled only if he orientates his production in the direction indicated by the programme. In France, for example, the tax on investment is reduced by 5 per cent for investments in accordance with the state programme. Subsidies and loans at a low rate of interest are granted in Italy for taking part in the programme of the industrial development of the South.

The system of state privileges as such existed long before the advent of capitalist programming. It is important to emphasise another point: the purposive character of this policy in which the centre of gravity lies in the selective state financing of private investments. The purposive state financing of capitalist enterprises called into being, along with the conventional forms of credit, new institutions financing private projects in accordance with the aims stated in the programmes. Such institutions are functioning in Norway, Italy, France, etc. From 30 to 40 per cent of all capital investments made in the Common Market countries (of which four practice state programming) are financed or controlled by the state.

The state's selection of the most important directions for private enterprise has created new relations between the capitalist state, defending the common interests of the capitalist class, and individual monopolies guided by their own separate interests. Formally, these relations appear as a working agreement between the state and the monopolies, and essentially, they express the struggle among monopolies for an additional rate of profit. This struggle is waged in the framework of special agencies concerned in the development of investment programmes and constituting an important element in the programming mechanism. In France these agencies are sectoral "modernisation commissions" whose activity is aimed, not at determining the targets to be met or the measures necessary for meeting them, but at combating price controls, deductions for social needs and large taxes on capital, on the one hand, and hanging on to financial benefits already secured and augmenting them if possible, on the other.

To sum up, the principal means for ensuring the operation of a programme is a system of purposive state benefits. If a capitalist refuses to follow the recommendations of a programme (which correspond to his general class interests but do not always suit his particular line of business), he is deprived partially or completely of substantial financial aid. Therefore, when the entrepreneur finds he cannot invest more profitably than in the direction recommended by the state, he complies with the state programme; and conversely, he is completely indifferent to state recommendations in the contrary case.

Thus, the capitalist law of seeking maximum profit furnishes objective conditions for economic programming within the framework of the attainment of certain aims of the monopoly bourgeoisie. However, the same law makes impossible in principle any real planning, in the sense that the scale and direction of production would always be maintained in accordance with the plan at each enterprise and hence throughout national production. As has been indicated above, the capitalist practice of programming incorporates no direct organisational-economic tie between even the most elaborate national programme and the programmes of individual enterprises. Therefore, even when an entrepreneur or a group of entrepreneurs channel their investments in accordance with the programme, they do so because they are interested in state benefits at that particular moment, whereas they have only a vague idea of what would be the reasonable volume of production at their enterprises. Under the stimulating influence of the treasury, the rate of profit increases, which impels the private owner to expand output; yet this expansion inevitably clashes with the limitations of capitalist production.

Finally, the national income at the disposal of the bourgeois state is sufficient to attract a certain number of enterprises to co-operate under economic programmes, but it is insufficient to reorientate the whole of capitalist production in the direction assigned by the programme. A case in point is the automobile industry of France or Italy. The financial position of the automobile monopolies in these countries coupled with a favourable market situation enabled them to ignore the state programme completely. As a result, the whole automobile industry of Western Europe is now experiencing considerable overproduction difficulties.

## 2. HOW ARE PROGRAMMES COMPILED?

The system of advisory programming is based on the capitalist market economy. It depends entirely on the capacity of the market subject to fluctuations of supply and demand. Therefore, the programme is calculated proceeding from an *expected* demand and not an *actual* need (and the resources necessary to satisfy it).

In particular, in France the search for equilibrium bulks large at all stages of programming, whether in the preliminary study of drafts, in the organisation of sectoral and *ad hoc* commissions, or in the Equilibrium Group set up specially for the purpose. A possible supply is thus brought in line with an expected demand—on paper but not in reality. Characteristic in this respect is the pronouncement of an "indicative planning" expert: "Indicative plans are not opposed to the market, they are part and parcel of the market economy which is subject if not to cyclic fluctuations then at least to the alternation of high and low reference marks. . . . It is quite evident that the lower reference marks are reflected in the indicators of a plan which have sometimes to be lowered compared with the originally adopted variant". (*Les problèmes de la planification*, Colloque de Janvier 1962 de l'Institut Sociologique. Brussels 1962, p. 55). This statement expresses very clearly one essential premise: the "indicative plan" is adjusted to supply and demand fluctuations. Moreover, the "plan" is made to fit these spontaneous fluctuations not only during its "realisation" but even at the very beginning of its development.

The development of an "indicative plan" is usually preceded by forecasts of the economic development of the country in the next four or five years. The forecasts are based on the conjuncture trends evolved in the previous period, by estimating which the average level for "high and low reference marks" is obtained. Calculated in this way, the average level of industrial growth in previous years is adopted, with insignificant corrections, as the rate of growth for the "planned" period.

The procedure for compiling and endorsing "plans" is roughly the same in all West European countries engaged in economic programming. First a draft is drawn up, on the basis of the official data, specifying the key direction of the government's economic policy. The draft is usually prepared by a special advisory agency (in the Ministry of Finance, etc.). Then the draft is examined by representatives of big business, who inform the government to what extent the expected results of the current economic policy suit them.

Proceeding from the assumption that the economic policy will not undergo any significant changes, the compilers of the "plan" determine three possible variants of growth: minimum, medium and maximum. After the government has settled on one of the three variants, the corresponding agencies begin to develop concrete items of the draft, and to elaborate it into a "plan" specifying the expected rate of production and of employment, the volume of expected investments in various sectors, and the measures to be provided by the government for realising the plan. The latter part of the "plan" is especially unreliable, for the government controls no more than 15 to 25 per cent of production capacity in the countries where economic programming is practised. Essentially, instead of targets, the "plan" consists of hypothesis or even merely recommendations for private owners (as is the case in Great Britain, for example).

The development of "plans" includes special models intended to reflect economic processes as a set of equations containing certain known economic quantities taken from the previous year's economic performance. The solution of these equations yields the values of unknown quantities. What actually takes place cannot be an accurate reproduction of such a model, since it is constantly subjected to numerous readjustments and corrections following from economic fluctuations inherent in capitalism. However, the model establishes the interdependence between economic quantities and indicates how some of them will vary if one of them changes.

The development of economic models and the application of mathematics are used especially extensively in France and the Netherlands. However, the progress of the techniques of "planning" does not correlate with their effectiveness. For example, in France economic modelling has been going on for more than twenty years, but forecasts in France correspond to realities hardly more frequently than in other West European countries.

In contrast to socialist planning, indicative programming is confined to determining (not always successfully) the general trend of economic development without being able to change deliberately its structural proportions. As a matter of fact, the initiators of indicative planning do not set themselves such an aim. Their aim lies elsewhere: on the one hand, to predict conjuncture trends and try to make adjustments to them and ensure the highest possible rates of profit for the monopoly bourgeoisie; and on the other hand, to channel capital investment into the most "dynamic" sectors with the aid of incentives specified in the programme.

France affords the best example to use in analysing the technique of drawing up an indicative plan, because there the problem has received the most extensive theoretical and practical treatment. It is true that in purely theoretical terms French econometrics is probably second to the econometric school of the Netherlands. However, France takes priority in the volume of practical measures.

The development of the "plan" in France is divided into two stages. At the first, preliminary, stage the Commissariat of the Equipment and Productivity Plan prepares the first "sketch", mapping out the volume of production and investment in the key sectors, estimates employment and foreign trade and sets down the volume of personal demand in approximate terms. Then the government chooses one of the variants, which leads to the second stage at which the "plan" is developed in detail for each sector, and general conditions are determined for "balanced growth".

The compilation of the "sketch" passes in turn through two phases: first, the quantities of goods and services are determined and a physical equilibrium is found (on paper, of course); and then, accepting it as a known quantity, financial conditions are determined for realising this physical equilibrium, and corrections are introduced into the original expected figures of production to attain a financial equilibrium as well —by which is meant the equilibrium between all cash flows (wages, profit, investment, taxation, savings, etc.).

The physical equilibrium is determined as follows. The point of departure is the calculation of final demand (consumer goods and services) for the last year of the "plan". For example, 1965 was set down as the last year of the Fourth Plan in France. Proceeding from the amount of ultimate demand, the developers prepare several variants of the average annual growth of gross national output. Then the ultimate demand calculated in millions of francs (in constant prices) for each variant is divided into three components: manufactured goods, farm products and services. The value relation between these components is established from the average proportions in the previous ten years.

Simultaneously the ultimate product is subdivided into five items corresponding to those used by the French system of national accounts: the gross capital investments of enterprises (all private and state investments, except for those in housing construction), housing construction, personal consumption (including, besides wages, the incomes of farmers, entrepreneurs, professional people, etc., spent on personal consumption), administrative consumption (the administrative expenses of all governmental offices, social insurance agencies, the managements of private companies and institutions, foreign and international organisations), and finally foreign trade (export). It is clear that this method of differentiating ultimate demand glosses over the social relations between classes and, in particular, it is impossible to isolate from the item "personal consumption" the wages and salaries of employees which are dissolved in the earnings of the entrepreneurs, tradesmen, high-ranking officials, etc.

But setting aside the question of class relations, let us concentrate on the technical aspect of the problem. How can the compilers of the "plan" determine each of the above five items for the last year of the period planned? Gross capital investments are calculated by means of capital coefficients. If it is known from the experience of previous years what volume of capital investment is necessary to produce a given volume of industrial output, the relation between the first and second quantities can readily be computed, Such coefficients exist for industries, farming and services which, in contrast to the Soviet system, are also included in the sphere of production.

Consequently, if the ultimate demand for these sectors is known (even in approximate terms) the total sum of capital investments can be calculated with the aid of the above coefficients. It is true that the capital coefficients determined by the data relating to the preceding period do not reflect the technical progress of the future and hence the use of the coefficients seriously distorts the estimate of the required volume of investment. However, this does not worry the compilers of the programme, since other items of the ultimate demand are also determined only approximately or simply by rule of thumb.

In particular, the volume of new building and administrative consumption is derived not from calculation but from purely empirical estimates following from conjectures of the ministries concerned, based on current state policy or their own current purchases. Nor are any calculations of a stricter kind made to determine exports. Contradictory estimates are obtained as a result. For example, the sum of French export between 1962 and 1965 was originally set at 5,100 million francs (or approximately 1,000 million dollars) and was then reduced by half!

Finally, personal consumption is outlined at the first stage. However, in a capitalist economy the volume of this vital factor of growth of production lends itself least of all to statistical calculation—it keeps fluctuating, depending on the level of business activity, the level of employment and the situation of the class struggle. Therefore, the compilers of the "indicative plan" are satisfied with subtracting from the total volume of ultimate demand the sum of the "known" four items of consumption. The method has no bearing on the determination of the level of personal consumption based on the real demand of the population.

Speaking formally, this statistical co-ordination of the five items of the ultimate demand is a simple economic model. It is used for developing a more complex model, first with 17 and then 28 sectors. The latter model is first calculated in constant prices, price-changes being taken into account in the concluding stage of developing the "plan".

The principle of constructing the model in constant prices, i.e. the attainment of a physical equilibrium, reduces to finding, proceeding from the five ultimate demand items already found, such an output for each sector as would meet the demand as a whole as well as each item of it. The authors of the "indicative plan" cannot solve this problem by relying on the technical coefficients alone, and resort to linear equations.

What functional dependencies do they deal with?

Each country engaged in economic programming has developed its own system of equations and functional dependencies, but the underlying principle is the same everywhere. In France formal econometrics deals with the following dependencies (or "proportions"). These are above all the dependence between the volume of total personal consumption and the consumption of each specific product. Then follows the relation between the production in those sectors whose goods are used for "ultimate consumption" (i.e. personal and administrative consumption) and those serving "intermediate" consumption. Other "proportions" are the dependence between the output of each sector and the contemplated capital investment in this sector (capital coefficient) as well as the relation between the output and manpower of each sector with allowances for expected changes in the productivity of labour. Finally, a dependence is established between the output of a sector and the import of the raw materials the sector consumes, as well as between personal consumption and imports intended for personal consumption.

These relations between different aspects of production are expressed by coefficients used for linear equations. Therefore, to evaluate the reliability of these economic forecasts, we need to know how the coefficients are determined.

For this purpose it is interesting to consider, for example, the dependence between the ultimate output and the output of intermediate sectors. A real chain-reaction of inter-relations occurs in this case. For example, the production of clothes requires fabrics, the production of fabrics requires yarn, electric power and labour, which in turn require a constant production of a number of other products. Similar ties originate in other sectors responsible for the ultimate output.

The input-output table is used to reflect all these dependencies between different sectors of production. The output of each intermediate section needed to obtain a given ultimate product can readily be calculated by this chessboard table. A similar table is also used in socialist planning; but in contrast to indicative planning, the social character of socialist production makes it possible to take definite technical changes into account. Besides, the input-output table in socialist planning contains many more sectors than the French table, for example.

The table used by the French economists in the development of the

Fourth Plan (1962 to 1965) contained coefficients calculated by the data of 1956 with very small corrections for technical progress. The extremely low effect of the corrections introduced in the coefficients is explained not only by the fact that these corrections were outdated but also by a number of other processes of the capitalist market, and in particular constant changes in the structure of prices which has a decisive effect on the entrepreneur's inclination to undertake technical innovations. In socialist production, technical progress can be seriously studied, projected and actively influenced with the aid of effective planned measures aimed at the introduction of new types of equipment and technology.

In some cases, having recognised their inability to cope with unpredictable market fluctuations, certain Western economists completely abstract themselves in their forecasts from objective factors (like the variation of prices, technical changes, etc.). This is what they do when estimating the balance of trade, which does not lend itself to any prediction. For example, in the development of the Fourth Plan in France the authors accepted a rather doubtful conjecture that imports would satisfy the same part of personal consumption as in the previous decades. But stiffer inter-imperialist competition on the foreign market, on the one hand, and much higher prices on the domestic market, on the other, made nonsense of this forecast in the second year (1963) of the programmed period.

Restricted possibilities for economic prediction under capitalism force Western economists to use, mainly, averages obtained by such unreliable methods as the extrapolation of annual data of the preceding period. As a result, old trends which might have been caused by unique economic or political circumstances are projected into the future and confuse all calculations. Any unexpected emergence of new trends leads to the same results.

Such are the adverse objective conditions under which the framework of the indicative plan is created: the model in constant prices which then serves for the government's choice of one out of the three variants of the average annual rate of expected economic growth. This model is also used by special planning sectoral or *ad hoc* committees, elaborating the model with allowances for investments in different sectors of production (as well as the interests of the ruling class as a whole).

At this stage the model is too abstract: it does not reflect the sphere of circulation with its constantly changing conditions of taxation, credit and finance operations, pricing, etc. It is in the sphere of circulation that there occurs the process of distribution and redistribution of the national income created in the sphere of production. The authors of the indicative plan intended to serve monopoly capital wish to channel financial resources in a desired direction. In which direction, exactly? This is known to them from the accounts of the sectoral committees, which reflect the desires of the largest industrial companies. All that remains is to find out what state controls should be used to what extent to redistribute national financial resources in favour of the industrial monopolies. For this purpose a complex fabric of financial relations is woven over the carcass of the physical equilibrium model, and the result is the model in changing prices.

It was used for the first time in 1961, in the development of the Fourth Plan of economic development of France. A striking feature of this model is the sharp contrast between the fragility of the assumptions on which it is based and the perfection of the mathematical techniques adopted for their treatment. This feature is typical of indicative planning in general, regardless of the national peculiarities of its use. It reflects objective economic conditions under capitalism which create immense difficulties for solving even formal problems of planning. Therefore, the Western economists engaged in the field have to use highly sophisticated techniques to obtain even the roughest approximation of projected balanced economic development.

As for the final results, they are not satisfactory even from the formal point of view. Professor M. van Meerhaege (Belgium) writes on this point: "The results of the use of these methods must be evaluated with great caution. The dependencies which we establish between economic facts and which we lay at the basis of equations or even models prove valid for a definite period only. . . . Quite often we lack sufficient statistical data, especially for a comparatively long period. . . . Therefore, the use of analytical methods rests on a number of hypotheses which by no means always correspond to reality" (*La planification indicative.* Les problèmes de Planification, Colloque de l'Institut Sociologique. Brussels, 1962).

Some Western economists realise very well under what unfavourable conditions they have to practise planning and set themselves a different aim, namely, to determine purely formal conditions of economic equilibrium at a given moment or, more specifically, they determine the level of current prices, wages, profits, saving and taxes at which the projections set down in the model in constant prices would be formally realised.

Leaving aside the description of the model in mathematical terms, let us note one of its essential defects. The authors of the indicative plan for 1962 to 1965 proceeded, as has been mentioned above, from the situation of the French economy in 1959. However, essential structural changes occurred in subsequent years. In particular, the growing concentration of production led to the disappearance of a considerable number of small individual enterprises swallowed by large monopolies. The sum of paid taxes changed essentially as a result, since the taxation of small enterprises and large corporations differs radically. The system of prices also changed. However, these changes were not taken into account in the final results of the calculation of prices.

It is not surprising, therefore, that when the model of the indicative plan had been compiled, the only ultimate inference to be drawn from it for practical activity was the requirement of an additional redistribution of the national income in favour of "productive enterprises", which means in effect the further growth of private industrial capital at the expense of working people's incomes. In 1963 it was demanded that indirect prices be raised and the growth of wages restricted. As for the rate of growth established by the model (24 per cent for 1962 to 1965), it too had to be revised in the second year of the programme period.

Thus, even the formal aspect of indicative planning shows that the capitalist system offers no possibilities for the development of definite targets of prospective economic development, and still less for ensuring adequate proportions between different parts of production.

### 3. ARE PROGRAMMES FULFILLED?

The West European economic programmists interpret the concept "fulfilment of a plan" in a way which has nothing in common with its meaning in the practice of socialist planning. In the West European countries engaged in indicative planning, there are no agencies which can effectively ensure the progress of indicative plans. The spontaneous nature of private enterprise and the absence of any special jurisdiction of programming agencies rules out any effective planning. Nevertheless, the terms "fulfilment" or "failure" of a "plan" often occur, for example in France, where special statistical accounts concerning the "execution of plans of modernisation and equipment" are published annually. What is the real meaning of these terms?

All or nearly all means for fulfilling programmes in the capitalist countries are indirect. They cannot make state recommendations binding on the capitalist, and therefore they expect to stimulate his interest in programmes by promising material rewards. The state offers him additional sources of profit which he may earn if he reorientates his capital investments in the direction recommended by the programme.

If a private entrepreneur (company) has not at the moment any more profitable possibilities of using investments, he accepts this reorientation. In this case, however, he is not concerned about the programme but is motivated exclusively by a higher rate of profit, which leads most often to overproduction—with the only difference that "planned products" prove to be among the products produced in excess of the current effective demand.

Overproduction leads to structural disproportions and this sets off a reverse process: the reduction of production. Usually, this depressional reduction is also "planned", which is expressed in restrictive instead of stimulating measures, these restrictive measures being aimed at restoring equilibrium.

The main tool of financial stimulus to private enterprise is state credit at a special rate of interest. A round dozen of large financial institutions now engaged in extensive issuing of credit on such terms was set up in France after the war. These include the Fund of Economic and Social Development as well as several specialised banks (National Credit, Land Credit, Agricultural Credit, etc.). Through the medium of these specialised banks as well as with the aid of the budget the French Government controls more than 50 per cent of all capital investments in industry. The state commercial banks (as well as four nationalised banks and the *Banque de France*) are linked organisationally by the state *Conseil national du crédit*. In Norway the largest of the four state banks is the Housing Construction Bank, financing more than 70 per cent of capital investments in housing construction. In recent years these four banks accounted for more than a third of Norway's national credits. The state loan operations are co-ordinated by the Ministry of Finance. A semi-state fund (the state accounted for 51 per cent of the stock) was set up immediately after the war in the Netherlands (the Financial Corporation of National Economic Restoration) and along with other state funds accounts for 40 to 50 per cent of industrial financing. The Bank of Sweden plays the most essential role in financing private investments in Sweden and the

National Society of Industrial Credit performs this function in Belgium.

Another important tool for fulfilling economic programmes is the reduction of taxation. This incentive exists in all countries engaged in economic programming and acts as a catalyst of capital investments required under a programme. However, the home and foreign demand for goods and services exercises a decisive influence on the dynamics of capital investment. During low-demand periods tax-relief injections into the organism of market production have no effect as a rule. On the other hand, under favourable conditions tax benefits may, just like loan facilities, accelerate (and often excessively) the growth of some sectors of industrial production. However, neither tool of indicative programming can rid production of structural disproportions or make it continuous, i.e. ensure a recession-free development of the capitalist economy.

There is ample evidence to show that belief in the disappearance of economic recessions with the advent of indicative planning is a case of wishful thinking. The example of France, whose economy has been subjected to very extensive "planning regulation", is again the most convincing example in this respect. The Monnet Plan (1946 to 1953), the Hirsch Plan (1954 to 1957) then the Third Plan (1958 to 1961) and finally the Fourth Plan (1962 to 1965) span the entire post-war period, which nevertheless has been marked by serious economic complications, originating cyclically, despite all these programmes.

The *Monnet Plan* was adopted in January 1946, when all the resources of the French economy had suffered enormous damage as a result of the war. French industry faced the dilemma recorded in the programme: "modernisation or decay". Against this background extensive state allocations were made to develop the key industries. One of the main problems was to provide the national economy with domestic resources of power and raw materials and solve in this way the currency problem.

The nationalisation of the production of electrical energy, coal and gas was accompanied by heavy state investment in these sectors. Out of the total volume of state capital investments made under the programme and totalling 1,620,000 million francs between 1947 and 1953 (in current prices), 799,700 million francs, i.e. nearly half, went into the development of power and fuel production.

French industry expanded appreciably thanks to the state's substantial financial aid, but the main factor was the considerable growth of industrial consumption caused by the restoration of the national economy. The generation of power showed an especially substantial growth. While the total volume of output increased by 43 per cent between 1947 and 1953 (minus construction and calculated for the base year of 1952), the generation of power showed more than a 50 per cent increase.

The pre-war level (1929) in total industrial output was attained in 1949, but that in machine building only in 1951. Contrary to the perspectives of the Plan, the French economy twice experienced serious trouble: for the first time in 1950, when there was a recession which also affected the "planned sectors"—the production of coal, steel and tractors.

It should be noted, however, that in the state sectors (coal, electric power) or in those sectors in which the participation of the state was considerable (oil) the plan targets were met almost 100 per cent. This result was attained owing to the fact that in the nationalised sectors the state's targets were compulsory. In other sectors, where the state's participation was insignificant (metallurgy, agricultural machine building), the production developed completely outside the provisions of the programme.

The Second Plan (1954 to 1957) coincided with a cyclical boom of industrial production. However, despite these favourable conditions, the state programme did not yield the expected results: the French economy landed into a deep currency crisis.

As for industrial production, its correlation with the programme was very remote. Because of the boom, the targets for some sectors were exceeded considerably: by 203 per cent on the average for agricultural machine building and by more than 146 per cent for the automobile industry; for other sectors the showing proved, on the contrary, to be lower than the targets: 70 per cent below them in machine building and 90 per cent in steel making. Disproportions immediately resulted: some goods were produced in excess of personal consumption, while others, semi-finished products, or example, were produced in too small quantities to meet the demands of industry. Breakdowns were in evidence already in 1958, especially in the automobile industry and in electrical engineering, the markets for which were over-saturated.

The next "planned period", covering 1958 to 1961, demonstrated the intrinsic limitations of French "economic planning". The first year of this period coincided with a world economic crisis as a result of which the programme was urgently sent for reprocessing and wandered from one centre of forecasts to another for nearly half of the "planned period" until it was endorsed by the government on March 19, 1959. However, business activity continued to decline and the French experts had to reprocess the "plan" again. The result was an "intermediate plan" for 1960 and 1961 in which the index of production envisaged for 1961 was decreased to 123 as against 127 in the original variant (1956 = 100), However, even thus reduced, the "intermediate plan" targets were not met by several sectors. For example, instead of the 9·6 per cent growth of automobile production envisaged by the "intermediate plan" for 1961, the sector's output actually dropped by 9·1 per cent. A similar process was in evidence in electrical engineering.

Paradoxically, even a spontaneous decline of production is officially styled "planned". For example, the economic crisis at the close of 1960 and the beginning of 1961 was keynoted to the "execution" of the "intermediate plan", which indeed specified a 3 per cent *decrease* of output in 1961. The industrial index in the "intermediate plan" had simply been corrected for the current slump. Between November 1960 and January 1961 the index of industrial production in France dropped 6 per cent and up to November 1961 registered complete economic stagnation.

To sum up, in the "planning" of capitalist production it is not the economy that follows the plan but, on the contrary, the plan is adjusted to fit the unpredictable vicissitudes of the economy.

The Fourth Plan was adopted in June 1962, and its weakest spot proved to be foreign trade. The French monopolies have spared no effort to get the upper hand over their Common Market rivals in foreign economic expansion. It is to aid them in this expansion that both the Fourth and Fifth Plans provide for state financing of the most "dynamic" industrial enterprises as well as new "structural reforms" to increase industrial concentration and bring down production costs. Analysing the principal aims of the Fourth Plan, François Perroux frankly admitted that the "French economy is being influenced to an increasing extent by monpolies and financial groups. This feature is universal for the process of industrialisation in the Twentieth Century (the capitalist world is meant—M.B.) which is accompanied by technical and organisational growth. The process is helped by Common Market activity as well, leading to a higher level of concentration and polarisation. Finally, operating in the same direction is the Fourth Plan intended to contribute to further concentration of production in both industry and agriculture" (*Le IV Plan*, Paris, 1962, p. 19).

The Fourth Plan provided for a 24 per cent increase of national output in France by 1965 against 1961. To understand the limitations of indicative planning as a whole, it is worth noting that in 1961 economic conditions were favourable to meeting this target. Yet the calculated forecast proved wrong. Industrial output began to decline in the second half of 1962, contrary to the "plan".

Between October 1962 and March 1963 industrial output dropped by 16·4 per cent; in subsequent months there was a certain improvement, but it remained below the 1962 level until May 1963. Mining was hit especially badly: its output dropped by 16·7 per cent over the same period.

Unemployment was rife. In February 1963 the number of officially registered unemployed in France reached 200,000, and the forecasts of the "plan" had to be revised again. The targets of the Fourth Plan were substantially changed. The originally contemplated growth of gross national output in 1963 was "planned" to be cut by 23 per cent. In particular, the output of steel was reduced from 24,500,000 tons (as was originally planned for 1965) to 22,300,000 tons, i.e. by 9 per cent. Surely, such manipulations would be more properly labelled "the adjustment of statistical forecasts to fit unexpected fluctuations" rather than "economic planning".

The Fourth Plan set the average annual growth of gross national output at 5·5 per cent. In 1962 the actual rate was 6·3 per cent, in 1963 4·7 per cent and in 1964 4·3 per cent. The rate of industrial growth had been planned to equal 6·6 per cent but actually was lower.

The Fifth Plan of economic development to be realised in 1966 to 1970 was put forward in France late in 1965. An essential characteristic of the present stage of programming in France is the problem of economic-financial equilibrium which emerged as a result of a comparatively long experience of application of medium-term programmes. This experience indicates that, even formally, it is not possible to determine the conditions for a statistical physical equilibrium in order to secure the conditions for a general economic equilibrium for a prolonged period without taking into account prospective variations of various financial values (the growth or fall of prices, the increase or decrease of taxation, changes in personal incomes and spending patterns, etc.). It was clear that the *financial equilibrium* conditions had to be found for the next three or four years, i.e. it was necessary to determine the level of prices, wages, profits, savings and taxes at which the assumptions on prospective outputs could be realised, at least in formal terms. It is for this purpose that the "model in changing prices", partially used under the Fourth Plan, was developed. The model made it possible to introduce corrections for the future dynamics of prices into the summary economic table of resources and expenditures.

The need to determine the production-finance equilibrium conditions called forth, along with "programming by volume" (the development of the table of physical inputs and outputs), "programming by value" intended to complement the physical equilibrium with the financial balance.

"Programming by value" not only involves the problem of the formal modelling or simulation of various financial flows corresponding to the movement of goods and services. It also needs to ensure (as far as possible in capitalist production) a real preliminarily assigned relation between these flows. Therefore, the text of the Fifth Plan postulates concrete levels of prices, incomes and some other financial parameters established in accordance with preliminarily determined proportions between saving and consumption, between production and consumption, and between production and saving. In particular, the starting proportion—the ratio between personal consumption and gross national output—is to amount to 64·4 per cent in 1967 against 66 per cent in 1964. The gross national product is to amount in 1970 to 432,000 million francs (in the prices of 1960) or 27·5 per cent larger than in 1965 with an average annual growth of 5 per cent. Investments into the economy together with "special capital outlays" are set at 68,000 millions francs for 1970, which amounts to some 17 per cent of the gross national product. The growth of non-production expenses is to set at 39 to 40 per cent for the 1965 to 1970 period.

To meet these targets of the Fifth Plan, the Ministry of Finance in co-operation with the Commissariat of the Equipment and Production Plan has defined the basic purposes and numerical projections for "programming by value".

*In the sphere of prices* it is proposed to restrict their overall level by an average annual growth not exceeding 1·5 per cent. Measures will be taken (mainly with the aid of taxation) to secure minimum price fluctuations for manufactured goods (i.e. to preserve their high price level); to establish prices and rates at state enterprises corresponding to production costs (so far the prices of goods and services produced at these enterprises have been below their production costs); and to raise the rent for old houses (so far it has been much lower than for new houses). *In the sphere of incomes* it is proposed, in order to ensure the programmed level of prices, to restrict the nominal increase of average annual wages per person of a constant skill to 2·8 per cent, of the average annual incomes from farming to 3·8 per cent and of the annual average industrial profit to 3.3 per cent. In real terms, i.e. taking into account the policy of prices, the gap between wages and profits will evidently be much more considerable than the nominal difference mentioned above.

### 4. IN WHAT RESPECTS IS ECONOMIC PROGRAMMING EFFECTIVE?

Since the practice of programming has a comparatively short record, its results can only be summed up for those sectors and countries in which at least one long-term programme has been completed. These countries are France (four programmes), the Netherlands (three programmes), Norway (three programmes) and partially Italy (one programme). The main difficulty lies in the fact that the socialist method of comparing targets and results does not apply to the analysis of the actual role of programming in the capitalist countries. The concepts of "fulfilment" or "failure" of a programme are meaningless when applied to programming: even the largest monopolies have never received concrete assignments under state programmes. With essential reservations, these concepts can only be applied to nationalised enterprises subsidised from the budget according to the current economic programme.

The Western programmers admit that their practice of programming is decisively influenced by the current condition of the capitalist economy.

Therefore, some additional criteria are necessary for determining the effectiveness of programming. An essential criterion is, in my view, the extent of the influence of a programme on the cyclical fluctuations of capitalist production. To determine this extent, we must calculate the stability of the rates of industrial growth according to the variation coefficient in 1954 to 1963 for several countries of Western Europe, Japan and the U.S.A. (see the table below). By the "variation coefficient" is meant the ratio of the mean square deviation to the mean characteristic of a given population. The average annual rate of growth is accepted as the average characteristic of the population under study (industrial growth rate indices). The smaller the coefficient the less the amplitude of fluctuations in a given population, in our example, i.e. in application to the rates of growth, this coefficient describes the instability of economic growth.

Q

The data thus obtained point no doubt to a certain advantage of the programming countries over the countries where programming is not practised. The most conclusive example in this respect is that of the U.S.A., where the stability of growth is much less than in Italy or in France. On the other hand, the data for 1958 point to a considerable depression not only in the U.S.A. but also in all the programming countries. In other words, neither the programming applied in the countries of Western Europe nor other forms of the state interference in economic activity can eliminate the cyclical character of capitalist economic development.

Nevertheless, the practice of programming capitalist production is expanding. The fact is that the state contributes to the solution of some of the nodal problems of monopoly capitalism by resorting to financing selected monopoly groups. With the aid of programmes the state redistributes investments, which accelerates the growth of the sectors which are especially important strategically and/or commercially. For example, in Norway, the proportion of investments in the sectors defined by the programme as "priority sectors" (mining and manufacturing industry, the generation of power, merchant marine and whaling) accounted for 39·4 per cent in 1937–39, 50·5 per cent in 1946–49, and 47·1 per cent in 1950–56 of the total volume of investments. In France, chemicals, electric power and oil have been developing especially rapidly in accordance with the programmes.

Under present-day conditions of state-monopoly capitalism the element of planning inherent in large-scale production becomes effective in some countries of Western Europe in those industries which are largely or completely controlled by the state. Programming works better in these sectors. When the level of business activity is high, the output of state-run enterprises deviates little as a rule from the figure recommended by the programme. Therefore, the scale of overproduction at these enterprises is less considerable than at private enterprises. However, when economic conditions deteriorate, the programmes have usually to be revised with respect to nationalised enterprises as well.

Economic programming plays a considerable role in the policy of eliminating "bottlenecks" emerging in the process of capitalist economic development. This applies above all to the development of the economic infrastructure. A case in point is the intense reorganisation of the fuel and power basis of the economy of Western Europe, the state playing a decisive role in this reorganisation. This process is intimately linked with economic programming, just as is the modernisation of transport. The problems of financing scientific and technical progress and the training of personnel bulk large in West European programmes. The "plans" of France, Great Britain, Belgium and some other countries provide for a considerable increase of outlays on education and, in particular, special emphasis is laid on the numerical growth of scientific and technical manpower. The programmes also map out certain measures for the retraining of manpower because of the growth of "technological unemployment".

More tangible results have been obtained under economic programmes in the levelling of regional differences. Many new industrial complexes which have absorbed vast investments have appeared in recent years in the southern areas of Italy, in the northern areas of Norway, in the eastern areas of the Netherlands, etc. The rate of industrial growth is higher in these less developed areas than the average for the country as a whole. In the southern areas of Italy, for example, the proportion of industrial production between 1951–52 and 1959–60 increased from 29·6 per cent to 33·0 per cent, while the proportion of farming decreased from 43·1 per cent to 32·6 per cent in the same period. The economic reclamation of these areas at the state's expense expands the national domestic market and gives a new impetus to the growth of capitalist production.

The importance of programming lies not only in its purely economic effects. The statistical information which entrepreneurs receive when they participate in the activity of the "planning agencies", and which they can glean from the extensive data published in connection with programmes, is of inestimable value to them. Characteristically, the French programmes have been defined as "giant market surveys". In this sense it can be said that programming plays a definite role in increasing the proportion of production serving private enterprise.

An essential factor in programming is the development and implementation of measures for "reorganising the economic structure", i.e. measures aimed at intensifying the process of concentration of production and capital. The competition in the West European Common Market requires from the member countries not just a passive approval of concentration, or indirect contribution to this process, but an active and purposive policy in this field intended for a long period. Characteristically, the French Fifth Plan provides for restrictions of credit to small entrepreneurs and farmers. As a result, it is intended to eliminate small farms, as well as a considerable number of small firms in trade and services. New supermarkets are expected to replace small shops. Similar measures are being taken in other countries. In the Netherlands twenty machine building enterprises have specialised and standardised their output, with the state's active interference and assistance.

However, the economic programming in the West European countries has a dual and contradictory character. The changes in the sectoral structure of industry, the reorganisation of the fuel and power infrastructure as well as transport, the elimination of unproductive enterprises and superfluous elements in distribution, the development of large-scale production in farming, etc., constitute, as such, a progressive process. But since this process takes the form of capitalist rationalisation, the partial solution of important problems of modern capitalism is paralleled by the aggravation of other aspects of these problems and the emergence of new difficulties. For example, the West European programmes do not provide for the employment of those miners, railwaymen, farmers, etc., who are left without any means of subsistence as a result of capitalist rationalisation. The result is the aggravation of the problem of unemployment.

The basic contradiction of West European programming is the incompatibility of stable high rates of growth (which is the pivotal problem) with the policy of restriction of mass consumption. Characteristic of the West European programmes is not only the reorientation of investments but also their overall expansion to raise the rates of growth and the yield of profit of national production. The reduction of production costs by restricting the growth of wages is regarded by the monopoly bourgeoisie as the most effective and quickest means for intensifying economic expansion into foreign markets. Therefore, an "incomes policy" has become an important integral part of all West European programmes. An attempt is made with the aid of this policy to place the growth of wages under the rigid control of the programming agencies.

Thus, the reverse side of the state and monopoly practice of programming is an increasing pressure on the living standards of working people. The authors of the Fourth Plan in France stated bluntly that its main tenet was the necessity of slowing down the growth of personal consumption in favour of the expansion of investments and exports. In compliance with this tenet a session of the *Conseil du plan* sponsored by the Finance Minister, Giscard d'Estaing, in July 1963 decided to reduce the projected growth of personal consumption by one-third,

*Instability of the Rates of Industrial Growth*

| | 1954 | 1955 | 1956 | 1957 | 1958 | 1959 | 1960 | 1961 | 1962 | 1963 | Average annual rate of growth | Variation coefficient |
|---|---|---|---|---|---|---|---|---|---|---|---|---|
| Italy | 10·0 | 9·1 | 7·1 | 6·7 | 4·2 | 11·0 | 15·3 | 10·9 | 9·9 | 9·0 | 9·3 | 30·0 |
| Norway | 8·0 | 7·4 | 4·4 | 5·3 | 0 | 6·0 | 10·4 | 6·8 | 4·0 | 6·2 | 5·75 | 45·7 |
| France | 8·1 | 8·1 | 11·0 | 10·9 | 16·2 | 1·0 | 8·9 | 5·5 | 6·0 | 4·9 | 6·45 | 45·9 |
| West Germany | 12·1 | 14·9 | 8·2 | 5·4 | 3·1 | 7·0 | 11·2 | 5·9 | 4·8 | 3·9 | 7·5 | 50·8 |
| Japan | 6·7 | 7·8 | 24·6 | 15·1 | 1·0 | 24·0 | 25·8 | 19·2 | 8·1 | 9·0 | 13·8 | 60·7 |
| The Netherlands | 5·1 | 12·0 | 5·4 | 2·0 | 0 | 9·8 | 13·8 | 1·6 | 3·2 | 4·6 | 5·6 | 78·6 |
| Belgium | 5·8 | 9·9 | 6·0 | 0 | −5·7 | 4·0 | 6·7 | 4·5 | 6·0 | 5·7 | 4·2 | 81·4 |
| Great Britain | 5·6 | 5·3 | 0 | 2·0 | −1·0 | 5·0 | 6·7 | 1·8 | 0·9 | 3·5 | 2·95 | 97·1 |
| U.S.A. | −5·2 | 11·2 | 3·9 | 0 | −6·5 | 13·0 | 2·7 | 0·9 | 7·7 | 5·6 | 3·2 | 189·0 |

Another well-tried measure in France was the introduction of new taxes augmenting the budget in 1963 by 1,200 million francs, which amounted to one-third of all fiscal revenues. Far from introducing any essential changes in the capitalist mode of production, programming only accentuates the class contradictions inherent in it.

# Index